THE BOOK OF™ XEN

THE BOOK OF™ XEN

A Practical Guide for the System Administrator

by Chris Takemura and Luke S. Crawford

no starch
press

San Francisco

13 12 11 10 09   1 2 3 4 5 6 7 8 9

ISBN-10: 1-59327-186-7
ISBN-13: 978-1-59327-186-2

Publisher: William Pollock
Production Editors: Magnolia Molcan and Philip Dangler
Cover and Interior Design: Octopod Studios
Developmental Editor: Tyler Ortman
Technical Reviewer: Rami Rosen
Copyeditor: Jeanne Hansen
Compositor: Riley Hoffman
Proofreader: Rachel Kai
Indexer: Valerie Haynes Perry

For information on book distributors or translations, please contact No Starch Press, Inc. directly:

No Starch Press, Inc.
555 De Haro Street, Suite 250, San Francisco, CA 94107
phone: 415.863.9900; fax: 415.863.9950; info@nostarch.com; www.nostarch.com

Library of Congress Cataloging-in-Publication Data

```
Takemura, Chris, 1981-
  The book of Xen : a practical guide for the system administrator / Chris Takemura and Luke S. Crawford.
      p. cm.
  Includes index.
  ISBN-13: 978-1-59327-186-2
  ISBN-10: 1-59327-186-7
 1.  Xen (Electronic resource) 2.  Virtual computer systems. 3. Computer organization. 4.  Parallel processing
(Electronic computers) I. Crawford, Luke S. (Luke Seidel), 1980- II. Title.
  QA76.9.V5C83 2009
  004'.35--dc22
                                         2009029566
```

This one's for my dad, who first introduced me to text-based adventure games on a Z80-based Heathkit computer, and whose fault, therefore, all of this is.
—Chris Takemura

To Sarah. I got what I wanted.
—Luke S. Crawford

BRIEF CONTENTS

CONTENTS IN DETAIL

4
STORAGE WITH XEN
43

5
NETWORKING
59

6
DOMU MANAGEMENT: TOOLS AND FRONTENDS 75

7
HOSTING UNTRUSTED USERS UNDER XEN:
LESSONS FROM THE TRENCHES 89

8
BEYOND LINUX:
USING XEN WITH OTHER UNIX-LIKE OSs 109

9
XEN MIGRATION 125

10
PROFILING AND BENCHMARKING UNDER XEN 141

11
CITRIX XENSERVER: XEN FOR THE ENTERPRISE 159

12
HVM: BEYOND PARAVIRTUALIZATION 175

13
XEN AND WINDOWS 187

14
TIPS 199

15
TROUBLESHOOTING

A
XM REFERENCE

B
THE STRUCTURE OF THE XEN CONFIG FILE

INDEX

FOREWORD

Virtualization is cool. I've always had a soft spot for virtualization, since as a lifelong sysadmin I get pretty tired of the endless fine-tuning that goes into building a successful network "host." Especially when that fine-tuning evolves into upgrades involving screwdrivers, recabling, and dust.

While Xen wasn't the first serious virtualization platform, it was the first serious *open source* virtualization platform, so it was the first that I was willing to invest my time in learning about, and the first I'd consider basing any production-level systems on. Open source isn't just a preference for me—I dislike lock-in, so I hardly ever buy or deploy or depend on something that I couldn't replace with a different product offered by a competing vendor sometime in the future.

Like any serious open source system, Xen has the power of an ecosystcm in which anybody who wants to vend can pick a spot and start hacking, but Xen also has the backing of a strong company whose employees contribute to the open source version of their product. This kind of vertical openness makes it possible for anyone (a hobbyist or a Fortune 500 company) to jump into Xen, buy only what they want or need (or just get it all for free), and have it remain compatible with the rest of the ecosystem. Thank you, XenSource and Citrix, for all this.

Confession time: I don't use Xen for any of my personal projects. I just don't have enough systems in any one location, nor can I plan far enough in advance—I'm too small to be able to afford virtualization's efficiencies.

Whenever I do need separation of privilege on the same physical servers, I've been able to get away with FreeBSD jails or User Mode Linux. I also do a fair amount of real-time work, in which I need my code to be close to the hardware for design—and sometimes performance—reasons.

For professional work, my company uses a mixture of proprietary (VMware) and open source (Xen) virtualization and the results are outstanding. Whether it's to save money on hardware, save money on sysadmin time, or enable new kinds of computing, virtualization is a winner and it's here to stay. I've seen Amazon and Google build gigantic clouds of virtualized servers for their own use and for rental to customers, and this method has driven down IT costs for both new and established companies of all sizes. It probably saves power and lowers the industry's carbon footprint as well.

I'm struggling to find a way to communicate how amazingly *cool* this is. We try to write programs that fit into a single process, but they end up taking a whole Unix system because of all the processes and databases and shell scripts and file systems and UIDs they slop over. So we end up dedicating physical servers to applications that have no performance- or security-related reason to be on dedicated servers; but each one takes up some rack space and some sysadmin time, and each one generates some minimum amount of heat, and so on. Then along comes virtualization, and we're back to adding physical servers only when we've got a good reason to do so, which usually means for capacity reasons.

Note that while I admire cloud computing, I also fear it. Amazon and Google have their own virtualization APIs, and anyone who builds "version 1" of a system to live inside one of these commercial clouds is probably signing up to put "version 2" into the same cloud. Competition requires differentiation and most vendors want to be different in capability, not just in cost efficiency. In other words, lock-in is great for sellers but not so great for buyers. Thus my attraction to enterprise virtualization—and specifically to open source enterprise virtualization, with the resulting vertically open ecosystem. I'll build my own clouds whenever I need them—and with Xen, so can you.

A word about Luke. He was a kid who lived down the street from my sister, and she asked me to give him a chance. So I hired him at an anti-spam company called MAPS (yes, that's spam spelled backwards, pretty neat, huh?), and he turned out to be a dumbass kid, like we all were at that age. In the time since then, he has distinguished himself as a virtualizer and now, with this book, as a writer. Xen is cool stuff, but it's also deep and wide and dense—that is to say, it's a hard topic. Luke and Chris have unscrambled Xen into the linear form of a printed book in about the best way I can imagine anybody doing it, and I learned quite a bit about Xen from reading my advance copy. The book is also fun to read without the fun being distracting or dilutive.

Go forth and virtualize!

Paul Vixie
La Honda, California
September 2009

ACKNOWLEDGMENTS

First, we would like to thank No Starch Press. Without them, this book would never have been imagined, much less published. In particular, we'd like to thank our editor, Tyler Ortman, who had the thankless tasks of making us write and cutting our dumb jokes. We'd also like to especially thank Rami Rosen, who provided us with an excellent technical review; Jeanne Hansen, our long-suffering copyeditor; and Bill Pollock, who paid for it all (and who made sure we actually finished it). And to everyone else on No Starch's team: we couldn't have done it without you. It was a humbling experience to see so many people scrutinizing our work, and the book is much, much better for it.

We also want to thank all the people who worked on prgmr.com during its checkered history. Without help from many skilled people willing to work at below market rates, the company would have folded long ago. So, heartfelt thanks go to Thuy Vu, Neal Krummell, Will Crawford, and Nick Schmalenberger, and to everyone else who has worked here for shorter periods of time. Neal deserves a special mention. Aside from introducing Chris and Luke, Neal provided encouragement and help during the critical early phases of the project.

Maybe most of all, we want to thank the customers of prgmr.com for giving us a lab with real users to test all this stuff.

Chris would like to add:

And to Alan, Chris, Ian, and Ken: The book's done now, so stop teasing me about it. Thanks for the encouragement, everyone.

Luke's personal acknowledgments:

I want to thank my dad. (Sorry you got beat out for the dedication. I'm sure you understand.) Without his encouragement, my natural entrepreneurial spark would never have developed into the flaming inferno it is. And I want to thank my other dad, too. When I make fun of enterprise software, I compare it to stuff I wrote with my stepfather's copy of FoxPro when I was 14.

And extra thanks to Paul Vixie, who both gave me my first real job and agreed to write the foreword for this book: If I'm a good sysadmin today, my time at MAPS has quite a lot to do with that.

INTRODUCTION

Being an account of the struggles and travails encountered by Our Hero in his zealous quest for performance: In which there is brief confusion and a beginning.

Once upon a time, in the land of Armonk-where-the-shadows-lie, a band of fiendish programmers were weaving their evil schemes. And it seemed that dark days were upon the earth at last, and for all time, for the programmers seemed so very clever that no one would ever be able to stand against them. And even if some hero were, through great fortune or unimaginable heroism, to bring one low, then there would still be an innumerable quantity remaining, each more fiendish and subtle than the last.

Wait. That's not right at all. In fact, that's the beginning of an entirely different book. Let's try that again.

This book is about Xen. It's not about Zen. It will not show you a path to enlightenment, expressed as a release from the floating world. We will not give you advice on the Eightfold Path, or enumerate the Four Noble Truths. Those are beyond our purview. But if all goes well, this book will make you happy.

Virtualization: A Brief History

In this case, the vehicle for happiness will be virtualization. It sounds bizarre, but people have attempted to become happy through virtualization since the Dawn Of Time. (In computing terms, that's the 1970s.) IBM's team of programmers in Armonk produced the first VM (virtual machine) solution that we know of, VM/370, to ensure that their new machine would be able to run programs developed for an older model. Customers loved it back in 1979, and the Xen developers credit it as a major inspiration. A similar, more modern example might be the Xbox 360's software emulation of the original Xbox.

For a while, not much came of it. Virtualization continued to play a part in computing, mostly in the very top end of the market, but people continued to obstinately require a complete machine for most tasks until about 2001.

2001, everyone had to admit, looked very different from 1979.[1] Computers had become small and ubiquitous. The great time-sharing machines had given way to PCs. Batch processing was a rarity, and fully interactive desktop applications had become the *raison d'etre* of computing. Most important, from our perspective, the single computer had been eclipsed by the network: Most computers worth having were connected to the Internet, and each of them required various services.

These services, in turn, were designed in such a way that they could be readily provided by even the cheapest and smallest server, often many times over.[2] Suddenly the people operating these services had a terrible surplus of computing power, devouring electricity all out of proportion to the actual services they provided. Something had to be done. The stage was set for virtualization to re-emerge, this time as a means of server *consolidation*.

Some clever gentlemen at Cambridge decided that this idea could be extended even further—if virtualization allows an individual or company to consolidate their machines, they reasoned, shouldn't it also enable *multiple* organizations to consolidate their machines and reap even bigger benefits? That's the goal of Xen. It treats virtualization as a technology that allows people to ignore the hardware entirely. Computing, in this model, becomes a service or a commodity, "creating a world in which XenoServer execution platforms are scattered across the globe and available for any member of the public."[3]

That's where we are today. Although the XenoServer platform was never released, its vision survives today as "cloud computing," made possible by Xen (and, admittedly, other virtualization systems). Xen fits into this grand cloud computing scheme by enabling sites to create "nodes" that can be managed, transferred, and billed in ways that aren't feasible with other computing-as-service mechanisms.

---

[1] And, to our great dismay, also very different from the movie.

[2] We know, there are many applications where this is not the case—but there are still a lot of small web servers (for example) out there.

[3] Hand et al., "Controlling the XenoServer Open Platform," (University of Cambridge, England, 2003). Abstract.

So What's Xen Again? (And Why Should I Use It?)

Even if you're not interested in this sort of grid computing thing, Xen offers some advantages to both the system administrator and the home user.

Xen is a piece of software that enables one machine to behave as if it were many *virtual* machines. Each of these machines can run its own operating system and exist almost independently of the other virtual machines running on the same hardware. Each virtual machine (an *instance*, or *domain* in Xen parlance) has its own apparent network interfaces, disks, and memory.

At first, this makes Xen seem no different from an *emulator*, such as VMware, Microsoft's Virtual PC, or the open source QEMU.[4] However, these traditional emulators work by running software on a simulated processor that is, itself, also software—a rather slow proposition. Xen actually runs all software directly on the processor at full speed, with only a very small overhead for some resource management tasks.

This leads to the first, and probably the most important, advantage of Xen: Xen runs *fast* in comparison with traditional emulators. Preliminary results in "Xen and the Art of Virtualization"—one of the seminal Xen papers— indicated performance degradation of less than 2 percent for a standard workload and between 10 and 20 percent for a worst-case scenario. Since then, Xen has improved. We usually just consider Xen's performance to be "sufficient" and leave it at that. (Readers desiring a more precise answer might want to read Chapter 10, which discusses benchmarking Xen's performance with your particular application.)

Xen's advantages also show up in contrast to a standalone machine, even beyond the consolidation argument mentioned earlier. Like a traditional emulator, Xen provides robust fault isolation—that is, any software problem that affects one virtual machine is unlikely to affect the real machine or other virtual machines running on the same hardware. This makes it especially useful in environments where you can't be certain of the intentions or skill level of the users.

Also like traditional emulators, Xen provides an additional layer of abstraction between the machine and the user, allowing the administrator increased flexibility—suddenly the application can be decoupled from the hardware almost completely; stopped, started, moved around; made into a genuine service.

But Xen's main advantage is, in a sense, psychological: It makes it possible to think of computer time as even more of a commodity than it already is.[5] With Xen, you can run your own virtual computer for as much or as little time as you need, with resources tailored to the desired application.

Further, Xen gives you the ability to run whatever configuration you happen to need at a given time. For example, the web developer who wants to test a new page against different versions of Microsoft's Internet Explorer doesn't have to maintain a farm of Windows boxes, each with

---

[4] In fact, Xen uses QEMU extensively, as we'll see.

[5] This is sort of like cell phones. People use them, not as a substitute for landlines, but as a substitute for traditional planning.

different Windows versions, different patch levels, and different versions of Internet Explorer. Instead, it's possible to just keep different OS images on the hard drive and start them as needed.

Xen's Limitations

All right, we're getting carried away. Xen's not perfect, nor is it any sort of computing panacea. It has both disadvantages and limitations.

Xen's main disadvantage is that it only works with operating systems that have been specifically modified to support it. (But note that unmodified guest OSs are possible with sufficiently advanced hardware. We'll talk about that later, in Chapter 12.)

Xen's also more work to set up than a pure software emulator, requiring the user to work entirely in a guest domain (albeit a special, privileged guest domain) rather than simply starting an external emulation program as desired.

Additionally, the state of the Xen documentation is pretty dreadful. (That's what we're here for, you might say.) People are, of course, working on it, but everyone knows it's more fun to write code than to document it. Also, Xen's under such active development that much of the documentation that exists is out of date.

These are significant disadvantages, but they aren't so bad that you should be discouraged from running Xen.

Finally, though there are also some situations in which Xen—and virtualization itself—simply isn't useful. Xen isn't especially useful to people with a constant, CPU-limited workload, for example. It's not great in large server farms, where individual nodes are already scaled to their jobs. In these situations, Xen is probably not what you want, although the developers (and the open source community) are working on compelling features even for environments like these.

But, in the end, it's not Xen itself that's interesting—it's what you can use it for.

So, Why Should I Use Xen?

The short answer is, *because it will make your life easier.* Don't trust a piece of software? Spin off a virtual machine and see how you like it. Need to test a network app? Start up a few machines and see how well they talk to each other. Have a cluster that you want to test some new software on but can't afford a second "test" cluster? Xen offers a solution. Want decent snapshot backups? Xen could be your answer, with its ability to pause and back up a running machine within, literally, seconds. Need to provide hosting for dozens of users, each of whom wants complete authority to mess with their configuration? Well, that's what we do, and Xen's the way we do it. (The astute reader might notice in our writing a certain bias toward that last application. That's why.)

On a more fundamental level, Xen lets you take a machine, stop it, send it somewhere else, and resume it at will. It's one less thing to think about—suddenly the hardware is no longer important. A good thing for both users and administrators!

Finally, there's one last good reason to run Xen, one that's so big and mundane it often gets ignored: Xen is simply cheaper than running multiple boxes. CPU usage in data centers ranges between 5 percent and 40 percent—a fairly unimpressive figure.[6] Xen lets you put some of those unused cycles to use, without sacrificing reliability, performance, or scalability.

Unlike the virtualization technologies of a few decades ago, Xen virtualizes cheap commodity hardware; this might not make sense at first, until you realize that much of the market is *very* price sensitive, and power is becoming quite expensive. It's much cheaper to run one big dual quad-core rig than it is to run eight single-core boxes, and with Xen, you can easily split that quad-core system into individual systems.

Overview of the Book

All right, enough hype. Now for nuts and bolts.

We've organized this book (mostly) alternating between theoretical and practical discussion. In our experience, an admin needs both practical experience and a firm theoretical grounding to effectively solve problems, and that's what we aim to provide.

Chapter 1 is an overview of Xen and virtualization technologies in general. We try to outline how Xen works, what distinguishes it from other virtualization packages, and why you might (or might not) want to use it. This one is theory-intensive.

Chapter 2 is a step-by-step quick start based on the rationale that there's no substitute for experience. We install Xen from base principles on a CentOS system.

Chapter 3 describes manually creating virtual machine images to use with Xen.

Chapter 4 covers storage. It sounds kind of mundane, but storage is actually a vital part of virtualization—if storage is tied to a particular machine or hardware configuration, then many of Xen's coolest features won't work. We cover various storage options, laying the groundwork for subsequent discussion of migration and snapshots.

We talk about networking in Chapter 5—how to set it up and what options you have when doing so. Both this chapter and the previous focus a bit more on theory.

Chapter 6 is about a couple of popular packaged frontends that can be used with the open source Xen hypervisor to automate the routine drudgery of VM administration. We also talk about scripting Xen, if you'd rather build your own frontend.

---

[6] This is a generally held belief, but one oft-cited source is the presentation "Virtualization: Taking Charge of Your Servers" by Thomas Bittman.

Chapter 7 goes back to the practical case studies to talk about Xen for shared hosting. It's one of the big applications that's driving early adoption of Xen, and we've got a lot of experience doing it.

Moving on from shared hosting, in Chapter 8 we discuss possible alternatives to Linux, both as a "host" and "guest" OS.

In Chapter 9 we describe migration, both in theory and practice.

Chapter 10 is about performance analysis with Xen. We discuss Xen's robust support in this area, which doesn't seem to get mentioned nearly as often as it deserves.

With Chapter 11 we diverge a bit to cover the commercial product that XenSource (now a division of Citrix) has built around Xen.

Chapter 12 is about Xen's HVM support—that is to say, the hardware virtualization supported by Intel's and AMD's newest processors.

Chapter 13 covers Windows. We talk about using it with Xen, making it play nicely, how you can expect to access it, and what you might expect to do with it once you've got it working.

Chapter 14 is a collection of extremely practical tips for Xen admins.

Chapter 15 is a troubleshooting chapter—a collection of problems that we've run into and how we've solved them.

We've also included appendixes on Xen's domain configuration files and xm's syntax.

But I Am Impatient!

If you're really impatient to get started with Xen, skip to Chapter 2 and follow our step-by-step instructions. Then skim the rest of the book as the fancy strikes you.

If you're planning to deploy Xen as a service provider, we suggest following the steps in Chapter 2, then reading Chapters 3, 4, 5, 6, 7, 8, and probably 11, and finally just reading the whole book.

For those of you who are contemplating a large deployment of Xen, you'll probably be most interested in Chapters 3, 4, 5, 6, and 7, with an excursion to 13 to consider the commercial XenSource product. But again, we think we've put useful information throughout the book.

NOTE   *We've tried to keep this book as distribution- and version-independent as possible, except in the tutorial sections, where we try to be extremely specific and detailed, and in the distro-specific notes, which are necessarily, er, distro-specific.*

Often we will get carried away and make some ridiculous broad generalization, like "only an idiot would use Linux as an NFS server."[7] Where reasonable, we've tried to add footnotes that qualify and temper the occasionally strident claims we make.

---

[7] Actually, we've seen morons and imbeciles do this too.

1

XEN: A HIGH-LEVEL OVERVIEW

We'll start by explaining what makes Xen different from other virtualization techniques and then provide some low-level detail on how Xen works and how its components fit together.

Virtualization Principles

First, we might want to mention that computers, even new and fast ones with modern multitasking operating systems, can perform only one instruction at a time.[1] Now, you say, "But my computer is performing many tasks at once. Even now, I can see a clock running, hear music playing, download files, and chat with friends, all at the same time." And this is true. However, what is *actually* happening is that the computer is switching between these different tasks so quickly that the delays become imperceptible. Just as a movie is a

---

[1] Of course, SMP and multicore CPUs make this not entirely true, and we are drastically simplifying pipelining, superscalar execution, and so forth, but the principle still holds—at any instant, each core is only doing one thing.

succession of still images that give the illusion of movement, a computer performs tasks that are so seamlessly interweaved as to appear simultaneous.

Virtualization just extends this metaphor a bit. Ordinarily, this multiplexing takes place under the direction of the operating system, which acts to supervise tasks and make sure that each receives its fair share of CPU time. Because the operating system must therefore *schedule* tasks to run on the CPU, this aspect of the operating system is called a *scheduler*. With Xen virtualization, the same process occurs, with entire operating systems taking the place of tasks. The scheduling aspect is handled by the Xen kernel, which runs on a level superior to the "supervising" guest operating systems, and which we thus call the *hypervisor*.

Of course, it's not quite so simple—operating systems, even ones that have been modified to be Xen-friendly, use a different, more comprehensive, set of assumptions than applications, and switching between them is almost by definition going to involve more complexity.

So let's look at an overview of how virtualization is traditionally done and how Xen's design is new and different. A traditional virtual machine is designed to mimic a real machine in every way, such that it's impossible to tell from within the virtual machine that it isn't real. To preserve that illusion, fully virtualized machines intercept attempts to access hardware and emulate that hardware's functionality in software—thus maintaining perfect compatibility with the applications inside the virtual machine. This layer of indirection makes the virtual machine very slow.

Xen bypasses this slowdown using an approach called *paravirtualization—para* as a prefix means *similar to* or *alongside*. As the name suggests, it's not "real" virtualization in the traditional sense because it doesn't try to provide a seamless illusion of a machine. Xen presents only a partial abstraction of the underlying hardware to the hosted operating system, exposing some aspects of the machine as *limitations* on the guest OS, which needs to know that it's running on Xen and should handle certain hardware interactions accordingly.

NOTE   *Newer processors incorporate support for hardware virtualization, allowing unmodified operating systems to run under Xen. See Chapter 12 for details.*

Most of these limitations—by design—aren't noticeable to the system's users. To run under Xen, the guest OS kernel needs to be modified so that, for example, it asks Xen for memory rather than allocating it directly. One of the design goals for Xen was to have these changes occur in the hardware-dependent bits of the guest operating system, without changing the interface between the kernel and user-level software.

This design goal reduces the difficulty of moving to Xen by ensuring that existing binaries will work unmodified on the Xen guest OS and that the virtual machine will, in most regards, act exactly like a real one, at least from the perspective of the system's end users.

Xen therefore trades seamless virtualization for a high-performance paravirtualized environment. The paper in which the original Xen developers initially presented this project, "Xen and the Art of Virtualization,"[2] puts this

---

[2] See *http://www.cl.cam.ac.uk/research/srg/netos/papers/2003-xensosp.pdf.*

in strong terms, saying "Paravirtualization is necessary to attain high performance and strong resource isolation on uncooperative machine architectures such as x86." It's not quite as simple as "paravirtualization makes a computer fast"—I/O, for example, can lead to expensive context switches—but it is generally faster than other approaches. We generally assume that a Xen guest will run at about 95 percent of its native speed on physical hardware, assuming that other guests on the machine are idle.

However, paravirtualization isn't the only way to run a virtual machine. There are two competing approaches: full virtualization and OS-level virtualization.

Virtualization Techniques: Full Virtualization

Not all virtualization methods use Xen's approach. Virtualization software come in three flavors. At one extreme you have *full virtualization*, or emulation, in which the virtual machine is a software simulation of hardware, real or fictional—as long as there's a driver, it doesn't matter much. Products in this category include VMware and QEMU.

NOTE *And what, you ask, is this fictional hardware? Apart from the obvious "not real" answer, one good example is the VTPM driver. TPM (Trusted Platform Module) hardware is relatively uncommon, but it has some potential applications with signing code—for example, making sure that the running kernel is the correct one, rather than a fake put on by a rootkit or virus. Xen therefore makes a virtual TPM available to the domUs.*

With full virtualization, an unmodified[3] OS "hosts" a userspace program that emulates a machine on which the "guest" OS runs. This is a popular approach because it doesn't require the guest OS to be changed in any way. It also has the advantage that the virtualized architecture can be completely different from the host architecture—for example, QEMU can simulate a MIPS processor on an IA-32 host and a startling array of other chips.

However, this level of hardware independence comes at the cost of an enormous speed penalty. Unaccelerated QEMU is an order of magnitude slower than native execution, and accelerated QEMU or VMware ESX server can only accelerate the emulated machine if it's the same architecture as the underlying hardware. In this context, for normal usage, the increased hardware versatility of a full emulator isn't a significant advantage over Xen.

VMware is currently the best-known vendor of full-virtualization products, with a robust set of tools, broad support, and a strong brand. Recent versions of VMware address the speed problem by running instructions in place where possible and dynamically translating code when necessary. Although this approach is elegant and doesn't require guest OS modification, it's not as fast as Xen, making it less desirable for production setups or for a full-time work environment.

---

[3] Or a slightly modified OS—QEMU, for example, has the KQEMU kernel module, which speeds up the emulated code by allowing it to run directly on the processor when possible.

Virtualization Techniques: OS Virtualization

On the other extreme is *OS-level virtualization*, where what's being virtualized is the operating environment, rather than the complete machine. FreeBSD jails and Solaris Containers take this approach.

OS virtualization takes the position that the operating system already provides, or at least can be made to provide, sufficient isolation to do everything that a normal VM user expects—install software systemwide, upgrade system libraries in the guest without affecting those in the host, and so forth. Thus, rather than emulating physical hardware, OS virtualization emulates a complete OS userspace using operating system facilities.

FreeBSD jails and Solaris Containers (or Zones) are two popular implementations of OS-level virtualization. Both derive from the classic Unix chroot jail. The idea is that the jailed process can only access parts of the filesystem that reside under a certain directory—the rest of the filesystem, as far as this process can tell, simply doesn't exist. If we install an OS into that directory, it can be considered a complete virtual environment. Jails and Zones expand on the concept by also restricting certain system calls and providing a virtual network interface to enhance isolation between virtual machines. Although this is incredibly useful, it's neither as useful or as versatile as a full-fledged virtual machine would be. Because the jails share a kernel, for example, a kernel panic will bring down all the VMs on the hardware.

However, because they bypass the overhead of virtualizing hardware, virtualized machines can be about as fast as native execution—in fact, they are native.

OS virtualization and Xen complement each other, each being useful in different situations, possibly even simultaneously. One can readily imagine, for example, giving a user a single Xen VM, which he then partitions into multiple Zones for his own use.

Paravirtualization: Xen's Approach

Finally, somewhere between the two, there's *paravirtualization*, which relies on the operating system being modified to work in concert with a sort of "super operating system," which we call the *hypervisor*. This is the approach Xen uses.

How Paravirtualization Works

Xen works by introducing a very small, very compact and focused piece of software that runs directly on the hardware and provides services to the virtualized operating systems.[4]

---

[4] Some would call the Xen hypervisor a microkernel. Others wouldn't.

Xen's approach to virtualization does away with most of the split between host OS and guest OS. Full virtualization and OS-level virtualization have a clear distinction—the host OS is the one that runs with full privileges. With Xen, only the hypervisor has full privileges, and it's designed to be as small and limited as possible.

Instead of this "host/guest" split, the hypervisor relies on a trusted guest OS (domain 0, the *driver domain*, or more informally, *dom0*) to provide hardware drivers, a kernel, and a userland. This privileged domain is uniquely distinguished as the domain that the hypervisor allows to access devices and perform control functions. By doing this, the Xen developers ensure that the hypervisor remains small and maintainable and that it occupies as little memory as possible. Figure 1-1 shows this relationship.

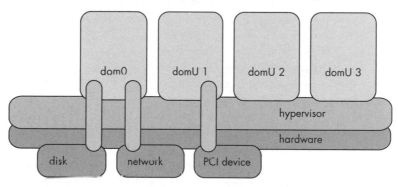

Figure 1-1: Shown here is the hypervisor with domains. Note that the hypervisor runs directly on the hardware but doesn't itself mediate access to disk and network devices. Instead, dom0 interacts directly with disk and network devices, servicing requests from the other domains. In this diagram, domU 1 also acts as a driver domain for an unnamed PCI device.

NOTE *See also "Safe Hardware Access with the Xen Virtual Machine Monitor," Fraser et al.[5] Also, non-dom0 driver domains can exist—however, they're not recommended on current hardware in the absence of an IOMMU (I/O Memory Management Unit) and therefore will not be covered here. For more on IOMMU development, see Chapter 12.*

Domain 0's privileged operations broadly fall into two categories. First, dom0 functions as an area from which to administer Xen. From the dom0, the administrator can control the other domains running on the machine—create, destroy, save, restore, etc. Network and storage devices can also be manipulated—created, presented to the kernel, assigned to domUs, etc.

Second, dom0 has uniquely privileged access to hardware. The domain 0 kernel has the usual hardware drivers and uses them to export abstractions of hardware devices to the hypervisor and thence to virtual machines. Think of the machine as a car, with the dom0 as driver. He's also a passenger but has privileges and responsibilities that the other passengers don't.

---

[5] See *http://www.cl.cam.ac.uk/research/srg/netos/papers/2004-oasis-ngio.pdf.*

Xen's Underpinnings: The Gory Details

So, with this concept of virtual devices firmly in mind, the question becomes: What does a computer need to provide at the most basic level? The Xen developers considered this question at length and concluded that Xen would have to manage *CPU time, interrupts, memory, block devices,* and *network.*

The hypervisor operates much like the very core of a traditional operating system, parceling out CPU time and resources to the operating systems that run under it, which in turn allocate resources to their individual processes. Just as modern operating systems can transparently pause a process, the Xen hypervisor can pause an operating system, hand control to another for a while, and then seamlessly restart the paused system.

Because Xen is designed to be small and simple, the hypervisor interacts with the OSs that run under it using a very few well-defined interfaces, which the Xen team refers to as *hypercalls.*

These hypercalls take the place of a standard operating system's system calls, with a similar interface. In effect, they have the same function—to allow user code to execute privileged operations in a way that can be controlled and managed by trusted code.

The hypercalls have several design goals and requirements. First, they are *asynchronous* so that hypercalls don't block other processes or other OSs— while one domain waits for a hypercall to finish, another domain can get some CPU time. Second, they are small, simple, and clearly defined—Xen has only about 50 hypercalls, in contrast with over 300 syscalls for Linux. Finally, the hypercalls use a common system of notifications to interact with the Xen hypervisor.

Scheduling

The CPU, regardless of Xen virtualization, is still a physical object, subject to all the messy and intractable laws of physical reality. It can perform only one instruction at a time, and so the various demands on its attention have to be scheduled. Xen schedules processes to run on the CPU in response to instructions from the guest OSs, subject to its own accounting of which guest should have access to the CPU at any given time.

Each guest maintains its own internal queues of which instructions to run next—which process gets a CPU time slice, essentially. In an ordinary machine, the OS would run the process at the head of a queue on the physical CPU. (Under Linux, the run queue.) On a virtual machine, it instead notifies Xen to run that process for a certain amount of time, expressed in domain-virtual terms.

The guest can also "make an appointment" with Xen, requesting an interrupt and CPU time at a later time, based on either a domain-virtual timer or system timer.

The domain-virtual timer is used mostly for internal scheduling between processes—the domU kernel can request that the hypervisor preempt a task and run another one after a certain amount of virtual time has passed. Note that the domain doesn't actually schedule processes directly on the CPU—that sort of hardware interaction has to be handled by the hypervisor.

The system timer is used for events that are sensitive to real-world time, such as networking. Using the system timer, the domain can give up the CPU for a while and request to be woken back up in time to refill the network buffer or send out the next ping.

The administrator can also tune the scheduling parameters that Xen uses to allocate resources to domains. There are a number of different algorithms, with varying degrees of usefulness. See Chapter 7 for more details on scheduling.

Interrupts

In computing terms, an *interrupt* is a request for attention. An interrupt usually occurs when some piece of hardware needs to interact with its control software (that is, drivers). Traditionally, interrupts must be handled immediately, and all other processes have to wait until the interrupt handler has finished. In the context of virtualization, this is patently unacceptable.

Xen therefore intercepts interrupts, rather than passing them directly through to guest domains. This allows Xen to retain control of the hardware, *scheduling* interrupt servicing, rather than merely reacting. Domains can register interrupt handlers with the hypervisor in advance. Then, when an interrupt comes in, Xen notifies the appropriate guest domain and schedules it for execution. Interrupts that occur while the domain is waiting to execute are coalesced into a nice package, avoiding unnecessary notifications. This also contributes to Xen's performance because context switches between domains are expensive.

Memory

The hypervisor has authority over memory that is both localized and absolute. It must allocate all memory used by the domains, but it only deals with physical memory and the page table—the guest OSs handle all other memory management functions.

This, as it turns out, is quite as much as any sensible implementor could desire. Memory, under x86, is difficult and arcane. The Xen authors point out, in a classic understatement, that "the x86 processors use a complex hybrid memory management scheme." Figure 1-2 shows an overview of address translation on the x86.

On the most fundamental, hardware-dependent level, or at least the lowest level we're willing to mention here, we have the machine memory. This can be accessed one word at a time, via numbered addresses. That's the final product, shown on the right in Figure 1-2.

However, this approach is too hardware dependent for a modern computer, which needs to be able to swap to disk, memory map I/O, use DMA, and so on. The processor therefore implements *virtual memory*, which provides two advantages for the programmer. First, it allows each process to access its own memory as if it were the only thing running on the computer— that is, as if it had the entirety of physical memory to itself. Second, virtual memory enables a process to access much more memory than is physically available, swapping to disk as necessary.

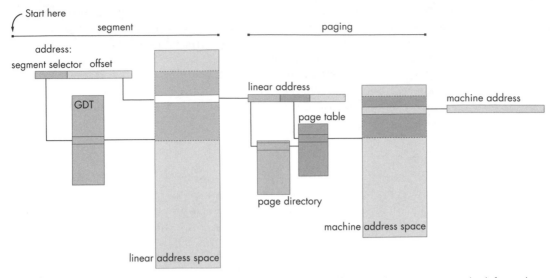

Figure 1-2: Let's take the example of translating an address given by an application. First, at the left, we have the address as given. This consists of a segment selector and offset. The MMU looks up the segment selector in the GDT (Global Descriptor Table) to find that segment's location in the linear address space, which is the complete address space accessible to the process (usually 4GB). The offset then acts as an address within that segment. This gives the processor a linear address relative to the process's address space. The MMU then decomposes that address into two indices and an offset—first it looks through the page directory to find the correct page table, then it finds the correct page in the page table, and finally it uses the offset to return a machine address—actual, physical memory.

Like physical memory, virtual memory is accessed one word at a time, via numbered addresses. The mapping between physical addresses and virtual addresses is handled by *page tables*, which associate chunks of physical memory with pages of virtual memory.

This level of abstraction applies even when there's only one operating system running on the machine. It's one of the basic forms of virtualization, so ubiquitous as to go unnoticed by most non-programmers.

Xen interposes itself at this point, acting as the sole gatekeeper of the page tables. Because applications have to go through Xen to update their mappings between virtual and physical memory, the hypervisor can ensure that domains only access memory within their reservation—memory that a domain doesn't have access to isn't mapped to any of its pages and therefore doesn't exist from the domain's perspective. Figure 1-3 shows the relationship between the hypervisor, physical memory, and pseudophysical mappings.

So far so good. x86 handles this partially in hardware, using an area of the processor called the *MMU*, or *Memory Management Unit*.

Although this mapping should be sufficient to provide memory protection and the *illusion* of contiguous virtual memory, the x86 architecture also uses segmentation to protect memory and increase the amount of addressable memory.[6] Application-level addresses are *logical addresses*, each of which

---

[6] This is untrue for AMD64, which does away with segmentation entirely. Instead, Xen on x86_64 uses page-level protection for its memory regions. Stranger things in Heaven and Earth, Horatio.

includes a 16-bit segment selector and a 32-bit segment offset, which the processor then maps to virtual (or *linear*) addresses, which are eventually turned into physical addresses.

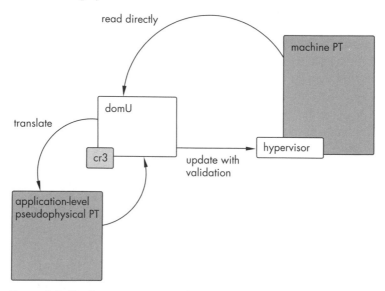

Figure 1-3: The hypervisor's main role is to validate the domU's updates to the page tables, ensuring that domU only maps memory allocated to it. The domU handles memory using physical pages directly, generating pseudophysical addresses where necessary.

In practice, however, modern software usually avoids the segment registers as much as possible—the segments are simply made equivalent to the entire address space, which has the practical effect of allowing processes to ignore their existence. However, the unused segmentation model provides a perfect way for Xen to protect its own memory reservation. The Xen hypervisor reserves a small amount of memory at the beginning of each domain's allocation and arranges the domain's segments so that they don't include the hypervisor's memory region.

NOTE   *This leads to the common* /lib/tls *problem. See Chapter 15 for more information.*

But wait! There's more. Each memory segment can also be protected by the system of *rings*, which specify the privilege levels that allow access to the memory on a per-process basis. Xen protects the hypervisor by allowing it to run in the privileged ring 0, while the guest OS uses privilege rings 1 through 3. This way, the processor can trap access attempts to the protected beginning of the segment.

Finally, Xen adds another layer to this memory-management tower of cards. Because the physical memory allocated to a domain is likely to be fragmented, and because most guest OSs don't expect to have to deal with this sort of thing, they must be modified to build a mapping between the hardware and the virtual machine, or *real physical* and *pseudophysical* addresses. This mapping is used for all other components of the guest OS so that they have the illusion of operating in a contiguous address space.

Thus, guest OS page tables still contain real machine addresses, which the guest itself translates to pseudophysical addresses for the benefit of applications. This helps Xen to remain fast, but it means that the guests cannot be trusted to manipulate page tables directly.

The internal update mechanisms are replaced by two hypercalls that request Xen to manipulate the page tables on the domain's behalf.

I/O Devices

Obviously, the domUs cannot be trusted to handle devices by themselves. Part of Xen's model is that even actively malicious guest domains should be unable to interfere with the hardware or other domains. All device access is through the hypervisor, with the aid of the dom0.

Xen handles domain I/O by using *device channels* and *virtual devices*. These are point-to-point links between a frontend device in the domU and a backend device in dom0, implemented as *ring buffers*, as shown in Figure 1-4. (Note that these are distinct from x86 privilege rings.)

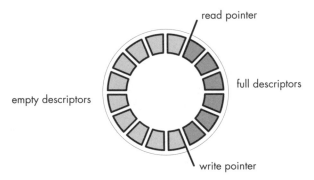

Figure 1-4: A ring buffer is a simple data structure that consists of preallocated memory regions, each tagged with a descriptor. As one party writes to the ring, the other reads from it, each updating the descriptors along the way. If the writer reaches a "written" block, the ring is full, and it needs to wait for the reader to mark some blocks empty.

The important qualities of these rings is that they're fixed size and lightweight—the domain operates directly on physical memory, without the need for constant hypervisor intervention. At opportune times, the virtual machine notifies the hypervisor that it's updated the ring, and the hypervisor then takes appropriate action (sending packets, replying with data, etc.).

For performance reasons, the rings generally contain I/O descriptors rather than actual data. The data is kept in separate buffers accessed through DMA, which Xen maintains control of using principles similar to those for memory allocation. The hypervisor also locks the pages in question, ensuring that the application doesn't try to give them away or use them incorrectly.

As the contents of a ring buffer are read, they're replaced by empty descriptors, indicating that the buffer has space for more data. Meanwhile, the reading process moves on to the next buffer entry. At the end of the buffer, it simply wraps around.

When a ring fills up, the backend device silently drops data intended for it. This is analogous to a network card or disk filling its buffer and usually results in a re-request for the data at a more convenient time.

Networking

The networking architecture (shown in Figure 1-5) of Xen is designed to reuse as much code as possible. Xen provides virtual network interfaces to domains and functions, via device channels, as a medium by which packets can move from a virtual interface in a guest domain to a virtual interface in the driver domain. Other functions are left to standard networking tools.

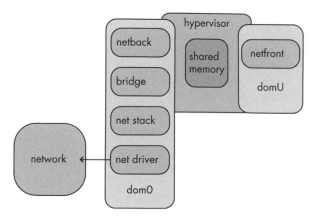

Figure 1-5: The domU uses the netfront *or network frontend driver as its network device, which then transparently flips packets to the* netback *driver in the dom0. The packets then go through the Linux software bridge, traverse Linux's network stack (including interaction with iptables and friends), and finally go to the network via Linux's network driver.*

The hypervisor functions solely as a data channel by which packets can move from the physical network interface to the domU's virtual interface. It mediates access between domains, but it doesn't validate packets or perform accounting—these are handled by iptables rules in dom0.

Accordingly, the virtual network interface is relatively simple—a buffer to receive packets, a buffer to send them, and a hypercall to notify the hypervisor that something has changed.

The other side of this is that there's a lot of configurability in Xen's networking because you can act on the virtual interfaces using all the standard Linux tools. For more information on networking and suggestions on how to use this nigh-unlimited power, see Chapter 5.

Block Devices

In practical terms, *block devices* are disks or disklike devices. MD arrays, filesystem images, and physical disks all fall under the general category of block devices.

Xen handles block devices in much the same way as network devices. The hypervisor exports *virtual block devices* (often referred to as VBDs) to the domUs and relies on the dom0 to provide backend drivers that map the functionality of the real block device to the VBD. The system of rings and limited hypercalls is also similar, as shown in Figure 1-6.

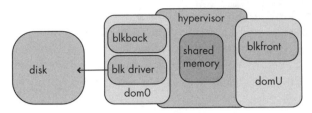

Figure 1-6: A domU's request for a block device begins with the blkfront or block frontend *driver, which uses a buffer in the hypervisor to interact with the* block backend *driver in domain 0. Blkback then reads or writes the requested blocks through dom0's block device driver (which can be a SCSI driver, IDE, fibre channel, etc.).*

Xen relies on the dom0 to create block devices and provide device drivers that map physical devices to Xen virtual devices.

For more information about this, see Chapter 4.

Putting It Together

In general, all of these implementation details demonstrate Xen's focus on simplicity and code reuse. Where possible, the Xen developers have chosen to focus on providing and managing channels between physical devices and virtual devices, letting Linux userspace tools and kernel mechanisms handle arbitration and device access. Also, the actual work is offloaded as much as possible to the dom0 so as to reduce the complexity of the hypervisor and maximize device support.

For the administrator, this means that Xen can be administered and monitored, by and large, with standard tools, and that most interactions with Xen take place at the level of the dom0. When Xen is installed and domains are running, the Xen domains act like normal, physical machines, running unmodified userspace programs, with some caveats. Let's move on to the next chapter to see how to set this up in practice.

2

GETTING STARTED

Fascinating though the theoretical under-pinnings and implementation details of Xen are, we should probably move on to working directly with Xen for a bit of practice. There is, after all, no substitute for experience.

So! Welcome to Xen. This chapter is an easy quick start aimed at gently introducing Xen to one of your machines. We will hold your hand and not let it go.

Because this is a detailed walk-through, we're going to give focused, specific instructions, deviating from our normal policy of being vague and distro-agnostic. For the purposes of this chapter, we'll assume you're installing CentOS 5.x with the *server* defaults and using its built-in Xen support.

If you're using something else, this chapter will probably still be useful, but you might have to improvise a bit—the goals will be the same but the steps will probably be different.

In general, the goals for this walk-through are as follows:

- Make sure your hardware can run Xen.
- Install a basic OS.
- Install Xen.
- Familiarize yourself with the Xen environment.
- Install a domU.
- Log in to your domU and configure it to make sure everything works.
- Rest.

Hardware Compatibility

First, make sure that your hardware's up to the task of running Xen. (It almost certainly is.)

All you need is a Pentium Pro or better, 512MiB of memory,[1] and a few hundred MiB of hard drive space. If you can't manage that, dig some change out of your couch cushions and buy a machine. The PPro came out in, what, 1996? Haven't you heard? This Is The Future.

---

[1] The absolute minimum would probably be 128MiB, but CentOS itself requires 256, and each domU will also require a significant amount of memory.

At present, Xen runs only on x86 (that is, Intel and AMD) processors and IBM's PowerPC. X86_64—the 64-bit extension to the x86 instruction set—is supported on both AMD and Intel processors. Xen also supports Intel's Itanium. For the sake of this walk-through, we'll assume that you're using an x86 or x86_64 machine.

Our test box, for example—chosen to be as common as possible—was a three-year-old Dell, with a Pentium 4, 1GB of RAM, and a quantity of hard drive space beyond my wildest imaginings. Personally, I think it's all so fast it makes me sick.

Anyway, so you've got a machine capable of running Xen. Congratulations. First, it needs a basic operating system that Xen can run on top of.

NOTE *Run on top of is probably not the best way of characterizing Xen's interaction with the dom0 OS, in view of the fact that the dom0 kernel runs on the hypervisor, but it is a convenient and frequently used phrase. We beg your patience, Constant Reader.*

Installing CentOS

First, we'll install CentOS in a completely ordinary way. Put the install medium in the drive, boot from it, and install it according to your preference. We opted to accept the default partitioning, which creates a small */boot* partition and devotes the rest of the drive to an LVM group, with a logical volume for swap and a volume for root. We also accepted the default configuration for the GRUB boot loader and the default network config.

NOTE *Now would also be a good time to make sure you have some sort of Internet access.*

Set your time zone and enter a root password. We're just running through the standard CentOS install process at this point—it's probably familiar territory. Follow the prompts as usual.

Next comes package selection. We chose the **virtualization server** package group, since that's the one that includes the Xen hypervisor and supporting tools, and left the rest blank. If you'd like to, you can also choose other package groups to install, like the GNOME desktop or server-gui set of packages, without modifying any of the steps in this section.

Select **Next**. Now the machine will install the packages you've selected. This may take a while, varying with package selection and install medium. It took us about 15 minutes to install from a DVD. When that's done, the machine will reboot and give you the chance to do postinstall configuration— firewall, services, SELinux, and so on.

At this point you may wish to do other system configuration related stuff, not directly related to Xen. Feel free.

Now, we're ready to create a virtual machine. But first let's look at Xen's boot messages and get familiar with the Xen environment.

Booting with Xen features extra Xen-specific boot output, as shown in Figure 2-1.

Figure 2-1: Success! The Xen kernel wants to have a conversation with us.

After GRUB loads, it loads the Xen hypervisor, which then takes control of the hardware and outputs its initialization lines (starting with (XEN)). Then it loads the dom0 kernel, which takes over and spews the familiar Linux boot messages that we know and tolerate. (Note that you may not see these messages if you're using the VGA console, since they go by rather quickly. You can type xm dmesg to see them at any time.)

After the system boots, you should be looking at the normal login prompt, with nary a sign that you're running in a Xen virtual machine. (Albeit a specially privileged virtual machine.) Now would be a great time to log in, if you haven't already.

Getting Familiar with Your Xen System

Before we start creating virtual machines, let's take a brief look at the Xen configuration files in the dom0. We'll be referring to these a lot in future chapters, so now might be a good time to take a quick tour.

First, there's the Xen configuration directory, */etc/xen*. Most, though not all, of the Xen configuration happens via files here or in the *scripts* subdirectory.

The main Xen config file is *xend-config.sxp*. This where you'd perform tasks like enabling migration or specifying the network backend. For now, we'll be content with the defaults.

NOTE   *If you're planning on using this Xen installation for anything besides this walk-through, now is a good time to set the* (dom-min-mem) *option in* xend-config.sxp *to something sensible. We use* (dom-min-mem 1024)*. See Chapter 14 for more details.*

The */etc/xen/scripts* directory contains scripts to handle tasks like setting up virtual devices.

Finally, domain configuration files live in */etc/xen*. For example, you can take a look at *xmexample1* to see a liberally commented sample config.

The */etc/init.d* directory contains scripts to start and stop Xen-related services. The Xen control daemon, xend, runs as a standard service from the */etc/init.d/xend* script. Although you probably won't need to modify it, this can be a handy place to change xend's parameters. It's also the easiest way to restart xend, by running /etc/init.d/xend restart. The *xendomains* script may also be of interest—it automatically saves domains when the system shuts down and restores them when it boots up.

There's also */boot/grub/menu.lst*. This file tells the bootloader, GRUB, to boot the Xen kernel, relegating the dom0 Linux kernel to a "module" line. Here you'd change the boot parameters for both Xen and Linux. For example, you might want to specify a fixed memory allocation for dom0 using the dom0_mem hypervisor option, or increase the number of network loopback devices via the Linux nloopbacks option.

domU data itself, if you're using file-backed virtual disks under CentOS and following the default prompts for virt-install, resides in */var/lib/xen/images*. Other distros and frontends are likely to have different defaults.

Management with xm

The main command that you'll use to interact with Xen is xm. This tool has a wide variety of subcommands. First, since we're still looking around the environment, try xm list:

```
# xm list
Name                                ID Mem(MiB) VCPUs State   Time(s)
Domain-0                             0     934     2 r-----    37.6
```

The output of xm list shows the running domains and their attributes. Here we see that only one domain is running, Domain-0 (abbreviated *dom0* throughout the book) with ID 0, 934MiB of memory, and two VCPUS. It's in the "running" state and has used 37.6 seconds of CPU time since boot.

NOTE *Red Hat doesn't officially support* xm, *although they unofficially expect it to continue working through RHEL 5.x. For this reason,* xm's *documentation may advertise capabilities that don't work on RHEL or CentOS. The supported management tool on RHEL and friends is* virsh, *for virtualization shell.*

You might also try xm info for more information on the hypervisor. We'll introduce more xm subcommands in later chapters, and there's a complete list in Appendix A.

Making a DomU

For the moment, since we want to create a domU, the xm subcommand we're most interested in is create. However, before we can create a domain, we need to create an OS image for it to boot from and use as storage.

Because this is an initial walk-through, we're going to install our Xen image using Red Hat's virt-install tool. For information on building your own domU images, take a look at Chapter 3.

Begin by starting virt-install. It'll start in interactive mode, and have a bit of a conversation with you, as shown. Our inputs are shown in bold. (If you decided to install the GUI, you can also use the graphical virt-manager tool. The prompts will look very similar.)

```
# virt-install

What is the name of your virtual machine? prospero
How much RAM should be allocated (in megabytes)? 256
What would you like to use as the disk (file path)? /var/lib/xen/images/prospero.img
How large would you like the disk (/var/lib/xen/images/prospero.img) to be (in gigabytes)? 4
Would you like to enable graphics support? (yes or no) no
What is the install location? http://mirrors.kernel.org/centos/5/os/i386
```

The machine then begins an interactive network install of CentOS. We won't go into the details of its operation for now—suffice it to say that great pains have been taken to preserve the appearance of installing an OS on a physical machine. As such, the install process should eerily resemble the one we performed at the start of this chapter. Follow its prompts. (For the curious, we discuss virt-install and its accompanying tools more thoroughly in Chapters 3 and 6.)

Once you've made your selections and gone through the install, the machine will reboot. Log in, and then shut the machine down via shutdown -h now (remember, it's an ordinary Linux box) so that we can look a bit more at things from the dom0 end.

Anatomy of a Domain Configuration File

Let's take a moment to examine the config file that virt-install generated for us. As we've mentioned already, the config file is *etc/xen/<domain name>* by convention.

```
# cat /etc/xen/prospero
name = "prospero"
uuid = "9f5b38cd-143d-77ce-6dd9-28541d89c02f"
maxmem = 256
memory = 256
vcpus = 1
bootloader = "/usr/bin/pygrub"
on_poweroff = "destroy"
on_reboot = "restart"
on_crash = "restart"
vfb = [   ]
disk = [ "tap:aio:/opt/xen/images/prospero.img,xvda,w" ]
vif = [ "mac=00:16:3e:63:b7:a0,bridge=xenbr0" ]
```

As you see, the file consists of simple name=value pairs, with Python-style lists in square brackets. Note the values that we specified in the virt-install session, plugged into appropriate places—the name, the memory amount, and the disk image. virt-install also fills in some network configuration, specifying a MAC address and dom0-level bridge device.

We'll examine many of the config file parameters more deeply in subsequent chapters. For now, let's just move on to seeing the effects of these values on our domain.

Configuring the DomU

Finally, start the image! We'll run xm with the create subcommand, which expects a config file name as an argument. We can omit the path, since it defaults to looking in *etc/xen*.

```
# xm create -c prospero
```

Since we passed the -c option to xm create, it'll immediately connect us to the domain's console, so that we can interact with the bootloader. Hit ENTER to boot with default options, and watch it go.

Once it boots, you should be looking at the console of a shiny new Xen domU, as illustrated in Figure 2-2. Log in as root and frolic.

Start by looking at the output of the dmesg command within the domU. Note that the disk and network devices are Xen's special paravirtualized devices.

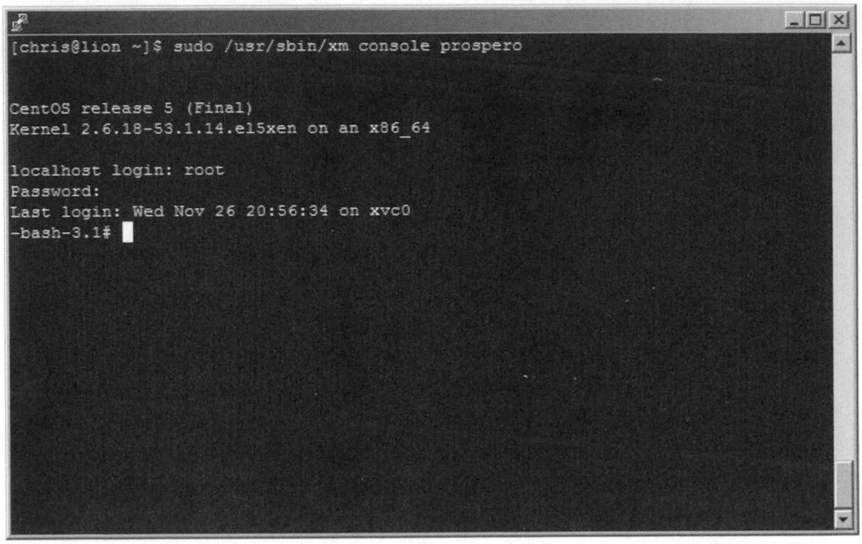

Figure 2-2: We assure you that this is the domU's console.

You can also take a look at the domU's networking, which is essentially indistinguishable from that of a normal Linux system:

```
# ifconfig eth0
eth0      Link encap:Ethernet  HWaddr 00:16:3E:63:B7:A0
          inet addr:216.218.223.74  Bcast:216.218.223.127  Mask:255.255.255.192
          inet6 addr: 2001:470:1:41:a800:ff:fe53:314a/64 Scope:Global
          inet6 addr: fe80::a800:ff:fe53:314a/64 Scope:Link
          UP BROADCAST RUNNING MULTICAST  MTU:1500  Metric:1

          RX packets:73650errors:0 dropped:0 overruns:0 frame:0
          TX packets:49731 errors:0 dropped:0 overruns:0 carrier:0
          collisions:0 txqueuelen:1000
          TX bytes:106033983 (101.1 MiB)     RX bytes:2847950 (2.7 MiB)
```

Note that we're using standard commands—one of the major features of Xen is that most of the management takes place via familiar Linux commands. This makes it easy to customize your Xen environment, usually by making changes to the support scripts. Furthermore, standard commands will generally behave in expected ways—for example, you can give yourself a new IP address via ifconfig, and it'll work just as it would on a physical machine.[2]

Let's return to the dom0 for a moment, just to take a look at the running domain from outside. To break out of the domU's console, type CTRL-]. You can reconnect at any time by running xm console <domU name or id> from the dom0.

---

[2] The administrator can disable this, however. You'll still be able to change the IP from the domU, but the dom0 will block traffic from the new IP. See Chapter 5 for details.

Now that we're back in the dom0, we can note that our new domain shows up in xm list, consuming memory and CPU time:

```
# xm list
Name                                ID Mem(MiB) VCPUs State   Time(s)
Domain-0                             0      739     2 r-----   136.7
prospero                             1      255     1 -b----   116.1
```

And that it's got a visible network device:

```
# ifconfig vif1.0
vif1.0    Link encap:Ethernet  HWaddr FE:FF:FF:FF:FF:FF
          inet6 addr: fe80::fcff:ffff:feff:ffff/64 Scope:Link
          UP BROADCAST RUNNING NOARP  MTU:1500  Metric:1
          RX packets:49731 errors:0 dropped:0 overruns:0 frame:0
          TX packets:73650 errors:0 dropped:0 overruns:0 carrier:0
          collisions:0 txqueuelen:32
          RX bytes:2847950 (2.7 MiB)  TX bytes:106033983 (101.1 MiB)
```

Some points to mention about the network device: First, it's got a dummy MAC address. You can see the actual MAC address of the virtual Ethernet device from within the domU. Second, the counters are reversed—the domain's actually downloaded 100MiB, and transmitted 2.7. Third, both IPv4 and IPv6 "just work" with the default setup. We go into further detail in Chapter 5.

From here you can treat the domain just like any other Linux box. You can set up users on it, SSH into it, or access its console via xm console. You can reboot it via the xm reboot command, and shut it down using xm shutdown.

You're Finished. Have a Cookie.

Now that you've got a domain, read the next chapter.

If it didn't work . . . what a fabulous opportunity to examine Chapter 15. We are sorry. Please email us and mention that our directions need work.

3

PROVISIONING DOMUS

You can suck Linux right out of the air, as it were, by downloading the right files and
putting them in the right places, but there probably are not more than a few hundred
people in the world who could create a functioning Linux system in that way.
—*Neal Stephenson,* In the Beginning Was the Command Line

Up until now, we've focused on administering the dom0, leaving the specifics of domU
creation up to the virt-install tool. However,
you'll probably need to build a domU image from
scratch on occasion. There are plenty of good reasons
for this—perhaps you want an absolutely minimal
Linux environment to use as a base for virtual private server (VPS) hosting
setups. Maybe you're deploying some custom application—a *server appliance*—
using Xen. It might just seem like a good way to keep systems patched.
Possibly you need to create Xen instances without the benefit of a network
connection.

Just as there are many reasons to want custom filesystem images, there
are many ways to make the images. We'll give detailed instructions for some
that we use frequently, and briefly mention some others, but it would be
impossible to provide an exhaustive list (and very boring besides). The goal
of this chapter is to give you an idea of the range of options you have in
provisioning domU filesystems, a working knowledge of the principles, and
just enough step-by-step instruction to get familiar with the processes.

A Basic DomU Configuration

All of the examples that we're presenting here should work with a basic—in fact, downright skeletal—domU config file. Something along the lines of this should work:

```
kernel = /boot/vmlinuz-2.6-xen.gz
vif = ['']
disk = ['phy:/dev/targetvg/lv,sda,w']
```

This specifies a kernel, a network interface, and a disk, and lets Xen use defaults for everything else. Tailor the variables, such as volume group and kernel name, to your site. As we mention elsewhere, we recommend including other variables, such as a MAC and IP address, but we'll omit them during this chapter for clarity so we can focus on creating domU images.

NOTE *This doesn't include a ramdisk. Either add a* ramdisk= *line or include* xenblk *(and* xennet *if you plan on accessing the network before modules are available) in your kernel. When we compile our own kernels, we usually include the* xenblk *and* xennet *drivers directly in the kernel. We only use a ramdisk to satisfy the requirements of the distro kernels.*

If you're using a modular kernel, which is very likely, you'll also need to ensure that the kernel has a matching set of modules that it can load from the domU filesystem. If you're booting the domU using the same kernel as the dom0, you can copy over the modules like this (if the domU image is mounted on */mnt*):

```
# mkdir -p /mnt/lib/modules
# cp -a /lib/modules/`uname -r` /mnt
```

Note that this command only works if the domU kernel is the same as the dom0 kernel! Some install procedures will install the correct modules automatically; others won't. No matter how you create the domU, remember that modules need to be accessible from the domU, even if the kernel lives in the dom0. If you have trouble, make sure that the kernel and module versions match, either by booting from a different kernel or copying in different modules.

Selecting a Kernel

Traditionally, one boots a domU image using a kernel stored in the dom0 filesystem, as in the sample config file in the last section. In this case, it's common to use the same kernel for domUs and the dom0. However, this can lead to trouble—one distro's kernels may be too specialized to work properly with another distro. We recommend either using the proper distro kernel, copying it into the dom0 filesystem so the domain builder can find it, or compiling your own generic kernel.

Another possible choice is to download Xen's binary distribution, which includes precompiled domU kernels, and extracting an appropriate domU kernel from that.

Alternatively (and this is the option that we usually use when dealing with distros that ship Xen-aware kernels), you can bypass the entire problem of kernel selection and use PyGRUB to boot the distro's own kernel from within the domU filesystem. For more details on PyGRUB, see Chapter 7. PyGRUB also makes it more intuitive to match modules to kernels by keeping both the domU kernel and its corresponding modules in the domU.

Quick-and-Dirty Install via tar

Let's start by considering the most basic install method possible, just to get an idea of the principles involved. We'll generate a root filesystem by copying files out of the dom0 (or an entirely separate physical machine) and into the domU. This approach copies out a filesystem known to work, requires no special tools, and is easy to debug. However, it's also likely to pollute the domU with a lot of unnecessary stuff from the source system and is kind of a lot of work.

A good set of commands for this "cowboy" approach might be:

```
# xm block-attach 0 duncan.img /dev/xvda1 w 0
# mke2fs -j /dev/xvda1
# mount /dev/xvda1 /mnt
# cd /
# tar -c -f - --exclude /home --exclude /mnt --exclude /tmp --exclude \
    /proc --exclude /sys --exclude /var | ( cd /mnt/ ; tar xf - )
# mkdir /mnt/sys
# mkdir /mnt/proc
```

NOTE   *Do all this as root.*

These commands, in order, map the backing file to a virtual device in the dom0, create a filesystem on that device, mount the filesystem, and tar up the dom0 root directory while omitting */home, /mnt, /tmp, /proc, /sys*, and */var*. The output from this tar command then goes to a complementary tar used to extract the file in */mnt*. Finally, we make some directories that the domU will need after it boots. At the end of this process, we have a self-contained domU in *duncan.img*.

Why This Is Not the Best Idea

The biggest problem with the cowboy approach, apart from its basic inelegance, is that it copies a lot of unnecessary stuff with no easy way to clear it out. When the domU is booted, you could use the package manager to remove things or just delete files by hand. But that's work, and we are all about avoiding work.

Stuff to Watch Out For

There are some things to note:

- You *must* mkdir /sys and /proc or else things will not work properly.

  The issue here is that the Linux startup process uses */sys* and */proc* to discover and configure hardware—if, say, */proc/mounts* doesn't exist, the boot scripts will become extremely annoyed.

- You may need to mknod /dev/xvda b 220 0.

  /dev/xvd is the standard name for Xen virtual disks, by analogy with the *hd* and *sd* device nodes. The first virtual disk is */dev/xvda*, which can be partitioned into */dev/xvda1*, and so on. The command

```
# /mknod /dev/xvda b 220 0
```

creates the node */dev/xvda* as a block device (b) with major number 220 (the number reserved for Xen VBDs) and minor number 0 (because it's *xvda*—the first such device in the system).

NOTE   *On most modern Linux systems, udev makes this unnecessary.*

- You may need to edit */etc/inittab* and */etc/securettys* so that */dev/xvc0* works as the console and has a proper getty.

  We've noticed this problem only with Red Hat's kernels: for regular XenSource kernels (at least through 3.1) the default getty on tty0 should work without further action on your part. If it doesn't, read on!

  The term *console* is something of a holdover from the days of giant time-sharing machines, when the system operator sat at a dedicated terminal called the *system console*. Nowadays, the console is a device that receives system administration messages—usually a graphics device, sometimes a serial console.

  In the Xen case, all output goes to the Xen virtual console, xvc0. The xm console command attaches to this device with help from xenconsoled. To log in to it, Xen's virtual console must be added to */etc/inittab* so that init knows to attach a getty.[1] Do this by adding a line like the following:

```
xvc:2345:respawn:/sbin/agetty -L xvc0
```

  (As with all examples in books, don't take this construction too literally! If you have a differently named getty binary, for example, you will definitely want to use that instead.)

  You might also, depending on your policy regarding root logins, want to add */dev/xvc0* to */etc/securetty* so that root will be able to log in on it. Simply append a line containing the device name, *xvc0*, to the file.

---

[1] getty gives you a login prompt. What, you didn't think they showed up by magic, did you?

Using the Package Management System with an Alternate Root

Another way to obtain a domU image would be to just run the setup program for your distro of choice and instruct it to install to the mounted domU root. The disadvantage here is that most setup programs expect to be installed on a real machine, and they become surly and uncooperative when forced to deal with paravirtualization.

Nonetheless, this is a viable process for most installers, including both RPM and Debian-based distros. We'll describe installation using both Red Hat's and Debian's tools.

Red Hat, CentOS, and Other RPM-Based Distros

On Red Hat–derived systems, we treat this as a *package* installation, rather than a *system installation*. Thus, rather than using anaconda, the system installer, we use yum, which has an installation mode suitable for this sort of thing.

First, it's easiest to make sure that SELinux is disabled or nonenforcing because its extended permissions and policies don't work well with the installer.[2] The quickest way to do this is to issue echo 0 >/selinux/enforce. A more permanent solution would be to boot with selinux=0 on the kernel command line.

NOTE *Specify kernel parameters as a space-separated list on the "module" line that loads the Linux kernel—either in /boot/grub/menu.lst or by pushing e at the GRUB menu.*

When that's done, mount your target domU image somewhere appropriate. Here we create the logical volume *malcom* in the volume group *scotland* and mount it on */mnt*:

```
# lvcreate -L 4096 -n malcom scotland
# mount /dev/scotland/malcom /mnt/
```

Create some vital directories, just as in the tar example:

```
# cd /mnt
# mkdir proc sys etc
```

Make a basic fstab (you can just copy the one from dom0 and edit the root device as appropriate—with the sample config file mentioned earlier, you would use */dev/sda*):

```
# cp /etc/fstab /mnt/etc
# vi /mnt/etc/fstab
```

---

[2] Although we don't really approve of the tendency to disable SELinux at the first hint of trouble, we decided to take the path of least resistance.

Fix *modprobe.conf,* so that the kernel knows where to find its device drivers. (This step isn't technically necessary, but it enables yum upgrade to properly build a new initrd when the kernel changes—handy if you're using PyGRUB.)

```
# echo "alias scsi_hostadapter xenblk\nalias eth0 xennet" > /mnt/etc/modprobe.conf
```

At this point you'll need an RPM that describes the software release version and creates the yum configuration files—we installed CentOS 5, so we used centos-release-5.el5.centos.i386.rpm.

```
# wget http://mirrors.prgmr.com/os/centos/5/os/i386/CentOS/centos-release-5.el5.centos.i386.rpm
# rpm -ivh --nodeps --root /mnt centos-release-5.el5.centos.i386.rpm
```

Normally, the CentOS release RPM includes the minor version number, but it is hard to find old versions. See the *README.prgmr* file in the same directory for a full explanation.

Next we install yum under the new install tree. If we don't do this before installing other packages, yum will complain about transaction errors:

```
# yum --installroot=/mnt -y install yum
```

Now that the directory has been appropriately populated, we can use yum to finish the install.

```
# yum --installroot=/mnt -y groupinstall Base
```

And that's really all there is to it. Create a domU config file as normal.

Debootstrap with Debian and Ubuntu

Debootstrap is quite a bit easier. Create a target for the install (using LVM or a flat file), mount it, and then use debootstrap to install a base system into that directory. For example, to install Debian Etch on an x68_64 machine:

```
# mount /dev/scotland/banquo /mnt
# debootstrap --include=ssh,udev,linux-image-xen-amd64 etch /mnt http://mirrors.easynews.com/
linux/debian
```

Note the --include= option. Because Xen's networking requires the hot-plug system, the domU must include a working install of udev with its support scripts. (We've also included SSH, just for convenience and to demonstrate the syntax for multiple items.) If you are on an i386 platform, add libc6-xen to the include list. Finally, to ensure that we have a compatible kernel and module set, we add a suitable kernel to the include= list. We use linux-image-xen-amd64. Pick an appropriate kernel for your hardware.

If you want to use PyGRUB, create */mnt/etc/modules* before you run debootstrap, and put in that file:

```
xennet
xenblk
```

Also, create a */mnt/boot/grub/menu.lst* file as for a physical machine.

If you're not planning to use PyGRUB, make sure that an appropriate Debian kernel and ramdisk are accessible from the dom0, or make sure that modules matching your planned kernel are available within the domU. In this case, we'll copy the sdom0 kernel modules into the domU.

```
# cp -a /lib/modules/<domU kernel version> /mnt/lib/modules
```

When that's done, copy over /etc/fstab to the new system, editing it if necessary:

```
# cp /etc/fstab /mnt/etc
```

Renaming Network Devices

Debian, like many systems, uses udev to tie eth0 and eth1 to consistent physical devices. It does this by assigning the device name (ethX) based on the MAC address of the Ethernet device. It will do this during debootstrap—this means that it ties eth0 to the MAC of the box you are running debootstrap on. In turn, the domU's Ethernet interface, which presumably has a different MAC address, will become eth1.[3] You can avoid this by removing */mnt/etc/udev/rules.d/z25_persistent-net.rules*, which contains the stored mappings between MAC addresses and device names. That file will be recreated next time you reboot. If you only have one interface, it might make sense to remove the file that generates it, */mnt/etc/udev/rules.d/z45_persistent-net-generator.rules*.

```
# rm /mnt/etc/udev/rules.d/z25_persistent-net.rules
```

Finally, unmount the install root. Your system should then essentially work. You may want to change the hostname and edit */etc/inittab* within the domU's filesystem, but these are purely optional steps.

```
# umount /mnt
```

Test the new install by creating a config file as previously described (say, */etc/xen/banquo*) and issuing:

```
# xm create -c /etc/xen/banquo
```

---

[3] Or another device, depending on how many Ethernet devices the original machine had.

QEMU Install

Our favorite way to create the domU image—the way that most closely simulates a real machine—is probably to install using QEMU and then take the installed filesystem and use that as your domU root filesystem. This allows you, the installer, to leverage your years of experience installing Linux. Because it's installing in a virtual machine as strongly partitioned as Xen's, the install program is very unlikely to do anything surprising and even more unlikely to interact badly with the existing system. QEMU also works equally well with all distros and even non-Linux operating systems.

QEMU does have the disadvantage of being slow. Because KQEMU (the kernel acceleration module) isn't compatible with Xen, you'll have to fall back to software-only full emulation. Of course, you can use this purely for an initial image-creation step and then copy the pristine disk images around as needed, in which case the speed penalty becomes less important.

QEMU'S RELATION TO XEN

You may already have noted that QEMU gets mentioned fairly often in connection with Xen. There's a good reason for this: The two projects complement each other. Although QEMU is a *pure*, or *classic*, full emulator, there's some overlap in QEMU's and Xen's requirements. For example, Xen can use QCOW images for its disk emulation, and it uses QEMU fully virtualized drivers when running in hardware virtualization mode. QEMU also furnishes some code for the hardware virtualization built into the Linux kernel, KVM (kernel virtual machine)[*] and win4lin, on the theory that there's no benefit in reinventing the wheel.

Xen and QEMU aren't the same, but there's a general consensus that they complement each other well, with Xen more suited to high-performance production environments, and QEMU is aimed more at exact emulation. Xen's and QEMU's developers have begun sharing patches and working together. They're distinct projects, but Xen developers have acknowledged that QEMU "played a critical role in Xen's success."[†]

---

[*] Although we don't cover KVM extensively, it's another interesting virtualization technology. More information is available at the KVM web page, *http://kvm.sf.net/*.

[†] Liguori, Anthony, "Merging QEMU-DM upstream," *http://www.xen.org/files/xensummit_4/ Liguori_XenSummit_Spring_2007.pdf*.

This technique works by running QEMU as a pure emulator for the duration of the install, using emulated devices. Begin by getting and installing QEMU. Then run:

```
# qemu -hda /dev/scotland/macbeth -cdrom slackware-11.0-install-dvd.iso -boot d
```

This command runs QEMU with the target device—a logical volume in this case—as its hard drive and the install medium as its virtual CD drive. (The Slackware ISO here, as always, is just an example—install whatever you like.) The -boot d option tells QEMU to boot from the emulated CD drive.

Now install to the virtual machine as usual. At the end, you should have a completely functional domU image. Of course, you're still going to have to create an appropriate domU config file and handle the other necessary configuration from the dom0 side, but all of that is reasonably easy to automate.

One last caveat that bears repeating because it applies to many of these install methods: If the domU kernel isn't Xen-aware, then you will have to either use a kernel from the dom0 or mount the domU and replace its kernel.

virt-install—Red Hat's One-Step DomU Installer

Red Hat opted to support a generic virtualization *concept* rather than a specific *technology*. Their approach is to wrap the virtualization in an abstraction layer, libvirt. Red Hat then provides support software that uses this library to take the place of the virtualization package-specific control software.[4] (For information on the management end of libvirt, virt-manager, see Chapter 6.)

For example, Red Hat includes virsh, a command-line interface that controls virtual machines. xm and virsh do much the same thing, using very similar commands. The advantage of virsh and libvirt, however, is that the virsh interface will remain consistent if you decide to switch to another virtualization technology. Right now, for example, it can control QEMU and KVM in addition to Xen using a consistent set of commands.

The installation component of this system is virt-install. Like virsh, it builds on libvirt, which provides a platform-independent wrapper around different virtualization packages. No matter which virtualization backend you're using, virt-install works by providing an environment for the standard network install method: First it asks the user for configuration information, then it writes an appropriate config file, makes a virtual machine, loads a kernel from the install medium, and finally bootstraps a network install using the standard Red Hat installer, anaconda. At this point anaconda takes over, and installation proceeds as normal.

Unfortunately, this means that virt-install only works with network-accessible Red Hat–style directory trees. (Other distros don't have the install layout that the installer expects.) If you're planning to standardize on Red Hat, CentOS, or Fedora, this is okay. Otherwise, it could be a serious problem.

Although virt-install is usually called from within Red Hat's virt-manager GUI, it's also an independent executable that you can

---

[4] There's nothing *inherently* Red Hat–specific about libvirt, but Red Hat is currently driving its adoption. See *http://libvirt.org/* for more information.

use manually in an interactive or scripted mode. Here's a sample virt-install session, with our inputs in bold.

```
# /usr/sbin/virt-install

Would you like a fully virtualized guest (yes or no)?  This will allow you to
run unmodified operating systems. no

What is the name of your virtual machine? donalbain

How much RAM should be allocated (in megabytes)? 512

What would you like to use as the disk (path)? /mnt/donalbain.img

How large would you like the disk (/mnt/donalbain.img) to be (in gigabytes)? 4

Would you like to enable graphics support? (yes or no) no

What is the install location?
ftp://mirrors.easynews.com/linux/centos/4/os/i386/
```

Most of these inputs are self-explanatory. Note that the install location can be *ftp://*, *http://*, *nfs:*, or an SSH-style path (*user@host:/path*). All of these can be local if necessary—a local FTP or local HTTP server, for example, is a perfectly valid source. *Graphics support* indicates whether to use the virtual framebuffer—it tweaks the vfb= line in the config file.

Here's the config file generated from that input:

```
name = "donalbain"
memory = "512"
disk = ['tap:aio:/mnt/donalbain.img,xvda,w', ]
vif = [ 'mac=00:16:3e:4b:af:c2, bridge=xenbr0', ]
uuid = "162910c8-2a0c-0333-2349-049e8e32ba90"
bootloader = "/usr/bin/pygrub"
vcpus = 1
on_reboot = 'restart'
on_crash  = 'restart'
```

There are some niceties about virt-install's config file that we'd like to mention. First, note that virt-install accesses the disk image using the tap driver for improved performance. (For more details on the tap driver, see Chapter 4.)

It also exports the disk as xvda to the guest operating system, rather than as a SCSI or IDE device. The generated config file also includes a randomly generated MAC for each vif, using the 00:16:3e prefix assigned to Xen. Finally, the image boots using PyGRUB, rather than specifying a kernel within the config file.

Converting VMware Disk Images

One of the great things about virtualization is that it allows people to distribute *virtual appliances*—complete, ready-to-run, preconfigured OS images. VMware has been pushing most strongly in that direction, but with a little work, it's possible to use VMware's prebuilt virtual machines with Xen.

PYGRUB, PYPXEBOOT, AND FRIENDS

The principle behind PyGRUB, pypxeboot, and similar programs is that they allow Xen's domain builder to load a kernel that isn't directly accessible from the dom0 filesystem. This, in turn, improves Xen's simulation of a real machine. For example, an automated provisioning tool that uses PXE can provision Xen domains without modification. This becomes especially important in the context of domU images because it allows the image to be a self-contained package—plop a generic config file on top, and it's ready to go.

Both PyGRUB and pypxeboot take the place of an analogous utility for physical machines: GRUB and PXEboot, respectively. Both are emulations written in Python, specialized to work with Xen. Both acquire the kernel from a place where the ordinary loader would be unable to find it. And both can help you, the hapless Xen administrator, in your day-to-day life.

For more notes on setting up PyGRUB, see Chapter 7. For more on pypxeboot, see "Installing pypxeboot" on page 38.

Other virtualization providers, by and large, use disk formats that do more than Xen's—for example, they include configuration or provide snapshots. Xen's approach is to leave that sort of feature to standard tools in the dom0. Because Xen uses open formats and standard tools whenever possible, its disk images are simply . . . filesystems.[5]

Thus, the biggest part of converting a virtual appliance to work with Xen is in converting over the disk image. Fortunately, qemu-img supports most of the image formats you're likely to encounter, including VMware's *.vmdk*, or Virtual Machine Disk format.

The conversion process is pretty easy. First, get a VMware image to play with. There are some good ones at *http://www.vmware.com/appliances/directory/*.

Next, take the image and use qemu-img to convert it to a QCOW or raw image:

```
# qemu-img convert foo.vmdk -o qcow hecate.qcow
```

This command duplicates the contents of *foo.vmdk* in a QCOW image (hence the -o qcow, for output format) called *hecate.qcow*. (*QCOW*, by the way, is a disk image format that originates with the QEMU emulator. It supports AES encryption and transparent decompression. It's also supported by Xen. More details on using QCOW images with Xen are in Chapter 4.) At this

---

[5] Except when they're QCOW images. Let's ignore that for now.

point you can boot it as usual, loading the kernel via PyGRUB if it's Xen-aware or if you're using HVM, or using a standard domU kernel from within the dom0 otherwise.

Unfortunately, this won't generate a configuration suitable for booting the image with Xen. However, it should be easy to create a basic config file that uses the QCOW image as its root device. For example, here's a fairly minimal generic config that relies on the default values to the extent possible:

```
name = "hecate"
memory = 128
disk = ['tap:qcow:/mnt/hecate.img,xvda,w' ]
vif = [ '' ]
kernel = "/boot/vmlinuz-2.6-xenU"
```

Note that we're using a kernel from the dom0 filesystem rather than loading the kernel from the VMware disk image with PyGRUB, as we ordinarily suggest. This is so we don't have to worry about whether or not that kernel works with Xen.

RPATH'S RBUILDER: A NEW APPROACH

RPath is kind of interesting. It probably doesn't merit extended discussion, but their approach to building virtual machines is cool. Neat. Elegant.

RPath starts by focusing on the application that the machine is meant to run and then uses software that determines precisely what the machine needs to run it by examining library dependencies, noticing which config files are read, and so on. The promise of this approach is that it delivers compact, tuned, refined virtual machine images with known characteristics—all while maintaining the high degree of automation necessary to manage large systems.

Their website is *http://rpath.org/*. They've got a good selection of prerolled VMs, aimed at both testing and deployment. (Note that although we think their approach is worth mentioning, we are not affiliated with rPath in any way. You may want to give them a shot, though.)

Mass Deployment

Of course, all this is tied up in the broader question of *provisioning infrastructure* and higher-level tools like Kickstart, SystemImager, and so on. Xen amplifies the problem by increasing the number of servers you own exponentially and making it easy and quick to bring another server online. That means you now need the ability to automatically deploy lots of hosts.

Manual Deployment

The most basic approach (analogous to *tarring up a filesystem*) is probably to build a single tarball using any of the methods we've discussed and then make a script that partitions, formats, and mounts each domU file and then extracts the tarball.

For example:

```
#!/bin/bash

LVNAME=$1

lvcreate -C y -L 1024 -n ${LVNAME} lvmdisk

parted /dev/lvmdisk/${LVNAME} mklabel msdos
parted /dev/lvmdisk/${LVNAME} mkpartfs primary ext2 0 1024

kpartx -p "" -av /dev/lvmdisk/${LVNAME}

tune2fs -j /dev/mapper/${LVNAME}1

mount /dev/mapper/${LVNAME}1 /mountpoint

tar -C /mountpoint -zxf /opt/xen/images/base.tar.gz

umount /mountpoinl

kpartx -d /dev/lvmdisk/${LVNAME}

cat >/etc/xen/${LVNAME} <<EOF

name = "$LVNAME"
memory = 128
disk = ['phy:/dev/lvmdisk/${LVNAME},xvda,w']
vif = ['']
kernel = "/boot/vmlinuz-2.6-xenU"

EOF

exit 0
```

This script takes a domain name as an argument, provisions storage from a tarball at */opt/xen/images/base.tar.gz*, and writes a config file for a basic domain, with a gigabyte of disk and 128MB of memory. Further extensions to this script are, as always, easy to imagine. We've put this script here mostly to show how simple it can be to create a large number of domU images quickly with Xen. Next, we'll move on to more elaborate provisioning systems.

QEMU and Your Existing Infrastructure

Another way to do mass provisioning is with QEMU, extending the QEMU installation we previously outlined. Because QEMU simulates a physical machine, you can use your existing provisioning tools with QEMU—in effect treating virtual machines exactly like physical machines. For example, we've done this using SystemImager to perform automatic installs on the emulated machines.

This approach is perhaps the most flexible (and most likely integrates best with your current provisioning system), but it's slow. Remember, KQEMU and Xen are not compatible, so you are running old-school, software-only QEMU. Slow! And needlessly slow because when a VM has been created, there's nothing to keep you from duplicating it rather than going through the entire process again. But it works, and it works the exact same way as your previous provisioning system.[6]

We'll describe a basic setup with SystemImager and QEMU, which should be easy enough to generalize to whichever other provisioning system you've got in place.

Setting Up SystemImager

First, install SystemImager using your method of choice—yum, apt-get, download from *http://wiki.systemimager.org/*—whichever. We downloaded the RPMs from SystemImager using the sis-install script:

```
# wget http://download.systemimager.org/pub/sis-install/install
# sh install -v --download-only --tag=stable --directory . systemconfigurator
\ systemimager-client systemimager-common  systemimager-i386boot-standard \
systemimager-i386initrd_template  systemimager-server
```

SystemImager works by taking a system image of a *golden client*, hosting that image on a server, and then automatically rolling the image out to targets. In the Xen case, these components—golden client, server, and targets—can all exist on the same machine. We'll assume that the server is dom0, the client is a domU that you've installed by some other method, and the targets are new domUs.

Begin by installing the dependency, systemconfigurator, on the server:

```
# rpm -ivh systemconfigurator-*
```

Then install the server packages:

```
# rpm -ivh systemimager-common-* systemimager-server-* \
    systemimager-i386boot-standard-*
```

Boot the golden client using xm create and install the packages (note that we are performing these next steps within the domU rather than the dom0):

```
# scp user@server:/path/to/systemimager/* .
# rpm -ivh systemconfigurator-*
# rpm -ivh systemimager-common-* systemimager-client-* \
systemimager-i386boot-initrd_template-*
```

---

[6] This can be made faster by using an HVM domU for the SystemImager install, rather than a QEMU instance. Not *blazing fast*, but an improvement.

SystemImager's process for generating an image from the golden client is fairly automated. It uses rsync to copy files from the client to the image server. Make sure the two hosts can communicate over the network. When that's done, run on the client:

```
# si_prepareclient --server <server address>
```

Then run on the server:

```
# si_getimage --golden_client <client address> --image porter --exclude /mnt
```

The server will connect to the client and build the image, using the name *porter*.

Now you're ready to configure the server to actually serve out the image. Begin by running the si_mkbootserver script and answering its questions. It'll configure DHCP and TFTP for you.

```
# si_mkbootserver
```

Then answer some more questions about the clients:

```
# si_mkclients
```

Finally, use the provided script to enable netboot for the requisite clients:

```
# si_mkclientnetboot --netboot --clients lennox rosse angus
```

And you're ready to go. Boot the QEMU machine from the emulated network adapter (which we've left unspecified on the command line because it's active by default):

```
# qemu --hda /xen/lennox/root.img --boot n
```

Of course, after the clients install, you will need to create domU configurations. One way might be to use a simple script (in Perl this time, for variety):

```perl
#!/usr/bin/perl
$name = $ARGV[0];
open(XEN, '>', "/etc/xen/$name");
print XEN <<CONFIG;
kernel = "/boot/vmlinuz-2.6.xenU"
memory = 128
name = "$name"
disk = ['tap:aio:/xen/$name/root.img,hda1,w']
vif = ['']
root = "/dev/hda1 ro"
CONFIG
close(XEN);
```

(Further refinements, such as generating an IP based on the name, are of course easy to imagine.) In any case, just run this script with the name as argument:

```
# makeconf.pl lennox
```

And then start your shiny new Xen machine:

```
# xm create -c /etc/xen/lennox
```

Installing pypxeboot

Like PyGRUB, pypxeboot is a Python script that acts as a domU bootloader. Just as PyGRUB loads a kernel from the domain's virtual disk, pypxeboot loads a kernel from the network, after the fashion of PXEboot (for Preboot eXecution Environment) on standalone computers. It accomplishes this by calling udhcpc (the micro-DHCP client) to get a network configuration, and then TFTP to download a kernel, based on the MAC address specified in the domain config file.

pypxeboot isn't terribly hard to get started with. You'll need the pypxeboot package itself, udhcp, and tftp. Download the packages and extract them. You can get pypxeboot from *http://book.xen.prgmr.com/mediawiki/index.php/ pypxeboot* and udhcp from *http://book.xen.prgmr.com/mediawiki/index.php/ udhcp*. Your distro will most likely include the tftp client already.

The pypxeboot package includes a patch for udhcp that allows udhcp to take a MAC address from the command line. Apply it.

```
# patch -p0 < pypxeboot-0.0.2/udhcp_usermac.patch
patching file udhcp-0.9.8/dhcpc.c
patching file udhcp-0.9.8/dhcpc.h
patching file udhcp-0.9.8/README.udhcpc
```

Build udhcp. A simple make followed by make install did the trick for us. Copy pypxeboot and *outputpy.udhcp.sh* to appropriate places:

```
# cp pypxeboot-0.0.2/pypxeboot /usr/bin
# cp pypxeboot-0.0.2/outputpy.udhcp.sh /usr/share/udhcpc
```

Next set up the TFTP server for network boot. The boot server can be essentially the same as a boot server for physical machines, with the caveat that the kernel and initrd need to support Xen paravirtualization. We used the setup generated by Cobbler, but any PXE environment should work.

Now you should be able to use pypxeboot with a domU configuration similar to the following:

```
bootloader="/usr/bin/pypxeboot"
vif=['mac=00:16:3E:11:11:11']
bootargs=vif[0]
```

The regex that finds the MAC address in pypxeboot is easily confused. If you specify other parameters, put spaces between the `mac=` *parameter and the surrounding commas, for example,* `vif = ['vifname=lady , mac=00:16:3E:11:11:11 , bridge=xenbr0'].`

Create the domain:

```
# xm create lady
Using config file "/etc/xen/lady".
pypxeboot: requesting info for MAC address 00:16:3E:11:11:11
pypxeboot: getting cfg for IP 192.168.4.114 (C0A80427) from server 192.168.4.102
pypxeboot: downloading initrd using cmd: tftp 192.168.4.102 -c
get /images/scotland-xen-i386/initrd.img /var/lib/xen/initrd.BEUTCy
pypxeboot: downloading kernel using cmd: tftp 192.168.4.102 -c
get /images/scotland-xen-i386/vmlinuz /var/lib/xen/kernel.8HJDNE
Started domain lady
```

Automated Installs the Red Hat Way

Red Hat uses Kickstart to provision standalone systems. A full discussion of Kickstart is probably best left to Red Hat's documentation—suffice it to say that Kickstart has been designed so that, with some supporting tools, you can install Xen domUs with it.

The tools you'll most likely want to use to install virtual machines are Cobbler and koan. Cobbler is the server software, while koan (*Kickstart over a network*)[7] is the client. With the --virt option, koan supports installing to a virtual machine.

This being a Red Hat tool, you can install it with yum.

No, sorry, we lied about that. First you'll need to add the *Extra Packages for Enterprise Linux* repository to your yum configuration. Install the package describing the additional repo:

```
rpm -ivh http://download.fedora.redhat.com/pub/epel/5/i386/epel-release-5-3.noarch.rpm
```

Now you can install Cobbler with yum:

```
# yum install cobbler
```

Then you'll want to configure it. Run cobbler check, which will give you a list of issues that may interfere with Cobbler. For example, out of the box, Cobbler reported these issues for us:

```
The following potential problems were detected:
#0: The 'server' field in /var/lib/cobbler/settings must be set to something
other than localhost, or kickstarting features will not work.  This should be
a resolvable hostname or IP for the boot server as reachable by all machines
that will use it.
```

---

[7] It begs the question of whether there are non-networked Kickstart installs, but we'll let that slide.

```
#1: For PXE to be functional, the 'next_server' field in /var/lib/cobbler/
settings must be set to something other than 127.0.0.1, and should match the
IP of the boot server on the PXE network.
#2: change 'disable' to 'no' in /etc/xinetd.d/tftp
#3: service httpd is not running
#4: since iptables may be running, ensure 69, 80, 25150, and 25151 are
unblocked
#5: reposync is not installed, need for cobbler reposync, install/upgrade yum-
utils?
#6: yumdownloader is not installed, needed for cobbler repo add with --rpm-
list parameter, install/upgrade yum-utils?
```

After you've fixed these problems, you're ready to use Cobbler. This involves setting up install media and adding profiles.

First, find some install media. Kickstart is a Red Hat–specific package, so Cobbler works only with Red Hat–like distros (SUSE is also supported, but it's experimental). Cobbler supports importing a Red Hat–style install tree via rsync, a mounted DVD, or NFS. Here we'll use a DVD—for other options, see Cobbler's man page.

```
# cobbler import --path/mnt/dvd --name=scotland
```

If you're using a network install source, this may take a while. A full mirror of one architecture is around 5GB of software. When it's done downloading, you can see the mirror status by running cobbler report. When you've got a directory tree, you can use it as an install source by adding a *profile* for each type of virtual machine you plan to install. We suggest installing through Cobbler rather than *bare* pypxeboot and Kickstart because it has features aimed specifically at setting up virtual machines. For example, you can specify the domU image size and RAM amount in the machine profile (in GB and MB, respectively):

```
# cobbler profile add -name=bar -distro=foo -virt-file-size=4 -virt-ram=128
```

When you've added profiles, the next step is to tell Cobbler to regenerate some data, including PXEboot menus:

```
# cobbler sync
```

Finally, you can use the client, koan, to build the virtual machine. Specify the Cobbler server, a profile, and optionally a name for the virtual machine. We also used the --nogfx option to disable the VNC framebuffer. If you leave the framebuffer enabled, you won't be able to interact with the domU via xm console:

```
# koan --virt --server=localhost --profile=scotland --virt-name=lady --nogfx
```

koan will then create a virtual machine, install, and automatically create a domU config so that you can then start the domU using xm:

```
# xm create -c lady
```

And Then . . .

In this chapter, we've gone through a bunch of install methods, ranging from the generic and brute force to the specialized and distro-specific. Although we haven't covered anything in exhaustive detail, we've done our best to outline the procedures to emphasize when you might want to, say, use yum, and when you might want to use QEMU. We've also gestured in the direction of possible pitfalls with each method.

Many of the higher-level domU management tools also include a quick-and-easy way to install a domU if none of these more generic methods strike your fancy. (See Chapter 6 for details.) For example, you're most likely to encounter virt-install in the context of Red Hat's virt-manager.

The important thing, though, is to tailor the install method to your needs. Consider how many systems you're going to install, how similar they are to each other, and the intended role of the domU, and then pick whatever makes the most sense.

4

STORAGE WITH XEN

Throughout this book, so far, we've talked about Xen mostly as an integrated whole, a complete virtualization *solution*, to use marketing's word. The reality is a bit more complex than that. Xen itself is only one component of a platform that aims to free users from having to work with real hardware. The Xen hypervisor virtualizes a processor (along with several other basic components, as outlined in Chapter 2), but it relies on several underlying technologies to provide seamless abstractions of the resources a computer needs. This distinction is clearest in the realm of storage, where Xen has to work closely with a virtualized storage layer to provide the capabilities we expect of a virtual machine.

By that we mean that Xen, combined with appropriate storage mechanisms, provides near total hardware independence. The user can run the Xen machine anywhere, move the instance about almost at will, add storage freely, save the filesystem state cleanly, and remove it easily after it's done.

Sounds good? Let's get started.

Storage: The Basics

The first thing to know about storage—before we dive into configuration on the dom0 side—is how to communicate its existence to the domain. DomUs find their storage by examining the domU config file for a `disk=` line. Usually it'll look something like this:

```
disk = [
        'phy:/dev/cleopatra/menas,sda,w',
        'phy:/dev/cleopatra/menas_swap,sdb,w'
]
```

This line defines two devices, which appear to the domU as `sda` and `sdb`. Both are physical,[1] as indicated by the `phy:` prefix—other storage backends have their own prefixes, such as `file:` and `tap:` for file-backed devices. You can mix and match backing device types as you like—we used to provide a pair of `phy:` volumes and a file-backed read-only "rescue" image.

We call this a line, but it's really more of a stanza—you can put the strings on separate lines, indent them with tabs, and put spaces after the commas if you think that makes it more readable. In this case, we're using LVM, with a volume group named *cleopatra* and a pair of logical volumes called *menas* and *menas_swap*.

NOTE *By convention, we'll tend to use the same name for a domain, its devices, and its config file. Thus, here, the logical volumes* menas *and* menas_swap *belong to the domain* menas, *which has the config file* /etc/xen/menas *and network interfaces with similar names. This helps to keep everything organized.*

You can examine the storage attached to a domain by using the `xm block-list` command—for example:

```
# xm block-list menas
Vdev  BE handle state evt-ch ring-ref BE-path
2049  0     0     4     6       8    /local/domain/0/backend/vbd/1/2049
2050  0     0     4     7       9    /local/domain/0/backend/vbd/1/2050
```

Now, armed with this knowledge, we can move on to creating backing storage in the dom0.

Varying Types of Storage

It should come as little surprise, this being the world of open source, that Xen supports many different storage options, each with its own strengths, weaknesses, and design philosophy. These options broadly fall into the categories of *file based* and *device based*.

---

[1] As you may gather, a *physical* device is one that can be accessed via the block device semantics, rather than necessarily a discrete piece of hardware. The prefix instructs Xen to treat the device as a basic block device, rather than providing the extra translation required for a file-backed image.

Xen can use a *file* as a block device. This has the advantage of being simple, easy to move, mountable from the host OS with minimal effort, and easy to manage. It also used to be very slow, but this problem has mostly vanished with the advent of the blktap driver. The file-based block devices differ in the means by which Xen accesses them (basic loopback versus blktap) and the internal format (AIO, QCOW, etc.).

Xen can also perform I/O to a *physical* device. This has the obvious drawback of being difficult to scale beyond your ability to add physical devices to the machine. The physical device, however, can be anything the kernel has a driver for, including hardware RAID, fibre channel, MD, network block devices, or LVM. Because Xen accesses these devices via DMA (direct memory access) between the device driver and the Xen instance, mapping I/O directly into the guest OS's memory region, a domU can access physical devices at near-native speeds.

No matter what, though, all storage backends look the same from within the Xen virtual domain. The hypervisor exports a Xen VBD (virtual block device) to the domU, which in turn presents the device to the guest OS with an administrator-defined mapping to traditional Unix device nodes. Usually this will be a device of the form hdx or sdx, although many distros now use xvdx for *xen virtual disk*. (The hd and sd devices generally work, as well.)

We recommend blktap (a specialized form of file backend) and LVM for storage backends. These both work, offer good manageability, can be resized and moved freely, and support some mechanism for the sort of things we expect of filesystems now that we Live In The Future. blktap is easy to set up and good for testing, while LVM is scalable and good for production.

None of this is particularly Xen-specific. LVM is actually used (outside of Xen) by default for the root device on many distros, notably Red Hat, because of the management advantages that come with an abstracted storage layer. blktap is simply a Xen-specific mechanism for using a file as a block device, just like the traditional block loop driver. It's superior to the loop mechanism because it allows for vastly improved performance and more versatile filesystem formats, such as QCOW, but it's not fundamentally different from the administrator's perspective.

Let's get to it.

Basic Setup: Files

For people who don't want the hassle and overhead of LVM, Xen supports fast and efficient file-backed block devices using the blktap driver and library.

blktap (blk being the worn-down stub of "block" after being typed hundreds of times) includes a kernel driver and a userspace daemon. The kernel driver directly maps the blocks contained by the backing file, avoiding much of the indirection involved in mounting a file via loopback. It works with many file formats used for virtual block devices, including the basic "raw" image format obtainable by dding a block device.

You can create a file using the dd command:

```
# dd if=/dev/zero of=/opt/xen/anthony.img bs=1M count=1024
```

NOTE   *Your version of dd might require slightly different syntax—for example, it might require you to specify the block size in bytes.*

Now dd will chug away for a bit, copying zeroes to a file. Eventually it'll finish:

```
1024+0 records in
1024+0 records out
1073741824 bytes (1.1 GB) copied, 15.1442 seconds, 70.9 MB/s
```

Thus armed with a filesystem image, you can attach it using the tap driver, make a filesystem on it, and mount it as usual with the mount command.

```
# xm block-attach 0 tap:aio:/opt/xen/anthony.img /dev/xvda1 w 0
# mkfs /dev/xvda1
# mount /dev/xvda1 /mnt/
```

First, we use the xm(8) command to attach the block device to domain 0. In this case the xm command is followed by the block-attach subcommand, with the arguments <domain id to attach the device to> <backend device> <frontend device> <mode> and optionally [backend domain id]. To decompose our example, we are attaching *anthony.img* read/write using the tap:aio driver to */dev/xvda1* in domain 0 using domain 0 to mediate access (because we tend to avoid using non-dom0 driver domains). When the file is attached as */dev/xvda1*, we can create a filesystem on it and mount it as with any block device.

Now that it's mounted, you can put something in it. (See Chapter 3 for details.) In this case, we'll just copy over a filesystem tree that we happen to have lying around:

```
# cp -a /opt/xen/images/centos-4.4/* /mnt/
```

Add a disk= line to the domU config (in our example, */etc/xen/anthony*) to reflect the filesystem:

```
disk = ['tap:aio:/opt/xen/anthony.img']
```

Now you should be able to start the domain with its new root device:

```
# xm create -c anthony
```

Watch the console and bask in its soothing glow.

LVM: Device-Independent Physical Devices

Flat files are well and good, but they're not as robust as simply providing each domain with its own physical volume (or volumes). The best way to use Xen's physical device support is, in our opinion, LVM.

LVM, short for *logical volume management*, is Linux's answer to VxFS's storage pools or Windows Dynamic Disks. It is what the marketing people call *enterprise grade*. In keeping with the software mantra that "all problems can be solved by adding another layer of abstraction," LVM aims to abstract away the idea of "disks" to improve manageability.

Instead, LVM (as one might guess from the name) operates on logical volumes. This higher-level view allows the administrator much more flexibility—storage can be moved around and reallocated with near impunity. Even better, from Xen's perspective, there's no difference between an LVM logical volume and a traditional partition.

Sure, setting up LVM is a bit more work up front, but it'll save you some headaches down the road when you have eight domUs on that box and you are trying to erase the partition for the third one. Using LVM and naming the logical volume to correspond to the domU name makes it quite a bit harder to embarrass yourself by erasing the wrong partition.[2]

---

[2] This example is not purely academic.

QCOW

Up to this point, we've talked exclusively about the "raw" file format—but it's not the only option. One possible replacement is the QCOW format used by the QEMU project. It's got a lot to recommend it—a fast, robust format that supports sparse allocation, encryption, compression, and copy-on-write. We like it, but support isn't quite mature yet, so we're not recommending it as your primary storage option.

Nonetheless, it might be fun to try. To start working with QCOW, it'll be convenient to have QEMU. (While Xen includes some of the QEMU tools, the full package includes more functionality.) Download it from *http://www.nongnu.org/qemu/download.html*. As usual, we recommend the source install, especially because the QEMU folks eschew standard package management for their binary distribution.

Install QEMU via the standard process:

```
# tar zxvf <qemu source package>
# cd <qemu source directory>
# ./configure
# make
# su
# make install
```

QEMU includes the qemu-img utility, which is used to create and manipulate the various sorts of image files that QEMU supports, including QCOW, vmdk, raw, and others.

```
# qemu-img create -f qcow enobarbus.qcow 1024M
```

This command creates an image in QCOW format (-f qcow) with a size of 1,024MB. Of course, you'll want to replace the filename and size with appropriate values for your application.

You can also convert a raw image to a QCOW image with the img2qcow utility, which is included as part of the Xen distribution:

```
# img2qcow enobarbus.qcow enobarbus.img
```

You can use the QCOW image directly as a domain's root disk with the tap driver. Configure the guest domain to use the QCOW image as its root filesystem. In the domain's config file under */etc/xen*, add a disk= line similar to:

```
disk = [ 'tap:qcow:/opt/xen/enobarbus/enobarbus.qcow,sda1,w' ]
```

You can extend this line with another disk, thus:

```
disk = [ 'tap:qcow:/opt/xen/enobarbus/enobarbus.qcow,sda1,w' ,
'tap:qcow:/opt/xen/enobarbus/enobarbus_disk2.qcow,sdb1,w']
```

Basic Setup: LVM

The high-level unit that LVM operates on is the *volume group*, or VG. Each group maps *physical extents* (disk regions of configurable size) to *logical extents*. The physical extents are hosted on what LVM refers to as *physical volumes*, or *PVs*. Each VG can contain one or more of these, and the PVs themselves can be any sort of block device supported by the kernel. The logical extents, reasonably enough, are on *logical volumes*, abbreviated *LVs*. These are the devices that LVM actually presents to the system as usable block devices.

As we're fond of saying, there really is no substitute for experience. Here's a five-minute illustrated tutorial in setting up logical volumes (see Figure 4-1).

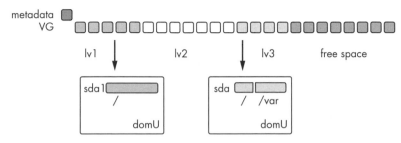

Figure 4-1: This diagram shows a single VG with two PVs. From this VG, we've carved out three logical volumes, lv1, lv2, and lv3. lv1 and lv3 are being used by domUs, one of which treats the entire volume as a single partition and one of which breaks the LV into subpartitions for / and /var.

Begin with some hard drives. In this example, we'll use two SATA disks.

NOTE   *Given that Xen is basically a server technology, it would probably be most sensible to use RAID-backed redundant storage, rather than actual hard drives. They could also be partitions on drives, network block devices, UFS-formatted optical media . . . whatever sort of block device you care to mention. We're going to give instructions using a partition on two hard drives, however. These instructions will also hold if you're just using one drive.*

WARNING   *Note that we are going to repartition and format these drives, which will destroy all data on them.*

First, we partition the drives and set the type to *Linux LVM*. Although this isn't strictly necessary—you can use the entire drive as a PV, if desired—it's generally considered good Unix hygiene. Besides, you'll need to partition if you want to use only a portion of the disk for LVM, which is a fairly common scenario. (For example, if you want to boot from one of the physical disks that you're using with LVM, you will need a separate */boot* partition.)

So, in this example, we have two disks, sda and sdb. We want the first 4GB of each drive to be used as LVM physical volumes, so we'll partition them with fdisk and set the type to 8e (Linux LVM).

If any partitions on the disk are in use, you will need to reboot to get the kernel to reread the partition table. (We think this is ridiculous, by the way. Isn't this supposed to be the future?)

Next, make sure that you've got LVM and that it's LVM2, because LVM1 is deprecated.[3]

---

[3] This is unlikely to be a problem unless you are using Slackware.

```
# vgscan --version
LVM version:        2.02.23 (2007-03-08)
Library version:    1.02.18 (2007-02-13)
Driver version:     4.5.0
```

You might need to load the driver. If vgscan complains that the driver is missing, run:

```
# modprobe dm_mod
```

In this case, dm stands for *device mapper*, which is a low-level volume manager that functions as the backend for LVM.

Having established that all three of these components are working, create physical volumes as illustrated in Figure 4-2.

```
# pvcreate /dev/sda1
# pvcreate /dev/sdb1
```

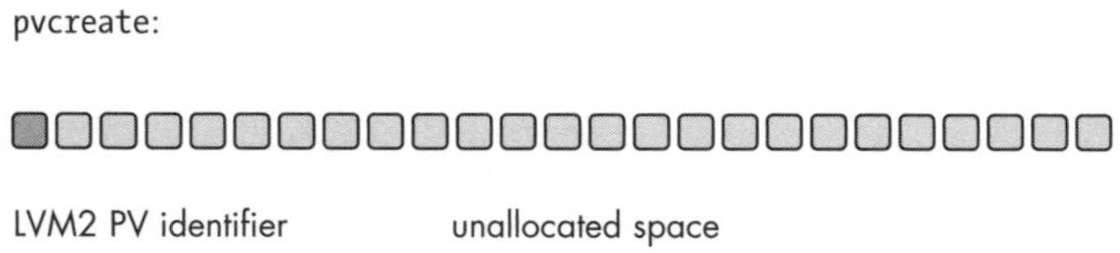

pvcreate:

LVM2 PV identifier   unallocated space

Figure 4-2: This diagram shows a single block device after pvcreate has been run on it. It's mostly empty, except for a small identifier on the front.

Bring these components together into a volume group by running vgcreate. Here we'll create a volume group named *cleopatra* on the devices sda1 and sdb1:

```
# vgcreate cleopatra /dev/sda1 /dev/sdb1
```

Finally, make volumes from the volume group using lvcreate, as shown in Figure 4-3. Think of it as a more powerful and versatile form of partitioning.

```
# lvcreate -L <length> -m1 --corelog -n menas cleopatra
```

Here we've created a mirrored logical volume that keeps its logs in core (rather than on a separate physical device). Note that this step takes a group name rather than a device node. Also, the mirror is purely for illustrative purposes—it's not required if you're using some sort of redundant device, such as hardware RAID or MD. Finally, it's an administrative convenience to give LVs human-readable names using the -n option. It's not required but quite recommended.

vgcreate:

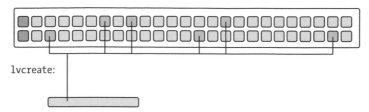

lvcreate:

Figure 4-3: lvcreate creates a logical volume, /dev/vg/lvol, by chopping some space out of the LV, which is transparently mapped to possibly discontinuous physical extents on PVs.

Create a filesystem using your favorite filesystem-creation tool:

```
# mkfs /dev/cleopatra/menas
```

At this point, the LV is ready to mount and access, just as if it were a normal disk.

```
# mount /dev/cleopatra/menas /mnt/hd
```

To make the new device a suitable root for a Xen domain, copy a filesystem into it. We used one from *http://stacklet.com/* —we just mounted their root filesystem and copied it over to our new volume.

```
# mount -o loop gentoo.img /mnt/tmp/
# cp -a /mnt/tmp/* /mnt/hd
```

Finally, to use it with Xen, we can specify the logical volume to the guest domain just as we would any physical device. (Note that here we're back to the same example we started the chapter with.)

```
disk = ['phy:/dev/cleopatra/menas,sda1,w']
```

At this point, start the machine. Cross your fingers, wave a dead chicken, perform the accustomed ritual. In this case our deity is propitiated by an xm create. Standards have come down in the past few millennia.

```
# xm create menas
```

Enlarge Your Disk

Both file-backed images and LVM disks can be expanded transparently from the dom0. We're going to assume that disk space is so plentiful that you will never need to shrink an image.

Be sure to stop the domain before attempting to resize its underlying filesystem. For one thing, all of the user-space resize tools that we know of won't attempt to resize a mounted filesystem. For another, the Xen hypervisor won't pass along changes to the underlying block device's size without restarting the domain. Most important, even if you were able to resize the backing store with the domain running, data corruption would almost certainly result.

File-Backed Images

The principle behind augmenting file-backed images is simple: We append more bits to the file, then expand the filesystem.

First, make sure that nothing is using the file. Stop any domUs that have it mounted. Detach it from the dom0. Failure to do this will likely result in filesystem corruption.

Next, use dd to add some bits to the end. In this case we're directing 1GB from our */dev/zero* bit hose to *anthony.img*. (Note that not specifying an output file causes dd to write to stdout.)

```
# dd if=/dev/zero bs=1M count=1024 >> /opt/xen/anthony.img
```

Use resize2fs to extend the filesystem (or the equivalent tool for your choice of filesystem).

```
# e2fsck -f /opt/xen/anthony.img
# resize2fs /opt/xen/anthony.img
```

resize2fs will default to making the filesystem the size of the underlying device if there's no partition table.

If the image contains partitions, you'll need to rearrange those before resizing the filesystem. Use fdisk to delete the partition that you wish to resize and recreate it, making sure that the starting cylinder remains the same.

LVM

It's just as easy, or perhaps even easier, to use LVM to expand storage. LVM was designed from the beginning to increase the flexibility of storage devices, so it includes an easy mechanism to extend a volume (as well as shrink and move).

If there's free space in the volume group, simply issue the command:

```
# lvextend -L +1G /dev/cleopatra/charmian
```

If the volume group is full, you'll need to expand it. Just add a disk to the machine and extend the vg:

```
# vgextend /dev/cleopatra /dev/sdc1
```

Finally, just as in the previous example, handle the filesystem-level expansion—we'll present this one using ReiserFS.

```
# resize_reiserfs -s +1G /dev/cleopatra/charmian
```

Copy-on-Write and Snapshots

One of the other niceties that a real storage option gives you is copy-on-write, which means that, rather than the domU overwriting a file when it's changed, the backend instead transparently writes a copy elsewhere.[4] As a corollary, the original filesystem remains as a *snapshot*, with all modifications directed to the copy-on-write clone.

This snapshot provides the ability to save a filesystem's state, taking a snapshot of it at a given time or at set intervals. There are two useful things about snapshots: for one, they allow for easy recovery from user error.[5] For another, they give you a checkpoint that's known to be consistent—it's something that you can conveniently back up and move elsewhere. This eliminates the need to take servers offline for backups, such as we had to do in the dark ages.

CoW likewise has a bunch of uses. Of these, the most fundamental implication for Xen is that it can dramatically reduce the on-disk overhead of each virtual machine—rather than using a simple file as a block device or a logical volume, many machines can share a single base filesystem image, only requiring disk space to write their changes to that filesystem.

CoW also comes with its own disadvantages. First, there's a speed penalty. The CoW infrastructure slows disk access down quite a bit compared with writing directly to the device, for both reading and writing.

If you're using sparse allocation for CoW volumes, the speed penalty becomes greater due to the overhead of allocating and remapping blocks. This leads to fragmentation, which carries its own set of performance penalties. CoW can also lead to the administrative problem of oversubscription; by making it possible to oversubscribe disk space, it makes life much harder if you accidentally run out. You can avoid all of this by simply allocating space in advance.

There's also a trade-off in terms of administrative complexity, as with most interesting features. Ultimately, you, the Xen administrator, have to decide how much complexity is worth having.

We'll discuss device mapper snapshots, as used by LVM because they're the implementation that we're most familiar with. For shared storage, we'll focus on NFS and go into more detail on shared storage systems in Chapter 9. We also outline a CoW solution with UnionFS in Chapter 7. Finally, you might want to try QCOW block devices—although we haven't had much luck with them, your mileage may vary.

---

[4] This is traditionally abbreviated CoW, partly because it's shorter, but mostly because "cow" is an inherently funny word. Just ask Wikipedia.

[5] It's not as hard you might suppose to rm your home directory.

LVM and Snapshots

LVM snapshots are designed more to *back up* and *checkpoint* a filesystem than as a means of long-term storage. It's important to keep LVM snapshots relatively fresh—or, in other words, make sure to drop them when your backup is done.[6]

Snapshot volumes can also be used as read-write backing store for domains, especially in situations where you just want to generate a quick domU for testing, based on some preexisting disk image. The LVM documentation notes that you can create a basic image, snapshot it multiple times, and modify each snapshot slightly for another domain. In this case, LVM snapshots would act like a block-level UnionFS. However, note that when a snapshot fills up, it's immediately dropped by the kernel. This may lead to data loss. The basic procedure for adding an LVM snapshot is simple: Make sure that you have some unused space in your volume group, and create a snapshot volume for it.

THE XEN LIVECD REVISITED: COPY-ON-WRITE IN ACTION

The Xen LiveCD actually is a pretty nifty release. One of its neatest features is the ability to automatically create copy-on-write block devices when a Xen domain starts, based on read-only images on the CD.

The implementation uses the device mapper to set up block devices and snapshots based on flat files, and is surprisingly simple.

First, the basic storage is defined with a line like this in the domain config file:

```
disk=['cow:/mnt/cdrom/rootfs.img 30,sda1,w']
```

Note the use of the cow: prefix, which we haven't mentioned yet. This is actually a custom prefix rather than part of the normal Xen package.

We can add custom prefixes like cow: because */etc/xen/scripts/create_block_device* falls through to a script with a name of the form *block-[type]* if it finds an unknown device type—in this case, cow. The *block-cow* script expects one argument, either create or destroy, which the domain builder provides when it calls the script. *block-cow* then calls either the *create_cow* or *destroy_cow* script, as appropriate.

The real setup takes place in a script, */usr/sbin/create_cow*. This script essentially uses the device mapper to create a copy-on-write device based on an LVM snapshot,[*] which it presents to the domain. We won't reproduce it here, but it's a good example of how standard Linux features can form the basis for complex, abstracted functions. In other words, a good hack.

---

[*] More properly, a device mapper snapshot, which LVM snapshots are based on. LVM snapshots are device mapper snapshots, but device mapper snapshots can be based on any pair of block devices, LVM or not. The LVM tools provide a convenient frontend to the arcane commands used by dmsetup.

---

[6] Even if you add no data to the snapshot itself, it can run out of space (and corrupt itself) just keeping up with changes in the main LV.

First, check to see whether you have the driver dm_snapshot. Most modern distros ship with this driver built as a loadable module. (If it's not built, go to your Linux kernel source tree and compile it.)

```
# locate dm_snapshot.ko
```

Manually load it if necessary.

```
# modprobe dm_snapshot
```

Create the snapshot using the lvcreate command with the -s option to indicate "snapshot." The other parameters specify a length and name as in an ordinary logical volume. The final parameter specifies the *origin*, or volume being snapshotted.

```
# lvcreate -s -L 100M -n pompei.snap /dev/cleopatra/pompei
```

This snapshot then appears to be a frozen image of the filesystem—writes will happen as normal on the original volume, but the snapshot will retain changed files as they were when the snapshot was taken, up to the maximum capacity of the snapshot.

When making a snapshot, the length indicates the maximum amount of changed data that the snapshot will be able to store. If the snapshot fills up, it'll be dropped automatically by the kernel driver and will become unusable.

For a sample script that uses an LVM snapshot to back up a Xen instance, see Chapter 7.

Storage and Migration

These two storage techniques—flat files and LVM—lend themselves well to easy and automated *cold migration*, in which the administrator halts the domain, copies the domain's config file and backing storage to another physical machine, and restarts the domain.

Copying over a file-based backend is as simple as copying any file over the network. Just drop it onto the new box in its corresponding place in the filesystem, and start the machine.

Copying an LVM is a bit more involved, but it is still straightforward: Make the target device, mount it, and move the files in whatever fashion you care to.

Check Chapter 9 for more details on this sort of migration.

Network Storage

These two storage methods only apply to locally accessible storage. Live migration, in which a domain is moved from one machine to another without being halted, requires one other piece of this puzzle: The filesystem must be accessible over the network to multiple machines. This is an area of active development, with several competing solutions. Here we'll discuss NFS-based storage. We will address other solutions, including ATA over Ethernet and iSCSI, in Chapter 9.

NFS

NFS is older than we are, and it is used by organizations of all sizes. It's easy to set up and relatively easy to administer. Most operating systems can interact with it. For these reasons, it's probably the easiest, cheapest, and fastest way to set up a live migration-capable Xen domain.

The idea is to marshal Xen's networking metaphor: The domains are connected (in the default setup) to a virtual network switch. Because the dom0 is also attached to this switch, it can act as an NFS server for the domUs.

In this case we're exporting a directory tree—neither a physical device nor a file. NFS server setup is quite simple, and it's cross platform, so you can use any NFS device you like. (We prefer FreeBSD-based NFS servers, but NetApp and several other companies produce fine NFS appliances. As we might have mentioned, we've had poor luck using Linux as an NFS server.) Simply export your OS image. In our example, on the FreeBSD NFS server at 192.0.2.7, we have a full Slackware image at */usr/xen/images/slack*. Our */etc/exports* looks a bit like this:

```
/usr/xen/images/slack  -maproot=0 192.0.2.222
```

We leave further server-side setup to your doubtless extensive experience with NFS. One easy refinement would be to make / read-only and shared, then export read-write VM-specific */var* and */home* partitions—but in the simplest case, just export a full image.

NOTE   *Although NFS does imply a performance hit, it's important to recall that Xen's network buffers and disk buffers are provided by the same paravirtualized device infrastructure, and so the actual network hardware is not involved. There is increased overhead in transversing the networking stack, but performance is usually better than gigabit Ethernet, so it is not as bad as you might think.*

Now configure the client (`CONFIG_IP_PNP=y`). First, you'll need to make some changes to the domU's kernel to enable root on NFS:

```
networking->
networking options->
ip: kernel level autoconfiguration
```

If you want to do everything via DHCP (although you should probably still specify a MAC address in your domain config file), add DHCP support under that tree: `CONFIG_IP_PNP_DHCP:` or `CONFIG_IP_PNP_BOOTP` if you're old school. If you are okay specifying the IP in your domU config file, skip that step.

Now you need to enable support for root on NFS. Make sure NFS support is Y and not M; that is, `CONFIG_NFS_FS=Y`. Next, enable root over NFS: `CONFIG_ROOT_NFS=Y`. In *menuconfig*, you can find that option under:

```
File systems ->
  Network File Systems ->
    NFS file system support ->
      Root over NFS
```

Note that *menuconfig* won't give you the option of selecting root over NFS until you select kernel-level IP autoconfiguration.

Build the kernel as normal and install it somewhere where Xen can load it. Most likely this isn't what you want for a dom0 kernel, so make sure to avoid overwriting the boot kernel.

Now configure the domain that you're going to boot over NFS. Edit the domain's config file:

```
# Root device for nfs.
root = "/dev/nfs"

# The nfs server.
nfs_server = '38.99.2.7'

# Root directory on the nfs server.
nfs_root   = '/usr/xen/images/slack'

netmask="255.255.255.0"
gateway="38.99.2.1"
ip="38.99.2.222"
```

Note that we're just adding extra Linux kernel configuration to the domain config—values not used by Xen will be passed to the kernel command line. You can also explicitly put this configuration in the "extra" parameter. If you want to set the IP address via DHCP, you can replace the last three lines above with:

```
dhcp="dhcp"
```

You can then use DHCP to specify the NFS server and NFS root as well in the usual manner. Boot the domain and you're done. Because the storage is accessible to any machine on the network, Xen's live migration should work as well.

Closing Suggestions

This might seem like a bewildering, or even excessive, variety of storage options, but all of these have their places—be it in a hosting environment, or on the desktop, or in a storage pool for utility computing. The recommendations we've made in this chapter are a start, but in the end the best advice we can offer is to try all of these and see what works best. Find the right trade-off between ease of administration and scalability.

Finally, you can combine and extend many of these options. For example, the Xen LiveCD uses flat images with LVM snapshots. Depending on your application, the best solution might be simple filesystem images or a combination of software RAID and LVM. Keep experimenting and see what fits best. These are all examples of the flexibility of Xen's standards-based architecture, which relies on user-extensible scripts to define available storage using easily understood semantics. In Chapter 5, we'll look at how these same principles apply to Xen's network setup.

5

NETWORKING

So you've got your nice, shiny Xen box all set up and running, and now you want it to talk to the outside world. This seems eminently reasonable. After all, Xen's primary use is server consolidation—and a non-networked server is a contradiction in terms. Well, you're in luck. Xen has a robust and well-tested network foundation, which is versatile and easy to set up.

Like much of the rest of Xen, the networking infrastructure reuses as many standard tools as possible. In this case, Xen uses the standard bridge utilities and the `ip` command[1] all glued together with some clever bash and Python scripts to handle traffic between the dom0 and domU network interfaces.

---

[1] The IP command */sbin/ip* is the modern (unfortunately named) replacement for `ifconfig`. Get it as part of the iproute2 tool set, which offers similar functionality to net-tools but with added features.

As an administrator, your primary interaction with Xen virtual net devices is through the various config files. As you might expect, global parameters and initial setup are mostly handled by directives in *xend-config.sxp*. Domain-specific configuration is done within the domain's config file.

More advanced configuration can be done by modifying Xen's network scripts, stored in */etc/xen/scripts*.

If you are the sort that avoids a reboot at all costs, you can often directly manipulate Xen's network infrastructure while the VM is running through `brctl`, `iptables`, and the `xm` command, but these changes don't always successfully propagate to the domU. We will focus on the "manipulate the config file and reboot the domU" method here because it works in all situations.

Xen's Network Setup Process

Xen runs its network scripts at two points: at xend startup and at domain startup. (There are corresponding scripts for domain shutdown and xend stop.)

The role of the script run at xend startup (usually either `network-bridge` or `network-route`) is to switch from standard, non-Xen networking to Xen-based networking. In the case of `network-bridge`, for example, this script creates a bridge and assigns the physical Ethernet device to it. Then it initializes dom0's networking, creates a virtual interface, adds it to the bridge, and copies the configuration over to the bridged network device.

When Xen starts a domain, it executes the appropriate vif-* script—for example, `vif-bridge` in the case of `network-bridge`. The following shows the various scripts that would be run with the default setup.

```
(xend startup)
    |
    |- network-bridge ❶
        |
        |-xen-script-common.sh
        |-xen-network-common.sh

(xm create)
    |
    |-vif-bridge ❶
        |
        |-vif-common.sh
            |
            |-xen-hotplug-common.sh
            |   |
            |   |-logging.sh
            |   |-xen-script-common.sh
            |   |-locking.sh
            |
            |-xen-network-common.sh
```

Most of these scripts aren't terribly important to our purposes at the moment. For example, *logging.sh* is just sourced to provide a log() function. The main points we're interested in are the ones marked with ❶. These are good scripts to edit or good places to introduce a wrapper script.

These scripts are bash shell scripts (rather than Python, as one might expect from the fact that many of the other Xen configuration files are in Python). They all live in the */etc/xen/scripts* directory by default, alongside scripts to support the other classes of Xen virtual devices.

Defining Virtual Interfaces

All of the Xen networking options work by creating virtual interfaces in dom0 to serve as targets for bridging, iptables rules, and so on. Each virtual interface is defined by a section in the vif= line of the config file, delimited by a pair of single quotes.

Xen 3 supports up to eight virtual interfaces per domain (three prior to 3.1.) For example,

```
vif=['','','']
```

defines three virtual interfaces and tells Xen to configure them with sensible defaults. Note that they're comma-separated *and* delimited, in accord with Python array syntax.

You can examine these virtual interfaces from the dom0 by typing

```
# ifconfig -a
```

This will output information for a bunch of devices of the form

```
vifx.y
```

where *x* and *y* are numbers. (You might see tap devices as well if you're using HVM. Just treat them like vifs for now.)

NOTE   *Under recent Red Hat–derived distros (including CentOS 5.1 and Fedora 8), libvirt will create another bridge called* virbr0. *This bridge is set up for NAT by default and should be considered part of libvirt, rather than Xen. It functions much like Xen's* network-nat *implementation: dom0 runs a dnsmasq server on* virbr0 *and NAT's packets for domUs. It's a sensible default for a desktop, but probably ill-suited to a server. Specify* bridge=xenbr0 *to use Xen's bridge, rather than libvirt's. For the curious,* virbr *is configured by* /etc/libvirt/qemu/networks/default.xml. *You can disable the* virbr *devices by removing the symlink in* /etc/libvirt/qemu/networks/autostart.

Xen's default behavior is to give each virtual interface a name based on the domain number, where *x* is the domain number and *y* is the sequential number of the interface in the domU. For example, vif2.0 is eth0 in domain 2; vif2.1 is eth1 in domain 2. In addition, each physical network card in the machine will show up as a peth device (for *physical Ethernet*). xend creates these virtual interfaces on behalf of domains on domain startup. Thus, you'll see a varying number of them, depending on how many domains are running and how many network devices they have.

As we've stated before, the dom0 is a domain just like the rest, except for its ability to perform control-plane functions and its access to PCI devices. Therefore, vif0.0 is domain 0's virtual eth0 interface, and vif0.1 is eth1 in the dom0. (Xen conveniently creates an alias from ethX to vif0.x.)

NOTE   *veth devices also show up in the dom0. Don't worry about them. They're just used as scratch paper while xend copies information around.*

Ordinarily you can ignore the vifs while interacting with dom0. However, there are a few things to note: Because eth0 in dom0 is actually an alias for a virtual interface, it only sees traffic directed at dom0—domU traffic never reaches the alias. If you want to see the traffic going to the domUs with tcpdump or similar in dom0, you must look at the physical Ethernet card— that is, the appropriate peth interface.

Also, the peth might have a strange MAC, usually FF:FF:FF:FF:FF:FF. Because no packets actually originate or terminate at the peth device, it doesn't need an actual MAC address.

Finally, the virtual devices are provided by the netloop driver, and it defaults to only allowing eight virtual devices at a time. This value can be raised by increasing the value of the nloopbacks parameter:

```
# modprobe netloop nloopbacks=128
```

If it's built into the kernel, you can boot the dom0 kernel with a higher value for loopback.nloopbacks. Simply append netloop.nloopbacks=128 (or a similarly large value) to the module line that loads the Linux kernel in */boot/grub/menu.lst.*

Naming Virtual Interfaces

Accounting for bandwidth usage with this elaborate scheme of virtual inter-faces can be tricky. Because the interface names are based on the domain number, and the domain number changes each time the domain reboots, it's impractical to simply monitor bandwidth using the dom0's internal counters—you'll wind up with stuff like this:

```
vif58.0 RX bytes:12075895 (11.5 MiB)  TX bytes:14584409 (13.9 MiB)
```

One way around this is to name the virtual interfaces so that the name becomes independent of the domain number. You can name virtual interfaces from within the domU config file by specifying the vifname parameter as part of the vif= configuration directive. For example,

```
vif=['vifname=http']
```

would cause the vif in the dom0 to become http rather than vif*x.y*. (Within the domain, of course, it just shows up as eth0.) If the domain has multiple interfaces, specify them as follows:

```
vif=['vifname=http1', 'vifname=http2']
```

As of this writing, you'll then need to stop and start the domain to force it to reread the config file; a simple reboot won't work.

With the vifname specified, we can stop and start the domain. Here we shut down a domain:

```
# xm list http.xen
Name ID Mem(MiB) VCPUs State Time(s)
http.xen 6 96 1 -b---- 11358.0
# xm shutdown http.xen
xenbr0: port 8(vif6.0) entering disabled state
device vif6.0 left promiscuous mode
xenbr0: port 8(vif6.0) entering disabled state
```

Note that the device is simply vif6.0. Now start it up.

```
# xm create http.xen
Using config file "http.xen".
device http entered promiscuous mode
```

```
xenbr0: port 8(http) entering learning state
xenbr0: topology change detected, propagating
xenbr0: port 8(http) entering forwarding state
Started domain http.xen.prgmr.com

# cat http.xen.prgmr.com | grep vifname
vif = [ 'vifname=http, bridge=xenbr0' ]
```

TRUNCATED VIFNAMES

Linux silently truncates the vifname to 15 characters—it'll ignore any input beyond that without raising an error. Thus, for a vif named wiki.xen.prgmr.com,

```
# ifconfig wiki.xen.prgmr.
```

(first 15 characters, including the dot) or

```
# ifconfig wiki.xen.prgmr.com
```

or

```
# ifconfig wiki.xen.prgmr.foo.bar.baz
```

will work, but

```
# ifconfig wiki.xen
```

will fail with an ENODEV (a "no such device" or "device not found" error).
   Note that 15-character vifnames cause problems with some versions of iptables. Keep your vifnames to 8 characters to be safe.

Autoconfiguration

You can just leave the vif= line blank and let xm generate the entire configuration automatically, like so:

```
vif = ['']
```

This scenario has the advantage of allowing the domU administrator to configure the network with complete freedom from within the domU, using whatever tools are most convenient. This is the most accurate way of simulating a physical machine. Xen can generate IP and MAC addresses itself, if need be, and configure them to work without administrator intervention.

However, we don't recommend this because it leaves configuration of the network interface up to the users. At a minimum, you should specify the IP address so that Xen can set up the antispoofing rules to prevent an attacker with a Xen instance faking the source or destination address in his IP header, and specify a MAC address to avoid the possiblity of conflict. An IP or MAC address conflict can take down your network! Avoid it if at all possible.

Specifying a MAC Address

Ordinarily, in the absence of virtualization, hardware manufacturers do a good job of ensuring that each Ethernet device has a unique MAC address. With Xen, however, it becomes the administrator's responsibility to ensure that each virtual interface has a unique hardware address.

First, think back for a moment to the 7-layer OSI network model. Xen interacts with this model at layers 2 and 3; that is, it provides a virtual layer 2 switch with `network-bridge` and functions as an IP router with `network-route`. Both of these layers require the Xen domain to have a unique address. The antispoof rules and ip directive can take care of that for layer 3; however, you are also likely going to want to specify a MAC address.

Xen can simply make one up, but this results in a relatively high probability of a collision. When Xen picks a MAC for you, it starts with the 00:16:3e prefix assigned to Xen by the IEEE registration authority, and it picks the remaining three bytes at random; this means you have 3 bytes of entropy. At 1,000 hosts on one network (most of a /22) this gives you something like a 3 percent chance of a collision. (You can calculate this using the birthday paradox—a good use for your obscure math trivia.) Considering the huge yuckiness of a MAC address conflict, we suggest always manually specifying the MAC address. Do this by changing your `vif=` line to include a `mac=` section, like so:

```
vif= ['ip="10.0.0.1",mac="ae:00:01:02:03:04"']
```

Here at prgmr.com, we pick a 2-byte prefix and append the IP address in hex because the IP address is already unique. There are some important rules when doing this, though: First, the most significant bit should be zero; second, the address should be part of the "locally assigned" block to avoid possible conflicts with real Ethernet hardware. Fortunately, these rules can be distilled into a basic formula: Make the second hex digit of the first octet (*e* in the above example) one of 2, 6, A, or E. (Of course, you can avoid having to worry about this by using the Xen prefix mentioned above.)

Manipulating vifs with xm

Although we ordinarily modify networking settings indirectly through the config files, it's also possible to make changes directly using xm.

The relevant commands are network-attach and network-detach. Using network-attach, you can create a new virtual NIC as if it had been specified in the config file, with options specified on the command line. For example,

```
xm network-attach wiki.xen.prgmr.com script=network-bridge mac=00:16:3e:02:ac:7d bridge=xenbr0
```

If you don't specify the various parameters, Xen will supply default values, just as if they'd been unspecified in the vif= line of the config file.

Similarly, network-detach will detach a vif from the domU and destroy it.

```
xm network-detach wiki.xen.prgmr.com 0
```

The preceding command will remove eth0 from the domain *wiki.xen .prgmr.com*.

Securing Xen's Virtual Network

From a security standpoint, there are two aspects of Xen networking that bear mentioning. First, we want to make sure that the users can't pretend to be someone they're not. This is addressed by specifying an IP address and enabling the antispoofing rules. Second, we want to protect the dom0 while letting traffic through to the domUs. This is easily handled by appropriate iptables rules.

Specifying an IP Address

The antispoofing rules use iptables to ensure that the Xen box will drop packets that don't match the expected address for the vif that they're coming from, thus protecting your network from a rogue domU. The network scripts set this up using iptables to add a rule to the FORWARD chain allowing packets that match that IP address to pass to the domU's network device. (The function that does this is in *vif-common.sh*, for the curious.) For this to work, your FORWARD chain should have a policy of DROP—network-bridge should handle that automatically.

We use antispoofing with network-bridge. network-route adds similar rules. It's known to not work with network-nat.

Add the following to */etc/xen/xend-config.sxp*:

```
(network-script 'network-bridge antispoof=yes')
```

and set the following in the domain config file:

```
vif=['ip=10.0.0.1',bridge=xenbr0]
```

(Use an appropriate IP and bridge for your site, obviously.)

You can also specify a range of IP addresses in CIDR format (*CIDR* stands for *Classless Inter-Domain Routing*); that is, with a slash and the number of bits set in the netmask, in decimal. For example, to allow 10. anything, the previous line could be rewritten as

```
vif=['ip=10.0.0.1/8']
```

This doesn't keep the domU administrator from changing the domU's IP address, but it does block any packets from that changed IP address.

Firewalling the Dom0

With Xen's networking, the INPUT and OUTPUT chains don't affect packets aimed at the domUs. Thus, standard firewalls on the INPUT chain, like Red Hat's, won't affect domU packets. (domUs themselves, of course, can firewall their own virtual network devices as needed.)

NOTE *Many systems, by default, don't send bridge traffic through the FORWARD chain as you would expect—RHEL/CentOS 5.1 is an example of this problem. This causes the antispoofing rules to not work. A simple* echo 1 > /proc/sys/net/bridge/bridge-nf-call-iptables *solves the problem. Add that line to* /etc/xen/scripts/network-bridge *to have it run automatically when Xen sets up its networking.*

The only problem that we've seen with sending domU packets through the FORWARD chain is that, by default, the dom0 includes them in its connection tracking. On heavily loaded machines, the connection table will fill up, and the machine will drop packets. Our solution is to edit the frob_iptable() function in vif-bridge to include a rule like the following:

```
iptables -t raw "$c" PREROUTING -m physdev --physdev-in "$vif" "$@" -j NOTRACK
```

This lets antispoof work and keeps the domU traffic from interfering with the dom0, while allowing the domUs to have unhindered access to their packets.

Networking with network-route

network-route is the original option chosen by the Xen team (and few have used it since). It works by creating an internal IP router, which forwards traffic to and from the guest domains. Note that it doesn't do address translation—for that you'll want network-nat, or virbr. It has largely been superseded by network-bridge, which allows considerably more flexibility.

network-route does have its place, however. For one thing, it is transparent to the upstream network hardware, unlike network-bridge. For another thing, it's much simpler. network-route simply enables IP forwarding and then creates iptables rules in the dom0 to forward traffic to the correct virtual interfaces.

To use `network-route`, just uncomment the lines

```
(network-script network-route)
(vif-script vif-route)
```

and comment out the corresponding `network-bridge` and `vif-bridge` lines. That's really all there is to it. Restart `xend`, and `iptables` will show a new rule that handles forwarding to the `vif`:

```
# iptables -L FORWARD
Chain FORWARD (policy ACCEPT)
target prot opt source           destination
ACCEPT 0     --  192.168.42.190  anywhere PHYSDEV match --physdev-in n1
ACCEPT udp   --  anywhere        anywhere PHYSDEV match --physdev-in n1 udp spt:bootpc dpt:bootps
```

One common "gotcha" with `network-route` is that it only works if the IP address is specified in the `vif=` line—otherwise the script doesn't know what rules to add. So, at minimum, the interface definition for the example above should look like this:

```
vif = ['ip="192.168.42.190",vifname="n1"']
```

Networking with network-bridge

`network-bridge` is the currently accepted standard way of handling networking for guest domains in Xen. It uses the bridge tools in Linux to create a virtual layer 2 switch, to which it "plugs in" Xen virtual interfaces, as shown in Figure 5-1. It has the advantage of working with protocols that expect unadulterated Ethernet frames. This includes AoE, the pre-TCP/IP version of AppleTalk, NetBEUI, IPX, and a host of other protocols that date from the dark ages. It'll also work seamlessly with DHCP, which relies on broadcast packets. It's simple, logical, and robust.

The biggest disadvantage of `network-bridge` (apart from its complexity) is that it tears down and rebuilds the real network interface when `xend` starts. In some scenarios (for example, when dom0 has an NFS root) this can be unacceptable. This isn't a limitation of bridging, per se, only of attaching the bridge to the dom0 network device using the Xen scripts—if a dedicated physical device is used for the bridge, the problem goes away.

Another issue with `network-bridge` is that it places the physical Ethernet device into promiscuous mode. This can be a tremendous resource hog on busy networks because the CPU has to intercept all packets rather than just those intended for its address. Finally, outgoing packets will have a different MAC address from the one on the physical card, which can lead to trouble with, for example, certain wireless networking hardware. This also throws many layer 2 http load balancers through a loop—anything that expects only one MAC address down each Ethernet port will be sorely confused.

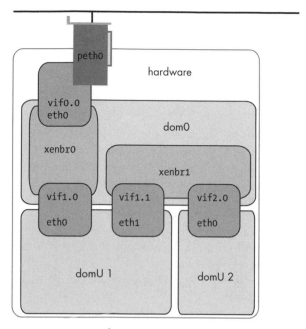

Figure 5-1: Some of network-bridge's capabilities

Even with these caveats, we recommend network-bridge for most Xen servers.

You can start the network-bridge script by hand if you like. For example, to manually create a bridge with the default name xenbr0 attached to eth0, type the following:

```
/etc/xen/scripts/network-bridge {start|stop} vifnum=0
```

NOTE   *If you have vifnum set above nloopbacks, even if you only have one bridge, Linux will complain as if you had more bridges than loopbacks. This is because Xen uses the vifnum to determine the number of the virtual device it uses for the frontend, which presupposes the existence of the preceding virtual devices. Increase nloopbacks, and everyone is happy.*

network-bridge is the default networking option, thus xend shouldn't need any configuration to use it. However, for completeness—to configure Xen to use network-bridge, modify *xend-config.sxp* to include the line

```
(network-script network-bridge)
```

NOTE   *OpenSUSE users might find that NetworkManager interferes with Xen's bridging. To fix this problem, go to **YaST ▸ Network Devices ▸ Network Card** and select the **Traditional Method with ifup** option.*

This script causes Xen to use a bridge setup much like the following:

```
# brctl show
bridge name     bridge id           STP enabled    interfaces
xenbr0          8000.feffffffffff   no             vif0.0
                                                   peth0
                                                   vif9.0
```

xenbr0 is, obviously, the name of the bridge. It bridges dom0's virtual Ethernet interface (vif0.0), the physical Ethernet card, and a domU's virtual interface. We can also see that STP (Spanning Tree Protocol) is disabled. In the default configuration, further domUs will simply have their interfaces added to this bridge.

STP is aimed at preventing loops in the network. You may want to turn STP on if you're doing anything complex with the virtual bridges. If you have multiple bridges and multiple network ports that you're using with Xen, it would probably be a good idea.

To rename the bridge, you can specify the bridge name as an option to the network-bridge script:

```
(network-script 'network-bridge bridge=foo')
```

Note also that network-bridge defaults to binding eth0 to the bridge. To change the physical network card, use

```
(network-script 'network-bridge bridge=foo netdev=eth1')
```

Then the bridge setup becomes

```
# brctl show
bridge name     bridge id           STP enabled    interfaces
foo             8000.feffffffffff   no             vif0.01
                                                   peth01
                                                   vif9.0
```

Networking with network-nat

network-nat is an extension of network-route that incorporates network address translation (NAT for short, or IP masquerade in some contexts).

The network-nat script supplied with Xen works around network-route's problem with DHCP in two ways. First, it can start a local DHCP server (so that guest domains can get addresses because they're now behind a router). If that's undesirable, it can create locally unique IP addresses using the domain ID. Then it sets up a standard iptables rule for IP masq:

```
Dom0 # iptables -t nat -n -L
Chain POSTROUTING (policy ACCEPT)
target prot opt source destination
MASQUERADE 0 -- 0.0.0.0/0 0.0.0.0/0
```

```
Dom0 # iptables -L FORWARD
Chain FORWARD (policy ACCEPT)
target prot opt source destination
ACCEPT 0 -- 10.0.0.0/16 anywhere PHYSDEV
match --physdev-in n1
ACCEPT udp -- anywhere anywhere PHYSDEV
match --physdev-in n1 udp spt:bootpc dpt:bootps
```

When a domain starts, it gets an IP address and adds appropriate iptables rules for itself. Xen passes the address to the kernel using the kernel-level IP autoconfiguration mechanism at boot (and isn't that a mouthful). network-nat can also integrate with your DHCP server.

```
DomU # ifconfig eth0 10.0.2.1/16
DomU # route add default gw 10.0.2.1
DomU # ping 192.168.42.60
PING 192.168.42.60 (192.168.42.60) 56(84) bytes of data.
64 bytes from 192.168.42.60: icmp_seq=1 ttl=63 time=1.94 ms
```

This shows the default configured IP address for eth0 in domain 2. Actual numbers will vary depending on your setup, of course.

Configuration Variables

As we've mentioned, the two basic places where the administrator interacts with Xen's networking are in */etc/xen/xend-config.sxp* and in the domain config file. In each of these, you focus on one line: the (network-script) line in the former case and the vif= line in the latter.

Each of these will fail horribly, without explanation, over trivial errors in syntax. (This is Python, after all. You can put arbitrary Python code right in your config files, if you like. Configuration files should always be written in a language that's Turing-complete. Just ask Eric Allman.)

The network-script line is wrapped in parentheses, with arguments in quotes and separated by spaces. For example, the following is valid:

```
(network-script 'network-bridge bridge=xenbr1')
```

We've already discussed the vif= line a bit. Note that the vif configuration uses a completely different syntax from the network script setting, though: brackets with commas between arguments.

```
vif = ['','bridge=xenbr1','bridge=xenbr2,ip="10.1.2.6"']
```

This line configures three interfaces, the first with default parameters, the second with a bridge argument, the third with bridge and IP. Note the commas between both separate interfaces and separate arguments.

Finally, in some examples you will see a dhcp=yes line. The dhcp= line isn't necessary unless the kernel needs to get its address at boot—for example, if it's mounting its root filesystem over NFS.

Custom Network Scripts

You might be thinking at this point that it's overkill to specify a configuration script in the Xen config file rather than simply selecting among built-in options. Take our word for it: The ability to specify your own network script is fantastically useful. Because Xen's networking is built on standard tools, the scripts are easy to understand and tailor to your particular needs.

The easiest way to do this, and a sufficient method for most configurations, is to create a small wrapper script that calls the standard Xen scripts with appropriate arguments. You can also modify the standard scripts to source additional functions and call those as necessary—for example, to modify firewall rules or attach monitoring scripts.

Multiple-Bridge Setups

Consider a scenario where you want inter-domU communication to occur on a purely virtual network, with a separate interface in each domain to communicate with the outside world.

In that case, you would create a pair of bridges, one with the default Xen setup, bridging the physical interface with the virtual ones, and one that bridges only virtual interfaces. Then you would specify both interfaces in the domain config file and configure them as normal from within the domain or the config file.

The wrapper would look something like this:

```
#!/bin/sh
dir=$(dirname "$0")
"$dir/network-bridge" "$@" vifnum=0
"$dir/network-bridge" "$@" vifnum=1 netdev=dummy0
```

This calls `network-bridge` twice, the first time as normal and the second time with a `netdev` argument, causing `network-bridge` to use a dummy network device rather than a real one.

To tell `xend` to run this script at startup, change the `network-script` line in *xend-config.sxp* as follows:

```
(network-script my-wrapper)
```

Make sure that the `my-wrapper` script is executable, or else nothing will work.

To use these bridges from the domUs, specify the correct bridge in the `vif=` line:

```
vif= ['mac= aa:0:1:2)11",bridge="xenbr1"']
```

Bridged and Routing

A slight modification to this scenario puts the domU communication on its own bridge, which is then routed via iptables rules in the dom0, as shown in Figure 5-2. (Arjen Runsink, who wrote a script that does this, calls this a *brouter*—a portmanteau of bridge and router.)

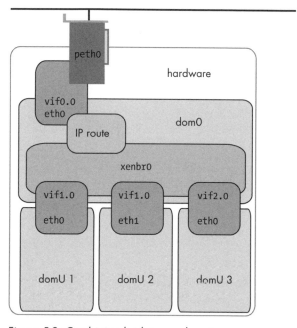

Figure 5-2: Combining bridging and routing

This creates a standard bridge, but it doesn't attach the physical device to it. Instead the bridge gets an IP address and a route. When a domU starts, its vif is attached to the bridge by the ordinary vif-bridge script.

Omitting the standard functions and such, the script looks something like this:

```
#!/bin/sh
dir=$(dirname "$0")
. "$dir/xen-script-common.sh"
. "$dir/xen-network-common.sh"

findCommand "$@"
evalVariables "$@"

op_start () {
    if [ ""${bridge}" = "null" ] ; then
        return
    fi

    create_bridge ${bridge}
```

```
    if link_exists "${bridge}" ; then
        ip address add dev $bridge $bridgeip
        ip link set ${bridge} up arp on
        ip route add to $brnet dev $bridge
    fi

    if [ ${antispoof} = 'yes' ] ; then
        antispoofing
    fi
}

op_stop () {
    ip route del to $brnet dev $bridge
    ip link set ${bridge} down arp off
    ip address del dev $bridge $bridgeip
    brctl delbr ${bridge}
}

case "$command" in
    start)
        op_start
        ;;
    stop)
        op_stop
        ;;
    *)
        echo "Unknown command: $command" >&2
        echo 'Valid commands are: start, stop' >&2
        exit 1
esac
```

We've cut out the show_status function to save space; the full version of this script is available at *http://en.opensuse.org/Xen3_and_a_Virtual_Network*. We've also removed the default values for parameters like $bridgeip because that's site specific, and we removed the declarations for create_bridge and add_to_bridge because those are provided by xen-network-common.

Call this script with a pair of lines like the following in */etc/xen/ xend-config.sxp*:

```
(network-script 'network-virtual bridgeip="10.0.0.1/24" brnet="10.0.0.1/24"')
(vif-script vif-bridge)
```

Further Thoughts

Variants of this same technique can be used to provide logging and accounting on a per-domain basis, or they can set up domain-specific firewall rules just by editing the network scripts. Ultimately, Xen's networking infrastructure is so flexible that you're able to do anything with a domU that you can with the dom0 (or, for that matter, with a non-Xen system), and there are enough script hooks to do it in an automated fashion.

6

DOMU MANAGEMENT: TOOLS AND FRONTENDS

Most of the material in this book focuses on fairly low-level administrative tasks. We've got a couple of reasons for this focus: first, because we feel that it's better to understand what the GUI tools are doing before trusting them with your data,[1] and second, because the add-on tools are not fully developed.

However, the true benefit of Xen is that it allows you to do things with a virtual machine that you can't do—or can't do easily—with a simple collection of physical machines. The main advantage of the more advanced management tools is that they exploit Xen virtualization to improve flexibility.

Besides, it gets kind of tedious to do everything from base principles all the time. In this chapter, we'll take an excursion from our usual fixation on doing things in the most laborious way possible and look at some of the labor-saving innovations available for Xen.

---

[1] A position unlikely to occasion much disagreement among sysadmins.

Broadly, we can categorize the various frontend packages by their intended audience; some tools are for the dom0 administrator and some are for the domU administrator (that is, the *customer* in Xen's computing-service model). The first group tends to focus on provisioning and destroying VMs, and the second group allows users who most likely don't have access to the dom0 to control their own VM at a higher level so they can, for example, give the domain a hard reboot or recover when the domU won't boot at all.

Despite this neat and theoretically useful division of labor, we're going to ignore the second category almost completely. There are two reasons for this: First, most end users won't want to do anything especially complex to their Xen instance. In our opinion, most of the Xen control panels are solutions in search of a problem. Second, almost none of the tools that we've tried in this category seem to have stabilized as of this writing.[2] Instead, we'll focus on the first category: software to simplify your life as a service provider, ranging from the simple to the elaborate. We'll end by briefly discussing the Xen-shell, which is a useful minimal customer-facing tool.

Tools for the VM Provider

When looking for a management tool, as with any piece of software, the first question to ask yourself is, What features do I need? Xen management tools run the gamut from simple provisioning scripts, like Xen-tools, to elaborate data-center-oriented packages, like OpenQRM.

The biggest factor influencing your choice of frontend, assuming that multiple ones provide the necessary functionality, is probably the dom0 operating system. Some frontends, such as Xen-tools, are designed and built with Debian in mind. Some work best with Red Hat. Slackware users, you're still on your own. Although you can install, say, virt-manager on Debian, it would be a difficult process, contrary to the dictates of nature.[3] In this chapter, we're going to focus on each tool in its native environment, beginning with Xen-tools for Debian.

Xen-tools

Xen-tools, at heart, consists of a cross-platform set of Perl scripts for automated installs, so it's fairly distro agnostic. Even though the authors develop on Debian, distribute *.deb* packages, and have an Apt repository, Xen-tools is relatively easy to install on other systems, so we encourage you to try it regardless of which distro you're running. Download a tarball at *http:// xen-tools.org/*.

---

[2] We blame Python's scorched-earth policy toward compatibility.

[3] Of course there are packages, but they're less closely integrated.

Installing Xen-tools

In the interest of keeping everything flowing smoothly, we installed Xen-tools on a Debian machine using Debian's Apt system. Because, like everything Xen-related, Xen-tools is under heavy development, we opted to get the package from the author's own repository to avoid getting an old version.

To do this, add his repo to your */etc/apt/sources.list*. For Etch, we appended:

```
#
#  Steve Kemp's repository:  Etch
#
deb     http://apt.steve.org.uk/etch etch main non-free contrib
deb-src http://apt.steve.org.uk/etch etch main non-free contrib
```

NOTE *Sometimes even the version in Apt is not as current as the one on the website. If all else fails, download the tar package, unpack it, and run make install to install it.*

Then run, as usual:

```
# apt-get update
# apt-get install xen-tools
```

Apt will then work its customary magic, installing the Xen-tools scripts and creating a configuration directory, */etc/xen-tools*.

For usage information, if you have `perldoc`, you can access any of the programs' embedded manual pages by running them with the `--manual` option. For example:

```
# xen-create-image --manual
```

will print out a long and intimidating man page. Don't be discouraged; it's just exposing the bewildering array of options Xen itself makes available. You can simplify things by specifying most of these options ahead of time in the Xen-tools config file rather than by command-line options.

Configuring Xen-tools

So let's make a config file. Trust us, it's much more pleasant to spend a bit of time setting some defaults rather than specifying global options every time you use the command.[4] Put your preferred options in */etc/xen-tools/xen-tools .conf*. We would use something like this:

```
lvm = verona
size = 2Gb
image = full
memory = 128Mb
swap = 128Mb
```

---

[4] Cdrecord, anyone?

```
fs = ext3
dist = sarge

initrd = /boot/initrd.img-2.6.16-2-xen-686
kernel = /boot/vmlinuz-2.6.16-2-xen-686

install-method = debootstrap
```

Fill in appropriate values, as always, and feel free to add from the liberally commented sample config anything that strikes your fancy. Some of these options, like initrd and kernel, specify literal directives that'll wind up in the final domU config file. Of the remaining options, most are self-explanatory; size specifies the filesystem size, swap is the amount of swap the domain will have, and so forth.

Because we've specified an LVM group, domains will be created with LVM volumes as backing store. You can also use filesystem images by specifying dir = /path/ rather than an LVM group. If you do that, make sure that the directory exists, otherwise the image creation step will fail silently and xen-create-image will populate the directory where the filesystem would have been mounted. This is almost certainly not what you want.

Also note the dist= line; this specifies which set of postinstall *hook* scripts xen-create-image will run to configure the new domain. If there isn't a directory under */usr/lib/xen-tools* corresponding to the dist value, xen-create-image will exit with an instructive error message. If you don't want to configure the domain at creation time, you can create an empty directory— say, */usr/lib/xen-tools/plan9*—and pass the name of the distribution (*plan9* in this case) as the dist value.

When you have the config file populated, actually creating domains is so easy as to be almost anticlimactic. Just specify a hostname, preferably fully qualified so that the postinstall scripts can configure the image correctly, on the command line, and the tool will do the rest. For example:

```
# xen-create-image mercutio.prgmr.com
```

NOTE   *Although setting a fully qualified domain name allows the postinstall scripts to handle domain configuration, it can cause trouble with the* xendomains *script on certain Red Hat derivatives, which assumes a domU name no longer than 18 characters.*

With the config file previously shown, this creates two logical volumes, */dev/verona/mercutio.prgmr.com-disk* and */dev/verona/mercutio.prgmr.com-swap*. It then mounts the disk volume and uses debootstrap to install sarge (Debian 3.1). Easy.

Xen tools and RPM-based DomU Images

The first versions of Xen-tools were developed with debootstrap installs of Debian in mind. However, the package has come a long way, and it's been generalized to support virtually every system out there. RPM-based distros are covered via a debootstrap-like tool. Other systems—even non-Linux systems—can be installed by copying a pristine filesystem image or extracting tarballs.

Although older versions of Xen-tools used RPMstrap, which we've used with some success in the past, the author of RPMstrap has ceased to develop it. Accordingly, the Xen-tools author has been working on a replacement called rinse. It's the recommended way of installing CentOS and Fedora with Xen-tools, and it's a fairly neat package by itself.

rinse's home page is at *http://xen-tools.org/software/rinse/*. Download it either from the download page at that site or by adding his apt repository and downloading via your package manager.

A full discussion of rinse's configuration options is probably out of place here. We enjoin you to read the fine manual. However, it works out of the box with an install method for xen-create-image, with a simple command line like the following:

```
# xen-create-image --hostname tybalt.prgmr.com --install-method=rinse
dist=centos-5
```

No problem.

Xen-tools Postinstall

After the image is installed, but before it's started for the first time, xen-create-image does some postinstall work. First it runs some scripts in the mounted domU filesystem to perform setup tasks, like setting the hostname and disabling unneeded gettys. Finally it creates a config file so that you can start the domain.

At this stage you can also have the machine configure itself with a role—specify the --role <script> command-line option to run the corresponding script located in */etc/xen-tools/role.d* at the end of the install, taking the mount point of the domU root filesystem as an argument. The roles that you'll want will depend on your needs. For example, you may want roles that differentiate between web, mail, and dns servers. The Xen-tools distribution comes with some samples that you can build upon.

After populating the domU image, the xen-create-image script will create a configuration file based on a template at */etc/xen-tools/xm.tmpl.* You can also specify a template on the command line using the --template option.

Extending the Config File Template

You can, as you might suppose, edit the template freely. Xen-tools passes options to the setup scripts by reading environment variables, which makes it easy to extend the template by passing in new variables and adding code to interpret them.

For example, because we like to use PyGRUB, we might edit the template by adding a bootloader option right beneath the kernel and initrd sections:

```
{ if ( $bootloader )
  {
    $OUT.= "bootloader       = '$bootloader'";
  }
}
```

Now we can create the image with the additional value specified as an environment variable:

```
# bootloader=/usr/bin/pygrub xen-create-image --hostname tybalt.prgmr.com
--install-method=rinse --dist=centos-5
```

and, as if by magic, the config file will have a bootloader entry.

We could also update the script that parses the config file and have it pass through the value as an environment variable, just as with the other options.

xen-list-images

Having created some domains, whether with xen-create-image or otherwise, it stands to reason that you might want to view a summary of domains that exist on the machine. The Xen-tools suite therefore also includes a tool to list existing domains, xen-list-images. Running it on our test system shows:

```
# xen-list-images
Name: mercutio.prgmr.com
Memory: 128
DHCP

Name: benvolio.prgmr.com
Memory: 96
IP: 192.168.1.93

Name: tybalt.prgmr.com
Memory: 128
DHCP
```

The tool parses Xen config files—both those created by Xen-tools and otherwise—and prints some information.

xen-delete-image

Finally we have xen-delete-image, which does exactly what the name suggests. It'll only work on images that follow the naming conventions used by xen-create-image, that is, it doesn't have the intelligence necessary to parse arbitrary domain definitions. Nonetheless, if you've standardized on Xen-tools or name disks in the format used by Xen-tools, it can be handy.

WARNING   *When run as root, this command will destroy data with no confirmation, even if you've specified the --test option.*

Run xen-delete-image like this, but very carefully:

```
# xen-delete-image --lvm verona mercutio.prgmr.com
```

This will delete *mercutio.prgmr.com-disk* and *mercutio.prgmr.com-swap* from the *verona* VG and delete the config file. If the data source option isn't specified, it defaults to the value in */etc/xen-tools/xen-tools.conf.*

libvirt, virsh, and virt-manager

On the RPM side, including SUSE, CentOS, and Fedora, we have a suite of tools based on libvirt. Although packages are available for Debian-based distros and Solaris, libvirt is primarily developed on, for, and largely by Red Hat, and it shows in the project's focus.

libvirt isn't a management tool per se, but it's worth mentioning here as a Xen frontend, part of a framework that sits in front of Xen and makes management tools easier to develop. The stated goal of the libvirt project (at *http://libvirt.org/*) is to "provide a long-term stable C API for virtualization." In other words, libvirt aims to allow a single tool to control any type of virtualization that libvirt supports, including Xen. This is wonderful, as far as it goes. However, the libvirt-based tools still aren't complete. In particular, their focus on Red Hat is sometimes inconvenient.

libvirt's main advantages are that it integrates very closely with Red Hat's tools and that the management tool, virt-manager, is excellent for interacting with live virtual machines.

The basic libvirt-based tool—or at least the first-generation, proof-of-concept version of this tool—is virsh, or *virtualization shell*. Right now it can perform most of the same operations as xm on Xen, QEMU, KVM, or OpenVZ domains.

This isn't the place to give a complete how-to on virsh; we're writing about Xen, and we've therefore focused on xm. However, virsh is the frontend of choice for Red Hat, so we'll provide some discussion and examples, but we're going to stick to Xen and virsh's capabilities as an xm replacement rather than emphasizing the new features virsh introduces.

The first thing to mention about virsh is that it uses a flagrantly different syntax from xm for domain definitions. virsh has a create command, just as xm does, but it expects an XML file as an argument.

Fortunately, virsh allows you to create the XML definition from a Xen domain. For example, to get an XML definition for the running domain *ophelia*:

```
# virsh dumpxml ophelia
<domain type='xen' id='8'>
<name>ophelia</name>
<uuid>162910c82a0c03332349049e8e32ba90</uuid>
<bootloader>/usr/bin/pygrub</bootloader>
<os>
  <type>linux</type>
  <kernel>/var/lib/xen/vmlinuz.8gmQDM</kernel>
  <initrd>/var/lib/xen/initrd.H3wHj2</initrd>
  <cmdline>ro root=/dev/VolGroup00/LogVol00 rhgb quiet</cmdline>
</os>
<memory>105472</memory>
<vcpu>1</vcpu>
<on_poweroff>destroy</on_poweroff>
<on_reboot>restart</on_reboot>
<on_crash>restart</on_crash>
<devices>
```

```
<interface type='bridge'>
  <source bridge='xenbr0'/>
  <mac address='00:16:3e:4b:af:c2'/>
  <script path='vif-bridge'/>
</interface>
<graphics type='vnc' port='5900'/>
<disk type='file' device='disk'>
  <driver name='tap' type='aio'/>
  <source file='/opt/xen/images/ophelia.img'/>
  <target dev='xvda'/>
</disk>
<console tty='/dev/pts/6'/>
</devices>
</domain>
```

You can see the correspondences between this XML definition and the domain config file; it defines the same basic resources in a different but still recognizable format. We can redirect this to a file, say *ophelia.xml*, shut down the original *ophelia*, and create a domain:

```
# virsh dumpxml ophelia > ophelia.xml
# virsh shutdown ophelia
# virsh create ophelia.xml
```

virsh can also list domains, just like xm:

```
# virsh list
 Id Name                 State
----------------------------------
  0 Domain-0             running
  4 ophelia              blocked
```

Finally, just as with xm, virsh can shutdown, restart, or destroy a domain, using the obvious command for each.

virt-manager

Apart from virt-install, which we discussed in Chapter 3, the most useful tool in the suite is probably virt-manager. It's pretty slick, and it's great in an area that's not covered by the Xen-tools scripts: interacting with live virtual machines. As Figure 6-1 shows, virt-manager provides a centralized location from which to view performance data, virtual framebuffers, and consoles. It also provides a quick overview of resource allocation. Like most GUI tools, virt-manager probably requires a bit more manual effort and clicking through dialog boxes than you'd like to use for everyday domU creation. Nonetheless, it's got support for Xen's basic life cycle: create and destroy. It also integrates with Red Hat's Kickstart deployment method for convenient semiautomated installs; you can just specify a *.ks* file when asked during the install dialog.

Getting Started with virt-manager

Because virt-manager comes with the operating system on Red Hat–based distros, assuming you selected the *virtualization* target during the install, you can invoke it without setting a finger to the keyboard. From the default GNOME desktop, click the **Applications** menu at the upper left, then **System Tools ▸ Virtual Machine Manager**. Enter your root password when prompted, and select **Local Hypervisor** to connect to the local instance of xend.[5] You'll be presented with something that looks vaguely like Figure 6-1.

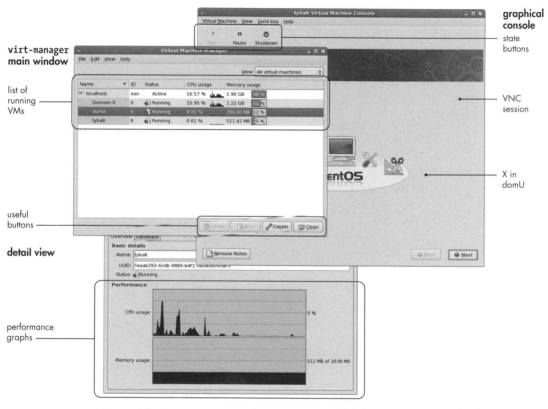

Figure 6-1: Here you can see the virt-manager *UI. It has a main screen that lists virtual machines; a detail view that shows VM resources, performance, and statistics; and a framebuffer console as well as a text console interface.*

To create an image using virt-manager, click the **File** menu, and select **New Machine**. virt-manager will then escort you through a set of friendly dialog boxes.

The first prompt asks for the name of the machine. Enter something appropriate, but make sure that it includes only letters, numerals, and underscores—fully qualified domain names won't work.

---

[5] Well, if you'd been logged in as root, you wouldn't have had to type anything. Not that we recommend that, of course.

Choose whether the new domain should be paravirtualized or fully virtualized. If you don't have HVM, the dialog will chide you for your inadequate hardware and gray out the Fully Virtualized option. For the purposes of this example, we're picking paravirtualization.

Then `virt-manager` asks for install media. Because it's calling `virt-install` behind the scenes, the same constraints apply; enter a network-accessible Red Hat–style directory tree. For example, *http://archive.fedoraproject.org/pub/ archive/fedora/linux/releases/7/Fedora/i386/os/* will install Fedora 7 from an HTTP Fedora mirror.

At this stage you can also specify a Kickstart file using the same syntax. This is a handy way to automate the install process. For example, to duplicate your dom0's install configuration, upload your */root/anaconda-ks.cfg* file somewhere convenient and specify it.

Select a backing store for the new virtual machine. The two choices map to `phy:` and `tap:aio:` devices. The GUI also gives you the option of creating a sparse file, but we don't recommend that for the reasons we described in some detail in Chapter 3.

Select a networking option. The two choices correspond to a `network-nat` work-alike and the standard `network-bridge`.

Finally, select memory and CPU allocation.

At the end, `virt-manager` will list your configuration and give you a chance to back out. Make sure everything looks right and click **Finish**. It'll validate your selections and then start creating the domain using `virt-install`.

The domain creation itself is probably the coolest feature of the libvirt suite. Rather than populating a filesystem from the dom0 and then booting a Xen instance, it downloads a Xen-aware net install image, immediately boots the domain from the installation kernel, and then uses that kernel to download the packages and populate the system. The install looks just like a normal install, using the framebuffer console to provide a completely ordinary Red Hat install experience. Because `virt-manager` integrates a VNC viewer, you can watch the install as it progresses from within the management application.

When the domain is running, you can pause it, shut it down, or examine its configuration from the main `virt-manager` window. Right-click the domain name to get a context menu with a list of operations, or select the domain by clicking it and use the button bar at the top.

NOTE   *Early versions of `virt-manager`, including the version shipped with Red Hat Enterprise Linux 5.0, suffered from the oversight that when a domain had stopped, it vanished from the GUI's list and thus couldn't be restarted without dropping to a command prompt. If you have an afflicted version, you can easily restart a domain configured with `virt-manager` using `xm` in the normal way.*

Still, though, virt-manager is too interactive and too limited to use for large installations. To address this, Red Hat's Emerging Technologies group (*http://et.redhat.com/*) is also working on a tool called oVirt, which aims to scale libvirt-based management across the entire data center. Another tool, the Puppet Recipe Manager, emphasizes the *software appliance* aspect of virtualization. It enables an administrator to build software recipes and automatically install them on virtual machines. We also mentioned Cobbler, an automated tool that can provision virtual machines, in Chapter 3.

One last libvirt-based tool that you might want to look at is `virt-clone`, which is capable of duplicating a domU image and its config file while altering any items that must be unique, such as the MAC address—a nice balance between convenience and control.

It's simple to run, taking most of its input from command-line options. For example, to clone the machine `sebastian` as `viola`:

```
# virt-clone -o sebastian -n viola -f /opt/xen/viola-root.img -f /opt/xen/
viola-swap.img preserve-data
```

Administering the Virtualized Data Center

The chief benefit of frontends like these is in doing things that are too large or complex for simpler tools, though some would hold that no problem is too large for a well-written shell script. The largest and best of these tools allow Xen to truly flex its capabilities, leading to giant automated systems such as we see in Amazon's EC2. In this category are several packages, including OpenQRM, ConVirt, and Enomalism. All three of these have their adherents. However, we've chosen to focus on lower-level, more commonly available tools while the more advanced management frontends stabilize.

Administration for the VM Customer

Although there are a number of packages aimed at allowing customers to manage their virtual machine, it's not clear to us that control-plane operations are really necessary in this context. Furthermore, most of the customer-facing tools are still in flux. It's difficult for us to recommend them at this point.

The best available solution, at least for now, seems to be to provide a reasonably simple menu through which customers can attach to the console, reboot their machines, shut down their machines, and re-create their domU image. There are many ways to do this. Our favorite is to allow customers to SSH to a console server, with sharply limited accounts.

Xen-shell

Although we like our home brew approach to management as described in Chapter 7, there are other options for those who believe that software can be perfectly adequate even if they didn't personally write it. Of these, our favorite is the Xen-shell. It's by the author of Xen-tools and is another example of his no-frills approach. We recommend it, not merely because we like Xen-tools or even because it's got a good feature set, because it doesn't have a giant list of dependencies. It's a simple product that does its job well.

It's available at *http://xen-tools.org/software/xen-shell/*. After you've downloaded it, use the standard unpack && make install process to install it.

At this point there's some configuration that needs to be done. Xen-shell works by taking user commands and running sudo xm in response to their input. You'll need to put xm into their path or, conversely, alter their path to include xm. We took the former approach:

```
# ln -s /usr/sbin/xm /usr/bin
```

We also need to configure */etc/sudoers* to make sure that the users are allowed to use sudo to run xm on their domain (and only their domain). This entails quite a number of additions to the file, one for each command we want to allow:

```
marlowe ALL=NOPASSWD:/usr/sbin/xm create goneril
marlowe ALL=NOPASSWD:/usr/sbin/xm create -c goneril
marlowe ALL=NOPASSWD:/usr/sbin/xm destroy goneril
marlowe ALL=NOPASSWD:/usr/sbin/xm shutdown goneril
marlowe ALL=NOPASSWD:/usr/sbin/xm list goneril
marlowe ALL=NOPASSWD:/usr/sbin/xm console goneril
marlowe ALL=NOPASSWD:/usr/sbin/xm reboot goneril
```

Then change the shell of the appropriate users to the Xen-shell. For example:

```
# chsh -s /usr/local/bin/xen-login-shell marlowe
```

To mark that a user is allowed to administer a domain, simply add the user to a line in the domain config file—an elegant and ingenious solution. We'll use the domain *goneril* as an example:

```
name = 'goneril'
xen-shell = 'marlowe'
```

Now, when marlowe logs in, he'll be presented with the Xen-shell interface from which he can execute various commands (get a list by typing **Help**).

NOTE *Although Xen-shell reads domain config files to find which domains can be administered by a user, it doesn't actually keep track of the config file's name, as of this writing. Domain configuration filenames, to work with Xen-shell's boot command, must be of the form <domU name>.cfg. Thus, goneril's config file must be /etc/xen/goneril.cfg.*

To extend the example, let's say that marlowe can administer multiple domains. Simply add the username to both domains, and use the control command in Xen-shell to switch between them. One of the niceties of Xen-shell is that the command only shows up if it's necessary.

```
xen-shell[goneril]> control regan
Controlling: regan
xen-shell[regan]>
```

Convenient, isn't it?

Really, though, this is just the beginning. The client software for Xen is still in turmoil, with constant development by multiple factions.

You may have noticed that we've left out a couple of prominent frontends. For one, we haven't even mentioned Citrix's offering because we cover it in Chapter 11. We also haven't addressed Amazon's EC2, which is probably the nearest thing to *utility computing* at present. As always, there's a big field of tools out there, and we're just aiming to make them seem manageable and talk about what works for us.

7

HOSTING UNTRUSTED USERS UNDER XEN: LESSONS FROM THE TRENCHES

Now that we've gone over the basics of Xen administration—storage, networking, provisioning, and management—let's look at applying these basics in practice. This chapter is mostly a case study of our VPS hosting firm, prgmr.com, and the lessons we've learned from renting Xen instances to the public.

The most important lesson of public Xen hosting is that the users can't be trusted to cooperate with you or each other. Some people will always try to seize as much as they can. Our focus will be on preventing this tragedy of the commons.

Advantages for the Users

There's exactly one basic reason that a user would want to use a Xen VPS rather than paying to colocate a box in your data center: it's cheap, especially for someone who's just interested in some basic services, rather than massive raw performance.

Xen also gives users nearly all the advantages they'd get from colocating a box: their own publicly routed network interface, their own disk, root access, and so forth. With a 128MB VM, they can run DNS, light mail service, a web server, IRC, SSH, and so on. For lightweight services like these, the power of the box is much less important than its basic existence—just having something available and publicly accessible makes life more convenient.

You also have the basic advantages of virtualization, namely, that hosting one server with 32GB of RAM is a whole lot cheaper than hosting 32 servers with 1GB of RAM each (or even 4 servers with 8GB RAM each). In fact, the price of RAM being what it is, I would argue that it's difficult to even economically justify hosting a general-purpose server with less than 32GB of RAM.

The last important feature of Xen is that, relative to other virtualization systems, it's got a good combination of light weight, strong partitioning, and robust resource controls. Unlike some other virtualization options, it's consistent—a user can rely on getting exactly the amount of memory, disk space, and network bandwidth that he's signed up for and approximately as much CPU and disk bandwidth.

Shared Resources and Protecting Them from the Users

> Xen's design is congruent to good security.
> —Tavis Ormandy, *http://taviso.decsystem.org/virtsec.pdf*

It's a ringing endorsement, by security-boffin standards. By and large, with Xen, we're not worried about keeping people from breaking out of their virtual machines—Xen itself is supposed to provide an appropriate level of isolation. In paravirtualized mode, Xen doesn't expose hardware drivers to domUs, which eliminates one major attack vector.[1] For the most part, securing a dom0 is exactly like securing any other server, except in one area.

That area of possible concern is in the access controls for shared resources, which are not entirely foolproof. The primary worry is that malicious users could gain more resources than they're entitled to, or in extreme cases cause denial-of-service attacks by exploiting flaws in Xen's accounting. In other words, we are in the business of enforcing performance isolation, rather than specifically trying to protect the dom0 from attacks via the domUs.

Most of the resource controls that we present here are aimed at users who aren't necessarily malicious—just, perhaps, exuberant.

Tuning CPU Usage

The first shared resource of interest is the CPU. While memory and disk size are easy to tune—you can just specify memory in the config file, while disk size is determined by the size of the backing device—fine-grained CPU allocation requires you to adjust the scheduler.

Scheduler Basics

The Xen scheduler acts as a referee between the running domains. In some ways it's a lot like the Linux scheduler: It can preempt processes as needed, it tries its best to ensure fair allocation, and it ensures that the CPU wastes as few cycles as possible. As the name suggests, Xen's scheduler schedules domains to run on the physical CPU. These domains, in turn, schedule and run processes from their internal run queues.

Because the dom0 is just another domain as far as Xen's concerned, it's subject to the same scheduling algorithm as the domUs. This can lead to trouble if it's not assigned a high enough weight because the dom0 has to be able to respond to I/O requests. We'll go into more detail on that topic a bit later, after we describe the general procedures for adjusting domain weights.

Xen can use a variety of scheduling algorithms, ranging from the simple to the baroque. Although Xen has shipped with a number of schedulers in the past, we're going to concentrate on the *credit scheduler*; it's the current default and recommended choice and the only one that the Xen team has indicated any interest in keeping.

The xm dmesg command will tell you, among other things, what scheduler Xen is using.

```
# xm dmesg | grep scheduler
(XEN) Using scheduler: SMP Credit Scheduler (credit)
```

If you want to change the scheduler, you can set it as a boot parameter—to change to the SEDF scheduler, for example, append sched=sedf to the kernel line in GRUB. (That's the Xen kernel, not the dom0 Linux kernel loaded by the first module line.)

---

[1] In HVM mode, the emulated QEMU devices are something of a risk, which is part of why we don't offer HVM domains.

VCPUs and Physical CPUs

For convenience, we consider each Xen domain to have one or more virtual CPUs (VCPUs), which periodically run on the physical CPUs. These are the entities that consume credits when run. To examine VCPUs, use xm vcpu-list <domain>:

```
# xm vcpu-list horatio
Name                        ID VCPUs   CPU State   Time(s) CPU Affinity
horatio                     16    0      0   ---   140005.6 any cpu
horatio                     16    1      2   r--   139968.3 any cpu
```

In this case, the domain has two VCPUs, 0 and 1. VCPU 1 is in the *running* state on (physical) CPU 1. Note that Xen will try to spread VCPUs across CPUs as much as possible. Unless you've pinned them manually, VCPUs can occasionally switch CPUs, depending on which physical CPUs are available.

To specify the number of VCPUs for a domain, specify the vcpus= directive in the config file. You can also change the number of VCPUs while a domain is running using xm vcpu-set. However, note that you can decrease the number of VCPUs this way, but you can't increase the number of VCPUs beyond the initial count.

To set the CPU affinity, use xm vcpu-pin <domain> <vcpu> <pcpu>. For example, to switch the CPU assignment in the domain *horatio*, so that VCPU0 runs on CPU2 and VCPU1 runs on CPU0:

```
# xm vcpu-pin horatio 0 2
# xm vcpu-pin horatio 1 0
```

Equivalently, you can pin VCPUs in the domain config file (*/etc/xen/ horatio*, if you're using our standard naming convention) like this:

```
vcpus=2
cpus=[0,2]
```

This gives the domain two VCPUs, pins the first VCPU to the first physical CPU, and pins the second VCPU to the third physical CPU.

Credit Scheduler

The Xen team designed the credit scheduler to minimize wasted CPU time. This makes it a *work-conserving* scheduler, in that it tries to ensure that the CPU will always be working whenever there is work for it to do.

As a consequence, if there is more real CPU available than the domUs are demanding, all domUs get all the CPU they want. When there is contention—that is, when the domUs in aggregate want more CPU than actually exists—then the scheduler arbitrates fairly between the domains that want CPU.

Xen does its best to do a fair division, but the scheduling isn't perfect by any stretch of the imagination. In particular, cycles spent servicing I/O by domain 0 are not charged to the responsible domain, leading to situations where I/O-intensive clients get a disproportionate share of CPU usage.

Nonetheless, you can get pretty good allocation in nonpathological cases. (Also, in our experience, the CPU sits idle most of the time anyway.)

The credit scheduler assigns each domain a *weight* and, optionally, a *cap*. The weight indicates the relative CPU allocation of a domain—if the CPU is scarce, a domain with a weight of 512 will receive twice as much CPU time as a domain with a weight of 256 (the default). The cap sets an absolute limit on the amount of CPU time a domain can use, expressed in hundredths of a CPU. Note that the CPU cap can exceed 100 on multiprocessor hosts.

The scheduler transforms the weight into a *credit* allocation for each VCPU, using a separate accounting thread. As a VCPU runs, it consumes credits. If a VCPU runs out of credits, it only runs when other, more thrifty VCPUs have finished executing, as shown in Figure 7-1. Periodically, the accounting thread goes through and gives everybody more credits.

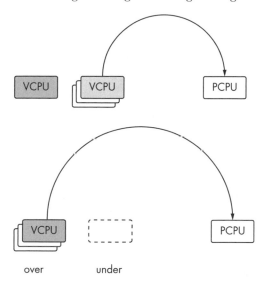

over   under

Figure 7-1: VCPUs wait in two queues: one for VCPUs with credits and the other for those that are over their allotment. Once the first queue is exhausted, the CPU will pull from the second.

In this case, the details are probably less important than the practical application. Using the xm sched-credit commands, we can adjust CPU allocation on a per-domain basis. For example, here we'll increase a domain's CPU allocation. First, to list the weight and cap for the domain horatio:

```
# xm sched-credit -d horatio
{'cap': 0, 'weight': 256}
```

Then, to modify the scheduler's parameters:

```
# xm sched-credit -d horatio -w 512
# xm sched-credit -d horatio
{'cap': 0, 'weight': 512}
```

Of course, the value "512" only has meaning relative to the other domains that are running on the machine. Make sure to set all the domains' weights appropriately.

To set the cap for a domain:

```
# xm sched-credit -d domain -c cap
```

Scheduling for Providers

We decided to divide the CPU along the same lines as the available RAM—it stands to reason that a user paying for half the RAM in a box will want more CPU than someone with a 64MB domain. Thus, in our setup, a customer with 25 percent of the RAM also has a minimum share of 25 percent of the CPU cycles.

The simple way to do this is to assign each CPU a weight equal to the number of megabytes of memory it has and leave the cap empty. The scheduler will then handle converting that into fair proportions. For example, our aforementioned user with half the RAM will get about as much CPU time as the rest of the users put together.

Of course, that's the worst case; that is what the user will get in an environment of constant struggle for the CPU. Idle domains will automatically yield the CPU. If all domains but one are idle, that one can have the entire CPU to itself.

NOTE   *It's essential to make sure that the dom0 has sufficient CPU to service I/O requests. You can handle this by dedicating a CPU to the dom0 or by giving the dom0 a very high weight—high enough to ensure that it never runs out of credits. At prgmr.com, we handle the problem by weighting each domU with its RAM amount and weighting the dom0 at 6000.*

This simple weight = memory formula becomes a bit more complex when dealing with multiprocessor systems because independent systems of CPU allocation come into play. A good rule would be to allocate VCPUs in proportion to memory (and therefore in proportion to weight). For example, a domain with half the RAM on a box with four cores (and hyperthreading turned off) should have at least two VCPUs. Another solution would be to give all domains as many VCPUs as physical processors in the box—this would allow all domains to burst to the full CPU capacity of the physical machine but might lead to increased overhead from context swaps.

Controlling Network Resources

Network resource controls are, frankly, essential to any kind of shared hosting operation. Among the many lessons that we've learned from Xen hosting has been that if you provide free bandwidth, some users will exploit it for all it's worth. This isn't a Xen-specific observation, but it's especially noticeable with the sort of cheap VPS hosting Xen lends itself to.

We prefer to use `network-bridge`, since that's the default. For a more thorough look at `network-bridge`, take a look at Chapter 5.

Monitoring Network Usage

Given that some users will consume as much bandwidth as possible, it's vital to have some way to monitor network traffic.[2]

To monitor network usage, we use BandwidthD on a physical SPAN port. It's a simple tool that counts bytes going through a switch—nothing Xen-specific here. We feel comfortable doing this because our provider doesn't allow anything but IP packets in or out, and our antispoof rules are good enough to protect us from users spoofing their IP on outgoing packets.

A similar approach would be to extend the *dom0 is a switch* analogy and use SNMP monitoring software. As mentioned in Chapter 5, it's important to specify a vifname for each domain if you're doing this. In any case, we'll leave the particulars of bandwidth monitoring up to you.

ARP CACHE POISONING

If you use the default network-bridge setup, you are vulnerable to ARP cache poisoning, just as on any layer 2 switch.

The idea is that the interface counters on a layer 2 switch—such as the virtual switch used by network-bridge—watch traffic as it passes through a particular port. Every time a switch sees an Ethernet frame or ARP is-at, it keeps track of what port and MAC it came from. If it gets a frame destined for a MAC address in its cache, it sends that frame down the proper port (and only the proper port). If the bridge sees a frame destined for a MAC that is not in the cache, it sends that frame to all ports.[*]

Clever, no? In most cases this means that you almost never see Ethernet frames destined for other MAC addresses (other than broadcasts, etc.). However, this feature is designed purely as an optimization, not a security measure. As those of you with cable providers who do MAC address verification know quite well, it is fairly trivial to fake a MAC address. This means that a malicious user can fill the (limited in size) ARP cache with bogus MAC addresses, drive out the good data, and force all packets to go down all interfaces. At this point the switch becomes basically a hub, and the counters on all ports will show all traffic for any port.

There are two ways we have worked around the problem. You could use Xen's network-route networking model, which doesn't use a virtual bridge. The other approach is to ignore the interface counters and use something like BandwidthD, which bases its accounting on IP packets.

---

[*] We are using the words *port* and *interface* interchangeably here. This is a reasonable simplification in the context of interface counters on an SNMP-capable switch.

Once you can examine traffic quickly, the next step is to shape the users. The principles for network traffic shaping and policing are the same as for standalone boxes, except that you can also implement policies on the Xen host. Let's look at how to limit both incoming and outgoing traffic for a particular interface—as if, say, you have a customer who's going over his bandwidth allotment.

---

[2] In this case, we're talking about bandwidth monitoring. You should also run some sort of IDS, such as Snort, to watch for outgoing abuse (we do) but there's nothing Xen-specific about that.

Network Shaping Principles

The first thing to know about shaping is that it only works on outgoing traffic. Although it is possible to *police* incoming traffic, it isn't as effective. Fortunately, both directions look like outgoing traffic at some point in their passage through the dom0, as shown in Figure 7-2. (When we refer to outgoing and incoming traffic in the following description, we mean from the perspective of the domU.)

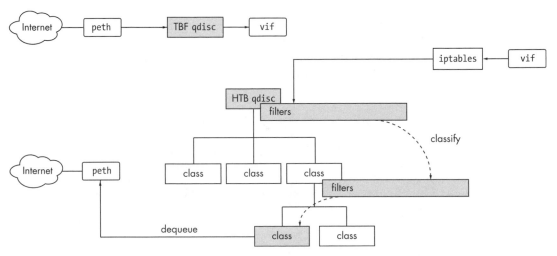

Figure 7-2: Incoming traffic comes from the Internet, goes through the virtual bridge, and gets shaped by a simple nonhierarchical filter. Outgoing traffic, on the other hand, needs to go through a system of filters that assign packets to classes in a hierarchical queuing discipline.

Shaping Incoming Traffic

We'll start with incoming traffic because it's much simpler to limit than outgoing traffic. The easiest way to shape incoming traffic is probably the *token bucket filter* queuing discipline, which is a simple, effective, and lightweight way to slow down an interface.

The token bucket filter, or TBF, takes its name from the metaphor of a bucket of tokens. Tokens stream into the bucket at a defined and constant rate. Each byte of data sent takes one token from the bucket and goes out immediately—when the bucket's empty, data can only go as tokens come in. The bucket itself has a limited capacity, which guarantees that only a reasonable amount of data will be sent out at once. To use the TBF, we add a qdisc (*queuing discipline*) to perform the actual work of traffic limiting. To limit the virtual interface osric to 1 megabit per second, with bursts up to 2 megabits and maximum allowable latency of 50 milliseconds:

```
# tc qdisc add dev osric root tbf rate 1mbit latency 50ms peakrate 2mbit maxburst 40MB
```

This adds a qdisc to the device osric. The next arguments specify where to add it (root) and what sort of qdisc it is (tbf). Finally, we specify the rate, latency, burst rate, and amount that can go at burst rate. These parameters correspond to the token flow, amount of latency the packets are allowed to have (before the driver signals the operating system that its buffers are full), maximum rate at which the bucket can empty, and the size of the bucket.

Shaping Outgoing Traffic

Having shaped incoming traffic, we can focus on limiting outgoing traffic. This is a bit more complex because the outgoing traffic for all domains goes through a single interface, so a single token bucket won't work. The policing filters might work, but they handle the problem by dropping packets, which is . . . bad. Instead, we're going to apply traffic shaping to the outgoing physical Ethernet device, peth0, with a *Hierarchical Token Bucket*, or HTB qdisc.

The HTB discipline acts like the simple token bucket, but with a hierarchy of buckets, each with its own rate, and a system of filters to assign packets to buckets. Here's how to set it up.

First, we have to make sure that the packets on Xen's virtual bridge traverse iptables:

```
# echo 1 > /proc/sys/net/bridge/bridge-nf-call-iptables
```

This is so that we can mark packets according to which domU emitted them. There are other reasons, but that's the important one in terms of our traffic-shaping setup. Next, for each domU, we add a rule to mark packets from the corresponding network interface:

```
# iptables -t mangle -A FORWARD -m physdev --physdev-in baldr -j MARK --set-mark 5
```

Here the number 5 is an arbitrary mark—it's not important what the number is, as long as there's a useful mapping between number and domain. We're using the domain ID. We could also use tc filters directly that match on source IP address, but it feels more elegant to have everything keyed to the domain's physical network device. Note that we're using physdev-in—traffic that goes out from the domU comes in to the dom0, as Figure 7-3 shows.

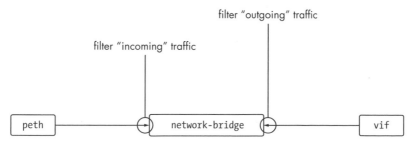

Figure 7-3: We shape traffic coming into the domU as it comes into the dom0 from the physical device, and shape traffic leaving the domU as it enters the dom0 on the virtual device.

Next we create a HTB `qdisc`. We won't go over the HTB options in too much detail—see the documentation at *http://luxik.cdi.cz/~devik/qos/htb/manual/userg.htm* for more details:

```
# tc qdisc add dev peth0 root handle 1: htb default 12
```

Then we make some classes to put traffic into. Each class will get traffic from one domU. (As the HTB docs explain, we're also making a parent class so that they can share surplus bandwidth.)

```
# tc class add dev peth0 parent 1: classid 1:1 htb rate 100mbit
# tc class add dev peth0 parent 1:1 classid 1:2 htb rate 1mbit
```

Now that we have a class for our domU's traffic, we need a filter that will assign packets to it.

```
# tc filter add dev peth0 protocol ip parent 1:0 prio 1 handle 5 fw flowid 1:2
```

Note that we're matching on the "handle" that we set earlier using iptables. This assigns the packet to the 1:2 class, which we've previously limited to 1 megabit per second.

At this point traffic to and from the target domU is essentially shaped, as demonstrated by Figure 7-4. You can easily add commands like these to the end of your `vif` script, be it `vif-bridge`, `vif-route`, or a wrapper. We would also like to emphasize that this is only an example and that the Linux Advanced Routing and Traffic Control how-to at *http://lartc.org/* is an excellent place to look for further documentation. The `tc` man page is also informative.

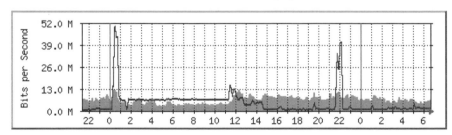

Figure 7-4: The effect of the shaping filters

Storage in a Shared Hosting Environment

As with so much else in system administration, a bit of planning can save a lot of trouble. Figure out beforehand where you're going to store pristine filesystem images, where configuration files go, and where customer data will live.

For pristine images, there are a lot of conventions—some people use */diskimages*, some use */opt/xen*, */var/xen* or similar, some use a subdirectory of */home*. Pick one and stick with it.

Configuration files should, without exception, go in */etc/xen*. If you don't give xm create a full path, it'll look for the file in */etc/xen*. Don't disappoint it.

As for customer data, we recommend that serious hosting providers use LVM. This allows greater flexibility and manageability than blktap-mapped files while maintaining good performance. Chapter 4 covers the details of working with LVM (or at least enough to get started), as well as many other available storage options and their advantages. Here we're confining ourselves to lessons that we've learned from our adventures in shared hosting.

Regulating Disk Access with *ionice*

One common problem with VPS hosting is that customers—or your own housekeeping processes, like backups—will use enough I/O bandwidth to slow down everyone on the machine. Furthermore, I/O isn't really affected by the scheduler tweaks discussed earlier. A domain can request data, hand off the CPU, and save its credits until it's notified of the data's arrival.

Although you can't set hard limits on disk access rates as you can with the network QoS, you can use the ionice command to prioritize the different domains into subclasses, with a syntax like:

```
# ionice -p <PID> -c <class> -n <priority within class>
```

Here -n is the knob you'll ordinarily want to twiddle It can range from 0 to 7, with lower numbers taking precedence.

We recommend always specifying 2 for the class. Other classes exist—3 is idle and 1 is realtime—but idle is extremely conservative, while realtime is so aggressive as to have a good chance of locking up the system. The within-class priority is aimed at proportional allocation, and is thus much more likely to be what you want.

Let's look at ionice in action. Here we'll test ionice with two different domains, one with the highest normal priority, the other with the lowest.

First, ionice only works with the CFQ I/O scheduler. To check that you're using the CFQ scheduler, run this command in the dom0:

```
# cat /sys/block/[sh]d[a-z]*/queue/scheduler
noop anticipatory deadline [cfq]
noop anticipatory deadline [cfq]
```

The word in brackets is the selected scheduler. If it's not [cfq], reboot with the parameter elevator = cfq.

Next we find the processes we want to ionice. Because we're using tap:aio devices in this example, the dom0 process is tapdisk. If we were using phy: devices, it'd be [xvd <domain id> <device specifier>].

```
# ps aux | grep tapdisk
root      1054  0.5  0.0  13588   556  ?   Sl  05:45   0:10   tapdisk
/dev/xen/tapctrlwrite1 /dev/xen/tapctrlread1
root      1172  0.6  0.0  13592   560  ?   Sl  05:45   0:10   tapdisk
/dev/xen/tapctrlwrite2 /dev/xen/tapctrlread2
```

Now we can ionice our domains. Note that the numbers of the tapctrl devices correspond to the order the domains were started in, not the domain ID.

```
# ionice -p 1054 -c 2 -n 7
# ionice -p 1172 -c 2 -n 0
```

To test ionice, let's run a couple of Bonnie++ processes and time them. (After Bonnie++ finishes, we dd a load file, just to make sure that conditions for the other domain remain unchanged.)

```
prio 7 domU tmp # /usr/bin/time -v  bonnie++  -u 1 && dd if=/dev/urandom of=load
prio 0 domU tmp # /usr/bin/time -v  bonnie++  -u 1 && dd if=/dev/urandom of=load
```

In the end, according to the wall clock, the domU with priority 0 took 3:32.33 to finish, while the priority 7 domU needed 5:07.98. As you can see, the ionice priorities provide an effective way to do proportional I/O allocation.

The best way to apply ionice is probably to look at CPU allocations and convert them into priority classes. Domains with the highest CPU allocation get priority 1, next highest priority 2, and so on. Processes in the dom0 should be ioniced as appropriate. This will ensure a reasonable priority, but not allow big domUs to take over the entirety of the I/O bandwidth.

Backing Up DomUs

As a service provider, one rapidly learns that customers don't do their own backups. When a disk fails (not *if—when*), customers will expect you to have complete backups of their data, and they'll be very sad if you don't. So let's talk about backups.

Of course, you already have a good idea how to back up physical machines. There are two aspects to backing up Xen domains: First, there's the domain's virtual disk, which we want to back up just as we would a real machine's disk. Second, there's the domain's running state, which can be saved and restored from the dom0. Ordinarily, our use of *backup* refers purely to the disk, as it would with physical machines, but with the advantage that we can use domain snapshots to pause the domain long enough to get a clean disk image.

We use xm save and LVM snapshots to back up both the domain's storage and running state. LVM snapshots aren't a good way of implementing full copy-on-write because they handle the "out of snapshot space" case poorly, but they're excellent if you want to preserve a filesystem state long enough to make a consistent backup.

Our implementation copies the entire disk image using either a plain cp (in the case of file-backed domUs) or dd (for phy: devices). This is because we very much want to avoid mounting a possibly unclean filesystem in the dom0, which can cause the entire machine to panic. Besides, if we do a raw device backup, domU administrators will be able to use filesystems (such as ZFS on an OpenSolaris domU) that the dom0 cannot read.

An appropriate script to do as we've described might be:

```perl
#!/usr/bin/perl
my @disks,@stores,@files,@lvs;

$domain=$ARGV[0];

my $destdir="/var/backup/xen/${domain}/";
system "mkdir -p $destdir";

open (FILE, "/etc/xen/$domain") ;
while (<FILE>) {
        if(m/^disk/) {
                s/.*\[\s+([^\]]+)\s*\].*/\1/;
                @disks = split(/[,]/);

                # discard elements without a :, since they can't be
                # backing store specifiers
                while($disks[$n]) {
                        $disks[$n] =~ s/['"]//g;
                        push(@stores,"$disks[$n]") if("$disks[$n]"=~ m/:/);
                        $n++;
                }
                $n=0;

                # split on : and take only the last field lf the first
                # is a recognized device specifier.
                while($stores[$n]) {
                        @tmp = split(/:/, $stores[$n]);
                        if(($tmp[0] =~ m/file/i) || ($tmp[0] =~ m/tap/i)) {
                                push(@files, $tmp[$#tmp]);
                        }
                        elsif($tmp[0] =~ m/phy/i) {
                                push(@lvs, $tmp[$#tmp]);
                        }
                        $n++;
                }
        }
}
close FILE;

print "xm save $domain $destdir/${domain}.xmsave\n";
system ("xm save $domain $destdir/${domain}.xmsave");

foreach(@files) {
    print "copying $_";
        system("cp $_ ${destdir}") ;
}

foreach $lv (@lvs) {
        system("lvcreate --size 1024m --snapshot --name ${lv}_snap $lv");
}

system ("xm restore $destdir/${domain}.xmsave && gzip $destdir/${domain}.xmsave");
```

```
foreach $lv (@lvs) {
    $lvfile=$lv;
    $lvfile=~s/\//_/g;
    print "backing up $lv";
        system("dd if=${lv}_snap | gzip -c > $destdir/${lvfile}.gz" ) ;
        system("lvremove ${lv}_snap" );
}
```

Save it as, say, *usr/sbin/backup_domains.sh* and tell cron to execute the script at appropriate intervals.

This script works by saving each domain, copying file-based storage, and snapshotting LVs. When that's accomplished, it restores the domain, backs up the save file, and backs up the snapshots via dd.

Note that users will see a brief hiccup in service while the domain is paused and snapshotted. We measured downtime of less than three minutes to get a consistent backup of a domain with a gigabyte of RAM—well within acceptable parameters for most applications. However, doing a bit-for-bit copy of an entire disk may also degrade performance somewhat.[3] We suggest doing backups at off-peak hours.

To view other scripts in use at prgmr.com, go to *http://book.xen.prgmr.com/*.

Remote Access to the DomU

The story on normal access for VPS users is deceptively simple: The Xen VM is exactly like a normal machine at the colocation facility. They can SSH into it (or, if you're providing Windows, rdesktop). However, when problems come up, the user is going to need some way of accessing the machine at a lower level, as if they were sitting at their VPS's console.

For that, we provide a console server that they can SSH into. The easiest thing to do is to use the dom0 as their console server and sharply limit their accounts.

NOTE *Analogously, we feel that any colocated machine should have a serial console attached to it.[4] We discuss our reasoning and the specifics of using Xen with a serial console in Chapter 14.*

An Emulated Serial Console

Xen already provides basic serial console functionality via xm. You can access a guest's console by typing xm console <domain> within the dom0. Issue commands, then type CTRL-] to exit from the serial console when you're done.

The problem with this approach is that xm has to run from the dom0 with effective UID 0. While this is reasonable enough in an environment with trusted domU administrators, it's not a great idea when you're giving an

---

[3] Humorous understatement.

[4] Our experience with other remote console tools has, overall, been unpleasant. Serial redirection systems work quite well. IP KVMs are barely preferable to toggling in the code on the front panel. On a good day.

account to anyone with $5. Dealing with untrusted domU admins, as in a VPS hosting situation, requires some additional work to limit access using ssh and sudo.

First, configure sudo. Edit /etc/sudoers and append, for each user:

```
<username> ALL=NOPASSWD:/usr/sbin/xm console <vm name>
```

Next, for each user, we create a ~/.ssh/authorized_keys file like this:

```
no-agent-forwarding,no-X11-forwarding,no-port-forwarding,command="sudo xm
console <vm name>" ssh-rsa <key> [comment]
```

This line allows the user to log in with his key. Once he's logged in, sshd connects to the named domain console and automatically presents it to him, thus keeping domU administrators out of the dom0. Also, note the options that start with no. They're important. We're not in the business of providing shell accounts. This is purely a console server—we want people to use their domUs rather than the dom0 for standard SSH stuff. These settings will allow users to access their domains' consoles via SSH in a way that keeps their access to the dom0 at a minimum.

A Menu for the Users

Of course, letting each user access his console is really just the beginning. By changing the command field in authorized_keys to a custom script, we can provide a menu with a startling array of features!

Here's a sample script that we call *xencontrol*. Put it somewhere in the filesystem—say /usr/bin/xencontrol—and then set the line in authorized_keys to call xencontrol rather than xm console.

```
#!/bin/bash
DOM="$1"
cat << EOF
`sudo /usr/sbin/xm list $DOM`


Options for $DOM
1. console
2. create/start
3. shutdown
4. destroy/hard shutdown
5. reboot
6. exit
EOF
printf "> "
read X
case "$X" in
```

```
*1*) sudo /usr/sbin/xm console "$DOM" ;;
*2*) sudo /usr/sbin/xm create -c "$DOM" ;;
*3*) sudo /usr/sbin/xm shutdown "$DOM" ;;
*4*) sudo /usr/sbin/xm destroy "$DOM" ;;
*5*) sudo /usr/sbin/xm reboot "$DOM" ;;
esac
```

When the user logs in via SSH, the SSH daemon runs this script in place of the user's login shell (which we recommend setting to /bin/false or its equivalent on your platform). The script then echoes some status information, an informative message, and a list of options. When the user enters a number, it runs the appropriate command (which we've allowed the user to run by configuring sudo).

PyGRUB, a Bootloader for DomUs

Up until now, the configurations that we've described, by and large, have specified the domU's boot configuration in the config file, using the kernel, ramdisk, and extra lines. However, there is an alternative method, which specifies a bootloader line in the config file and in turn uses that to load a kernel from the domU's filesystem.

The bootloader most commonly used is PyGRUB, or Python GRUB. The best way to explain PyGRUB is probably to step back and examine the program it's based on, GRUB, the GRand Unified Bootloader. GRUB itself is a traditional bootloader—a program that sits in a location on the hard drive where the BIOS can load and execute it, which then itself loads and executes a kernel.

PyGRUB, therefore, is like GRUB for a domU. The Xen domain builder usually loads an OS kernel directly from the dom0 filesystem when the virtual machine is started (therefore acting like a bootloader itself). Instead, it can load PyGRUB, which then acts as a bootloader and loads the kernel from the domU filesystem.[5]

PyGRUB is useful because it allows a more perfect separation between the administrative duties of the dom0 and the domU. When virtualizing the data center, you want to hand off virtual hardware to the customer. PyGRUB more effectively virtualizes the hardware. In particular, this means the customer can change his own kernel without the intervention of the dom0 administrator.

NOTE *PyGRUB has been mentioned as a possible security risk because it reads an untrusted filesystem directly from the dom0. PV-GRUB (see "PV-GRUB: A Safer Alternative to PyGRUB?" on page 105), which loads a trusted paravirtualized kernel from the dom0 then uses that to load and jump to the domU kernel, should improve this situation.*

---

[5] This is an oversimplification. What actually happens is that PyGRUB copies a kernel from the domU filesystem, puts it in /tmp, and then writes an appropriate domain config so that the domain builder can do its job. But the distinction is usually unimportant, so we've opted to approach PyGRUB as the bootloader it pretends to be.

PV-GRUB: A SAFER ALTERNATIVE TO PYGRUB?

PV-GRUB is an excellent reason to upgrade to Xen 3.3. The problem with PyGRUB is that while it's a good simulation of a bootloader, it has to mount the domU partition in the dom0, and it interacts with the domU filesystem. This has led to at least one remote-execution exploit. PV-GRUB avoids the problem by loading an executable that is, quite literally, a paravirtualized version of the GRUB bootloader, which then runs entirely within the domU.

This also has some other advantages. You can actually load the PV-GRUB binary from within the domU, meaning that you can load your first *menu.lst* from a read-only partition and have it fall through to a user partition, which then means that unlike my PyGRUB setup, users can never mess up their *menu.lst* to the point where they can't get into their rescue image.

Note that Xen creates a domain in either 32- or 64-bit mode, and it can't switch later on. This means that a 64-bit PV-GRUB can't load 32-bit Linux kernels, and vice versa.

Our PV-GRUB setup at prgmr.com starts with a normal xm config file, but with no bootloader and a kernel= line that points to PV-GRUB, instead of the domU kernel.

```
kernel = "/usr/lib/xen/boot/pv-grub-x86_64.gz"
extra = "(hd0,0)/boot/grub/menu.lst"
disk = ['phy:/dev/denmark/horatio,xvda,w','phy:/dev/denmark/rescue,xvde,r']
```

Note that we call the architecture-specific binary for PV-GRUB. The 32-bit (PAE) version is *pv-grub-x86_32*.

This is enough to load a regular *menu.lst*, but what about this indestructible rescue image of which I spoke? Here's how we do it on the new prgmr.com Xen 3.3 servers. In the xm config file:

```
kernel = "/usr/lib/xen/boot/pv-grub-x86_64.gz"
extra = "(hd1,0)/boot/grub/menu.lst"
disk = ['phy:/dev/denmark/horatio,xvda,w','phy:/dev/denmark/rescue,xvde,r']
```

Then, in */boot/grub/menu.lst* on the rescue disk:

```
default=0
timeout=5

title Xen domain boot
        root (hd1)
        kernel /boot/pv-grub-x86_64.gz (hd0,0)/boot/grub/menu.lst

title CentOS-rescue (2.6.18-53.1.14.el5xen)
        root (hd1)
        kernel /boot/vmlinuz-2.6.18-53.1.14.el5xen ro root=LABEL=RESCUE
        initrd /boot/initrd-2.6.18-53.1.14.el5xen.img

title CentOS installer
        root (hd1)
        kernel /boot/centos-5.1-installer-vmlinuz
        initrd /boot/centos-5.1-installer-initrd.img

title NetBSD installer
        root (hd1)
        kernel  /boot/netbsd-INSTALL_XEN3_DOMU.gz
```

(continued)

The first entry is the normal boot, with 64-bit PV-GRUB. The rest are various types of rescue and install boots. Note that we specify (hd1) for the rescue entries; in this case, the second disk is the rescue disk.

The normal boot loads PV-GRUB and the user's */boot/grub/menu.lst* from (hd0,0). Our default user-editable *menu.lst* looks like this:

```
default=0
timeout=5

title CentOS (2.6.18-92.1.6.el5xen)
        root (hd0,0)
        kernel /boot/vmlinuz-2.6.18-92.1.6.el5xen console=xvc0
root=LABEL=PRGMRDISK1 ro
        initrd /boot/initrd-2.6.18-92.1.6.el5xen.img
```

PV-GRUB only runs on Xen 3.3 and above, and it seems that Red Hat has no plans to backport PV-GRUB to the version of Xen that is used by RHEL 5.x.

Making PyGRUB Work

The domain's filesystem will need to include a */boot* directory with the appropriate files, just like a regular GRUB setup. We usually make a separate block device for */boot*, which we present to the domU as the first disk entry in its config file.

To try PyGRUB, add a bootloader= line to the domU config file:

```
bootloader = "/usr/bin/pygrub"
```

Of course, this being Xen, it may not be as simple as that. If you're using Debian, make sure that you have libgrub, e2fslibs-dev, and reiserfslibs-dev installed. (Red Hat Enterprise Linux and related distros use PyGRUB with their default Xen setup, and they include the necessary libraries with the Xen packages.)

Even with these libraries installed, it may fail to work without some manual intervention. Older versions of PyGRUB expect the virtual disk to have a partition table rather than a raw filesystem. If you have trouble, this may be the culprit.

With modern versions of PyGRUB, it is unnecessary to have a partition table on the domU's virtual disk.

Self-Support with PyGRUB

At prgmr.com, we give domU administrators the ability to repair and customize their own systems, which also saves us a lot of effort installing and supporting different distros. To accomplish this, we use PyGRUB and see to it that every customer has a bootable read-only rescue image they can boot into if their OS install goes awry. The domain config file for a customer who doesn't want us to do mirroring looks something like the following.

```
bootloader = "/usr/bin/pygrub"

memory = 512
name = "lsc"
vif = [ 'vifname=lsc,ip=38.99.2.47,mac=aa:00:00:50:20:2f,bridge=xenbr0' ]

disk = [
        'phy:/dev/verona/lsc_boot,sda,w',
        'phy:/dev/verona_left/lsc,sdb,w',
        'phy:/dev/verona_right/lsc,sdc,w',
        'file://var/images/centos_ro_rescue.img,sdd,r'
]
```

Note that we're now exporting four disks to the virtual host: a */boot* partition on virtual sda, reserved for PyGRUB; two disks for user data, sdb and sdc; and a read-only CentOS install as sdd.

A sufficiently technical user, with this setup and console access, needs almost no help from the dom0 administrator. He or she can change the operating system, boot a custom kernel, set up a software RAID, and boot the CentOS install to fix his setup if anything goes wrong.

Setting Up the DomU for PyGRUB

The only other important bit to make this work is a valid */grub/menu.lst*, which looks remarkably like the *menu.lst* in a regular Linux install. Our default looks like this and is stored on the disk exported as sda:

```
default=0
timeout=15

title centos
        root (hd0,0)
        kernel /boot/vmlinuz-2.6.18-53.1.6.el5xen console=xvc0 root=/dev/sdb ro
        initrd /boot/initrd-2.6.18-53.1.6.el5xen.XenU.img

title generic kernels
        root (hd0,0)
        kernel /boot/vmlinuz-2.6-xen root=/dev/sdb
        module /boot/initrd-2.6-xen

title rescue-disk
        root (hd0,0)
        kernel /boot/vmlinuz-2.6.18-53.1.6.el5xen console=xvc0 root=LABEL=RESCUE
ro
        initrd /boot/initrd-2.6.18-53.1.6.el5xen.XenU.img
```

NOTE   /boot/grub/menu.lst *is frequently symlinked to either* /boot/grub/grub.conf *or* /etc/grub.conf. /boot/grub/menu.lst *is still the file that matters.*

As with native Linux, if you use a separate partition for */boot*, you'll need to either make a symlink at the root of */boot* that points boot back to . or make your kernel names relative to /boot.

Here, the first and default entry is the CentOS distro kernel. The second entry is a generic Xen kernel, and the third choice is a read-only rescue image. Just like with native Linux, you can also specify devices by label rather than disk number.

WORKING WITH PARTITIONS ON VIRTUAL DISKS

In a standard configuration, partition 1 may be */boot*, with partition 2 as */*. In that case, partition 1 would have the configuration files and kernels in the same format as for normal GRUB.

It's straightforward to create these partitions on an LVM device using fdisk. Doing so for a file is a bit harder. First, attach the file to a loop, using `losetup`:

```
# losetup /dev/loop1 claudius.img
```

Then create two partitions in the usual way, using your favorite partition editor:

```
# fdisk /dev/loop1
```

Then, whether you're using an LVM device or loop file, use kpartx to create device nodes from the partition table in that device:

```
# kpartx -av /dev/loop1
```

Device nodes will be created under */dev/mapper* in the format *devnamep#*. Make a filesystem of your preferred type on the new partitions:

```
# mke2fs /dev/mapper/loop1p1
# mke2fs -j /dev/mapper/loop1p2

# mount /dev/mapper/loop1p2 /mnt
# mount /dev/mapper/loop1p1 /mnt/boot
```

Copy your filesystem image into */mnt*, make sure valid GRUB support files are in */mnt/boot* (just like a regular GRUB setup), and you are done.

Wrap-Up

This chapter discussed things that we've learned from our years of relying on Xen. Mostly, that relates to how to partition and allocate resources between independent, uncooperative virtual machines, with a particular slant toward VPS hosting. We've described why you might host VPSs on Xen; specific allocation issues for CPU, disk, memory, and network access; backup methods; and letting customers perform self-service with scripts and PyGRUB.

Note that there's some overlap between this chapter and some of the others. For example, we mention a bit about network configuration, but we go into far more detail on networking in Chapter 5, Networking. We describe xm save in the context of backups, but we talk a good deal more about it and how it relates to migration in Chapter 9. Xen hosting's been a lot of fun. It hasn't made us rich, but it's presented a bunch of challenges and given us a chance to do some neat stuff.

8

BEYOND LINUX: USING XEN WITH OTHER UNIX-LIKE OSs

One major benefit of paravirtualization which we've thus far ignored is the ability to run multiple operating systems on a single paravirtualized physical machine. Although Linux is the most popular OS to run under Xen, it's not the only option available. Several other Unix-like OSs can run as a dom0, and rather more have been modified to run as paravirtualized domUs.

Apart from Linux, only Solaris and NetBSD are capable of functioning as a dom0 with current versions of Xen. Some work has been done with the other BSDs and with Plan9, but these OSs either can only work as a domU or can only work with older Xen versions. Support is evolving rapidly, however. (FreeBSD seems especially close to having functional Xen bits.)

In this chapter, we'll focus on Solaris and NetBSD. Partially this is because they have mature Xen support, with active community involvement and ongoing development. Most importantly, though, it's because we have run them in production. In a later chapter, we'll discuss Windows.

Solaris

Sun has been pushing Xen virtualization heavily in recent community releases of OpenSolaris, and their effort shows. Solaris works well as both a dom0 and a domU, with closely integrated Xen support. The only caveat is that, as of this writing, OpenSolaris does not support Xen 3.3 and paravirt_ops domUs.

NOTE *Sun doesn't actually call their shipping version of Xen Xen. They use the term xVM for marketing purposes, and include the unrelated VirtualBox under the xVM label. We're going to continue to call it Xen, however, because it's the name we're used to.*

Only the x86 version of Solaris supports Xen—Solaris/SPARC uses alternate virtualization technologies.

VIRTUALIZATION WITH SOLARIS

Sun, being traditionally a "medium iron" company, has emphasized virtualization for a long time, with a few different, complementary technologies to implement virtualization at different levels. Here's an overview of their non-Xen virtualization offerings.

On new UltraSparc Niagara-based systems, pure hardware virtualization is provided by means of Logical Domains, or LDoms. These are a successor to the *Dynamic System Domains* found on earlier Sun Enterprise platforms, which allowed you to devote CPU and memory boards to independent OS instances. Similarly, on a reasonably new SPARC box, you can partition the CPU and memory to run multiple, independent operating systems, using the processor's hardware virtualization support.

On x86, Sun addresses full virtualization by way of their VirtualBox product. VirtualBox executes guest code directly where possible and emulates when necessary, much like VMware.

Finally, Sun addresses OS-level virtualization through Solaris Zones,* which are themselves an interesting, lightweight virtualization option. Like other OS-level virtualization platforms, Zones provide a fair amount of separation between operating environments with very little overhead.

Sun even offers the option to run Linux binaries under Solaris on x86_64, via *lx* branded Zones. (These *lx* branded Zones provide a thin compatibility layer between the Solaris kernel and Linux userspace. Pretty cool.) However, the Linux emulation isn't perfect. For example, since *lx* branded Zones use the same Solaris kernel that's running on the actual hardware, you can't load Linux device drivers.

---
* We tend to use the terms *Zone* and *Container* interchangeably. Technically, a Solaris Container implements system resource controls on top of Zones.

Getting Started with Solaris

To run Solaris under Xen, you'll need to get a copy of Solaris. There are several versions, so make sure that you pick the right one.

You do not want Solaris 10, which is the current Sun version of Solaris. Although it's a fine OS, it doesn't have Xen support because its development lags substantially behind the bleeding edge. (In this it caters to its market segment. We are personally acquainted with people who are running Solaris 8—a welcome contrast to the prevailing Linux view that software more than six months old is some sort of historical curiosity.)

Fortunately, Solaris 10 isn't the only option. Solaris Express acts as a preview of the next official Solaris version, and it's a perfectly capable OS for Xen in its own right. It incorporates Xen, but is still a bit behind the latest development. It's also not as popular as OpenSolaris.

Finally, there's OpenSolaris. Sun released huge tracts of Solaris source code a while ago under the Common Development and Distribution License[1] (CDDL), and the community's been pounding on it ever since. OpenSolaris is the result—it's much like Sun's release of Solaris but with new technology and a much faster release cycle. Think of the relationship between the two as like Red Hat Enterprise Linux and Fedora, only more so.

Both Solaris Express and OpenSolaris incorporate Xen support. Solaris Express has the Xen packages included on the DVD, while OpenSolaris requires you to download Xen as an add-on. Both of them provide a fairly polished experience. Although there are other distros based on the released Solaris code, none of them are particularly Xen-oriented, so the officially blessed distros are probably the best place to start.

RUNNING SOLARIS EXPRESS

We had some trouble deciding whether to focus on OpenSolaris or Solaris Express while we were writing this chapter. We decided to go with OpenSolaris because it seemed more popular, based on a completely unscientific poll of our friends.

However, Solaris Express is still a perfectly fine OS with excellent Xen support, so we've also included some notes on setting it up.

Believe it or not, Xen support should exist pretty much out of the box.* When you install Solaris Express on a system that supports Xen, it installs a Xen kernel and gives you the option to boot it from GRUB—just select **Solaris xVM** and off you go. (The included Xen version is 3.1.4 as of snv_107.)

From there, you can install domUs normally. It's even got virt-manager. Take a look at the next section for more details on setting up domUs. Most of these steps will apply to Solaris Express and OpenSolaris equally well.

---
* That's another reason we gloss over Solaris Express: Focusing on it would not, in the words of Douglas Adams, "make for nice fat books such as the American market thrives on."

In general, there are three possible configurations of (Open)Solaris that are of interest in our discussion of Xen.

- First, we have the Solaris dom0.
- Second, there's the Solaris domU on a Solaris dom0. This is a fairly straightforward setup.

---
[1] The CDDL is a free software license that's GPL-incompatible but generally inoffensive.

- Finally, you can run a Solaris domU under Linux with a minimum[2] of fuss.

Solaris Dom0

Let's start by setting up an OpenSolaris dom0, since you'll need one for the next section. (Although we suppose this applies only if you're doing something crazy like running through all our examples in order.)

Note that we're going to be using pfexec, the Solaris equivalent of sudo,[3] for these examples, so it's not necessary to be root for these steps.

First, download the distribution from *http://opensolaris.org/os/downloads/*. Follow the directions to unpack and burn it, and boot from the CD, just like virtually any other OS install.

The OpenSolaris LiveCD will probably be a familiar experience to anyone who's installed Ubuntu. It's really quite similar, with a standard GNOME desktop, some productivity software, and a cute *Install OpenSolaris* icon on the desktop. Double-click the **Install OpenSolaris** icon to launch the installer, then follow its directions.

When the installer finishes, it'll prompt you to reboot.

Setting Up Xen

If, once you reboot, you notice that you don't have Xen available, don't panic. OpenSolaris, unlike Solaris Express, doesn't include the Xen packages in the initial install. (Everything had to fit on a CD, after all.) You will have to install and set them up manually.

First, we create a ZFS boot environment. (If you're not familiar with boot environments, substitute the word *snapshot*. The idea is, if you break your system trying to install Xen, you can reboot into the original environment and try again.)

```
$ pfexec beadm create -a -d xvm xvm
$ pfexec beadm mount xvm /tmp/xvm
```

Next, we use the OpenSolaris pkg command to install the Xen packages in the new boot environment.

```
$ pfexec pkg -R /tmp/xvm install xvm-gui
```

As of OpenSolaris 2008.11, the xvm-gui package cluster provides all the necessary Xen packages. Previous versions may require you to install the

---

[2] The temptation exists to write "elegant minimum," but it's simply not so.

[3] Anyone planning to take offense to the comparison of pfexec and sudo: Please assume that we have been utterly convinced by your rhetoric and carry on with your day-to-day life.

packages individually. If you need to do that, you should be able to get away
with running:

```
# pkg install SUNWxvmhvm
# pkg install SUNWvirtinst
# pkg install SUNWlibvirt
# pkg install SUNWurlgrabber
```

These packages provide Xen (with HVM), virt-install, and virt-install's dependencies.

Next, we need to update GRUB to boot the Xen kernel properly.

Under OpenSolaris, *menu.lst* is at */rpool/boot/grub/menu.lst*. Edit the xvm menu item to look something like the following:

```
title xvm
findroot (pool_rpool,0,a)
bootfs rpool/ROOT/xvm
kernel$ /boot/$ISADIR/xen.gz
module$ /platform/i86xpv/kernel/$ISADIR/unix /platform/i86xpv/kernel/$ISADIR/
unix -B $ZFS-BOOTFS,console=text
module$ /platform/i86pc/$ISADIR/boot_archive
```

Note that we're using extensions to GRUB that enable variables in *menu.lst*, such as $ISADIR (for Instruction Set Architecture). Apart from that, it's a fairly normal Xen GRUB config, with the hypervisor, kernel, and ramdisk.

Reboot.

Solaris SMF

When you begin to configure a Solaris dom0, you'll probably notice immediately that some files aren't quite where you expect. For one thing, Solaris doesn't have an */etc/xen* directory, nor does it have the customary scripts in */etc/init.d*. The various support scripts in */etc/xen/scripts* instead live in */usr/lib/xen/scripts*. You can keep domain configurations wherever you like. (We actually make an */etc/xen* directory and put domain configurations in it.)

Instead of relying on the standard Xen config files, Solaris handles configuration and service startup via its own management framework, SMF (Service Management Facility). You can examine and change xend's settings using the svccfg command:

```
# svccfg -s xend listprop
```

This will output a list of properties for the xend service. For example, to enable migration:

```
# svccfg -s xend setprop config/xend-relocation address = \"\"
# svcadm refresh xend
# svcadm restart xend
```

You may have to enable the Xen-related services manually using svcadm, particularly if you initially booted the non-Xen kernel. To look at which services are stopped, use svcs:

```
# svcs -xv
```

If the Xen services are stopped for maintenance or disabled, you can enable them using svcadm:

```
# svcadm enable store
# svcadm enable xend
# svcadm enable virtd
# svcadm enable domains
# svcadm enable console
```

From that point, you should be able to use Solaris as a perfectly normal dom0 OS. It's even got libvirt. Have fun.

Creating a Solaris DomU

You didn't really think it would be that easy, did you? There are a couple of small caveats to note—things that make Xen under Solaris a slightly different animal than from under Linux. We'll start by creating a Solaris domU on a Solaris dom0, then extend our discussion to a Solaris domU on a Linux dom0.

ZFS Backing Devices

First, we suggest handling virtual block devices a bit differently under Solaris. Although you can create domU filesystems as plain loopback-mounted files, ZFS is probably a better option. It's been praised far and wide, even winning some grudging accolades from Linus Torvalds. It is, in fact, ideal for this sort of thing, and the generally accepted way to manage disks under Solaris— even more so now that OpenSolaris uses a ZFS root filesystem.

ZFS is pretty simple, at least to get started with. Users of LVM should find that creating a pool and filesystem are familiar tasks, even though the commands are slightly different. Here we'll make a pool, create a ZFS filesystem within the pool, and set the size of the filesystem:

```
# zpool create guests c0d0
# zfs create guests/escalus
# zfs set quota=4g guests/escalus
```

Now we can define a domain that uses the phy: device */dev/zvol/dsk/guests/ escalus* for its backing store, as shown in the config file.

We'll leave further subtleties of ZFS administration to Sun's documentation.

Installing a DomU via PyGRUB

The last thing to do before creating the domU is to write an appropriate config file. Here's ours:

```
# cat /etc/xen/escalus
name = "escalus"
memory = 512
disk = [
     'file:/opt/xen/install-iso/os200805.iso,6:cdrom,r',
     'phy:/dev/zvol/dsk/guests/escalus,0,w'
]
vif = ['']
bootloader = 'pygrub'
kernel = '/platform/i86xpv/kernel/unix'
ramdisk = 'boot/x86.microroot'
extra = /platform/i86xpv/kernel/unix -B console=ttya,livemode=text
on_shutdown = 'destroy'
on_reboot = 'destroy'
on_crash = 'destroy'
```

Note that the disk specifier works differently than with Linux domUs. Rather than using symbolic device names, as under Linux:

```
disk = ['file:/export/home/xen/solaris.img,sda1,w']
root = "/dev/sda1"
```

we instead specify the disk number:

```
disk = ['phy:/dev/zvol/dsk/guests/ecalus,0,w']
root = "/dev/dsk/c0d0s0"
```

Here we're installing Solaris from an ISO image (*os200805.iso*) using PyGRUB to pull the correct kernel and initrd off the CD image, boot that, and proceed with a normal install.

NOTE *One thing to watch out for is that domU networking will only work if you're using a GLD3-based network driver. The drivers that ship with Solaris are all fine in this regard—however, you may have trouble with third-party drivers.*

Once the install's done, we shut the machine down and remove the disk entry for the CD.

At this point your Solaris domU should be ready to go. Setting up a Linux domU is equally straightforward, since standard Linux domU images and kernels should work unmodified under Solaris.

Next, we'll look at setting up a Solaris domU under Linux.

Creating a Solaris DomU Under Linux

For the most part, a domU is independent of the dom0 OS, and thus the install under Linux uses much the same installation procedure as under Solaris. There are only a few pitfalls for the unwary.

First, you might have a bit more work to do to ensure that the domain can find an appropriate kernel. The Solaris image will complain bitterly, and in fact will not boot, with a Linux kernel.

If you're using PyGRUB on a Xen 3.1 or later system, you shouldn't need to do anything special. PyGRUB itself will load the appropriate files from OpenSolaris installation media without further intervention, just as in the previous example.

If you're not using PyGRUB, or if you're using the stock RHEL5.1 hypervisor, you'll need to extract the kernel and miniroot (initrd, for Linux people) from the OpenSolaris install package and place them somewhere that Xen can load them.

```
# mount -o loop,ro osol200811.iso
# cp /mnt/cdrom/boot/platform/i86pv/kernel/unix /xen/kernels/solaris/
# cp /mnt/cdrom/x86.miniroot /xen/kernels/solaris/
# umount /mnt/cdrom
```

Just as under Solaris, begin by writing a config file. We'll set up this config file to load the installer from the CD, and later alter it to boot our newly installed domU. Note that we're grabbing the kernel from the ISO, using the kernel and ramdisk options to specify the files we need.

```
bootloader = '/usr/bin/pygrub'
kernel = "/platform/i86xpv/kernel/amd64/unix"
ramdisk = "/boot/x86.microroot"
extra = "/platform/i86xpv/kernel/amd64/unix -- nowin -B install_media=cdrom"

cpu_weight=1024
memory = 1024
name = "rosaline"
vif = ['vifname=rosaline,ip=192.0.2.136,bridge=xenbr0,mac=00:16:3e:59:A7:88' ]
disk = [
        'file:/opt/distros/osol-0811.iso,xvdf:cdrom,r',
        'phy:/dev/verona/rosaline,xvda,w'
]
```

Make sure to create your backing store (*/dev/verona/rosaline* in this case). Now create the domain. Next step, installation.

Although OpenSolaris has a perfectly functional console when running as a domU, it unfortunately does not include a text mode installer. It does, however, include a VNC server and SSH server, either of which can be used to get a remote graphical display. Here's how to set up VNC.

Log in at the domU console with username *jack* and password *jack*.

Once you're in locally, set up your network. (If you're using DHCP, it'll probably already be set up for you, but it doesn't hurt to make sure.)

```
# pfexec ifconfig xnf0
xnf0: flags=201000843<UP,BROADCAST,RUNNING,MULTICAST,IPv4,CoS> mtu 1500 index 2
        inet 192.0.2.128 netmask ffffff00 broadcast 192.0.2.255
        ether aa:0:0:59:a7:88
```

You can see that our network is in fine shape, with the address 192.168.2.128. If it's not set up already, assign an address manually:

```
pfexec ifconfig xnf0 192.0.2.128/24
```

The VNC server should already be running. To enable remote access to it, run the vncpasswd command:

```
pfexec vncpasswd /etc/X11/.vncpasswd
```

vncpasswd will ask you to make up a password and enter it twice. Use this password to connect to the VNC server using your favorite VNC client. You should be greeted with an OpenSolaris desktop.

Finally, click the **Install OpenSolaris** icon on the desktop and proceed with the graphical install.

OpenSolaris DomU Postinstall Configuration

Once the installer has done its work, you'll be ready to shut down the domain and move to the next step: setting up the dom0 to load a kernel from a ZFS filesystem.

The problem is that in Xen 3.3, PyGRUB's version of libfsimage isn't able to handle recent versions of ZFS directly. Our solution was to download the Xen-unstable source tree (as of this writing, Xen 3.4-rc) from *http://xenbits .xen.org/* and build PyGRUB from that. (Alternatively, you can mount the install media, extract the kernel and microroot, specify these manually in the config file, and pass the correct "extra" line to the kernel—that works just as well.)

```
# hg clone http://xenbits.xen.org/xen-unstable.hg
# cd xen-unstable
# make tools
# cd xen-unstable.hg/tools/pygrub; make install
# cd xen-unstable.hg/tools/libfsimage; make install
```

Now we update the domain config file. Since we went to all the trouble of updating PyGRUB, we'll use it directly here:

```
bootloader='pygrub'
cpu_weight=1024
memory = 1024
```

```
name = "rosaline"
vif = ['vifname=rosaline,ip=192.0.2.136,bridge=xenbr0,mac=00:16:3e:59:A7:88' ]
disk = [
        #'file:/opt/distros/osol-0811.iso,xvdf:cdrom,r',
        'phy:/dev/verona/rosaline,xvda,w'
]
```

NOTE   *PV-GRUB, at this time, isn't able to load an OpenSolaris kernel properly. Use PyGRUB instead.*

Start your new domain as usual with xm:

```
# xm create rosaline
```

NetBSD

NetBSD is a popular choice for a dom0 OS because of its small and versatile design, which is a good match for the *dedicated virtualization server* model that Xen encourages. In our experience, a dom0 running NetBSD will use less memory and be at least as stable as one running Linux.

However, Linux people often make the mistake of assuming that NetBSD is exactly like Linux. It's not—it's kind of close, but NetBSD is the product of an evolution as long as Linux's, and it requires some practice to work with. In this section, we're going to assume that you're familiar with NetBSD's idiosyncrasies; we're only going to cover the Xen-related differences.

NetBSD's Historical Xen Support

NetBSD has supported Xen for a very long time—since NetBSD version 3.0, which incorporated support for Xen2 as dom0 and as a domU. This Xen2 support is quite stable. However, it has the obvious drawback of being Xen2, which lacks the Xen3 features like live migration and HVM. It's also 32 bit only, and doesn't support PAE (Physical Address Extension). (We've used this version quite a bit. The first Xen setup we used for hosting at prgmr.com was a dual Xeon running NetBSD 3.1 and Xen2, supporting Linux and NetBSD domUs.) NetBSD 3.1 introduced support for Xen 3.0.*x*—but only as a domU.

NetBSD 4.0 added Xen 3.1 support as both a domU and a dom0, and it also introduced support for HVM. The only remaining problem with NetBSD 4.0 was that it, like its predecessors, it did not support PAE or x86_64, which means that it was unable to use more than 4GB of memory. It also could not run as a domU on a 64-bit or PAE system, such as is used by Amazon's EC2. That last bit was the real killer—it meant NetBSD 4 required a non-PAE 32-bit hypervisor, which in turn limited you to 4GB of address space, which translates about 3.5GB of physical memory. (This limitation is so significant that Xen.org doesn't even distribute a non-PAE binary package anymore.)

Finally, the new and shiny NetBSD 5 adds PAE support for NetBSD domUs, x86-64 support for both dom0 and domUs, and support for 32-bit domUs on 64-bit dom0s (*32-on-64* in Xen parlance). Work is still being done to add features to bring NetBSD Xen support into feature parity with Linux's Xen support, but NetBSD is already a perfectly viable platform.

Installing NetBSD as a Dom0

The basic steps to get started using NetBSD with Xen are pretty much the same as for any other OS: Download it, install it, and make it work. Again, we're assuming that you're familiar with the basic NetBSD install procedure, so we're just going to outline these directions briefly.

Begin by downloading NetBSD and installing it as usual. (We opted to download and burn the ISO at *http://mirror.planetunix.net/pub/NetBSD/iso/ 5.0/amd64cd-5.0.iso.*) Configure the system according to your preference.

NOTE   *ftp:// and* http:// *are interchangeable on all of the* ftp.netbsd.org *URLs.* http:// *gets through firewalls better, and* ftp:// *is slightly faster. Pick one. Also, you often get significantly better speeds using a mirror rather than the netbsd.org site. If your FTP install fails partway through, the first thing to do is to try another mirror.*

However you install NetBSD, go through the installer and reboot into your new system. Next, install the Xen kernel and supporting tools using the NetBSD ports system, pkgsrc. Get pkgsrc at *http://ftp.netbsd.org/pub/NetBSD/ packages/pkgsrc.tar.gz.* Untar *pkgsrc.tar.gz*, then install Xen:

```
# cd pkgsrc/sysutils/xenkernel3 ; make install
# cd pkgsrc/sysutils/xentools3 ; make install
```

After installing the Xen tools, NetBSD will remind you to create the Xen device nodes:

```
# cd /dev ; sh MAKEDEV xen
```

Now that Xen is installed, our next task is to install GRUB in place of the standard NetBSD bootloader so that we can perform the multistage boot that Xen requires:

```
# cd pkgsrc/sysutils/grub ; make install
```

Our next step is to download and install NetBSD Xen kernels—we're already running off standard NetBSD kernels, and we've got the hypervisor installed, but we still need kernels for the dom0 and domUs. Download *netbsd-XEN3_DOM0.gz*, *netbsd-XEN3_DOMU.gz*, and *netbsd-INSTALL_XEN3 _DOMU.gz* from your favorite NetBSD mirror. (We used *http://mirror .planetunix.net/pub/NetBSD/NetBSD-5.0/.*)

Now that we have suitable Xen kernels to go with the hypervisor and supporting tools that we installed in the previous step, we can set up GRUB in the usual way:

```
# grub-install --no-floppy sd0a
```

Edit */grub/menu.lst* so that it boots the Xen kernel and loads NetBSD as a module. Here's a complete file, with comments (adapted from a NetBSD example at *http://www.netbsd.org/ports/xen/howto.html*):

```
# Boot the first entry by default
default=1

# after 10s, boot the default entry if the user didn't hit keyboard
timeout=10

# Configure serial port to use as console. Ignore this bit if you're
# not using the serial port.
serial --unit=0 --speed=115200 --word=8 --parity=no --stop=1

# Let the user select which console to use (serial or VGA). Default
# to serial after 10s
terminal --timeout=10 console serial
# An entry for NetBSD/xen, using /xen/kernels/xen.gz as the domain0
# kernel, with serial console. Domain0 will have 64MB RAM allocated.
# Assume NetBSD is installed in the first MBR partition.
title Xen 3.3 / NetBSD (sd0a, serial) root(hd0,0) kernel
(hd0,a)/xen/kernels/xen.gz dom0_mem=65536 com1=115200,8n1 module
(hd0,a)/xen/kernels/XEN3_DOM0 root=sd0a ro console=ttyS0

# Same as above, but using VGA console
# We can use console=tty0 (Linux syntax) or console=pc (NetBSD syntax)
title Xen 3.3 / NetBSD (sd0a, vga)
root(hd0,0)
kernel (hd0,a)/xen/kernels/xenkernel3-3.1.0nb2 dom0_mem=65536 noreboot
module (hd0,a)/xen/kernels/XEN3_DOM0 root=sd0a ro console=pc

# Load a regular NetBSD/i386 kernel. Can be useful if you end up with a
# nonworking /xen.gz
title NetBSD 5
root (hd0,a)
kernel (hd0,a)/netbsd-GENERIC
```

The important bits are the kernel name, XEN3_DOM0, and the root device, which we specify using NetBSD syntax.

NOTE *We've also set up this config file to use the serial console. No matter which operating system you use, we strongly recommend using a serial console with Xen, even if you prefer to use a KVM or other method of remote management normally. See Chapter 14 for more discussion of the many and varied uses of the serial console.*

Copy over the basic Xen config files to the directory where the Xen tools will expect to find them:

```
# cp /usr/pkg/share/examples/xen/* /usr/pkg/etc/xen/
```

Now that we have all the parts of a NetBSD dom0, we need to start xenbackendd and xend (in that order, or it won't work).

```
# cp /usr/pkg/share/examples/rc.d/xen* /etc/rc.d/

# echo "xenbackendd=YES">>/etc/rc.conf
# echo "xend=YES">>/etc/rc.conf
```

Finally, to get networking to work, create */etc/ifconfig.bridge0* with these contents:

```
create
!brconfig $int add fxp0 up
```

At this point you're most likely done. Reboot to test, or start the Xen services manually:

```
# /ctc/rc.d/xenbackendd start
Starting xenbackendd.
# /etc/rc.d/xend start
Starting xend
```

You should now be able to run `xm list`:

```
# xm list
Name ID Mem VCPUs State Time(s)
Domain-0 0 64 1 r----- 282.1
```

Installing NetBSD as a DomU

Installing NetBSD as a domU is easy, even with a Linux dom0. In fact, because NetBSD's INSTALL kernels include a ramdisk with everything necessary to complete the installation, we can even do it without modifying the configuration from the dom0, given a sufficiently versatile PyGRUB or PV-GRUB setup.

For this discussion, we assume that you've got a domU of some sort already set up—perhaps one of the generic prgmr.com Linux domains. In this domU, you'll need to have a small boot partition that GRUB[4] can read. This is where we'll store the kernel and GRUB configuration.

---

[4] More accurately, of course, your GRUB simulator. If this is PyGRUB, it relies on `libfsimage`.

First, from within your domain, download the NetBSD kernels:

```
# wget http://mirror.planetunix.net/pub/NetBSD/NetBSD-5.0/amd64/binary/kernel/
netbsd-INSTALL_XEN3_DOMU.gz
# wget http://mirror.planetunix.net/pub/NetBSD/NetBSD-5.0/amd64/binary/kernel/
netbsd-XEN3_DOMU.gz
```

Then, edit the domain's GRUB menu (most likely at */boot/grub/menu.lst*) to load the INSTALL kernel on next reboot. (On the reboot after that, when the installation's done, you'll select the NetBSD run option.)

```
title NetBSD install
      root (hd0,0)
      kernel /boot/netbsd-INSTALL_XEN3_DOMU

title NetBSD run
      root (hd0,0)
      kernel /boot/netbsd-XEN3_DOMU root=xbd1a
```

Reboot, selecting the **NetBSD install** option.

As if by magic, your domain will begin running the NetBSD installer, until you end up in a totally ordinary NetBSD install session. Go through the steps of the NetBSD FTP install. There's some very nice documentation at *http://netbsd.org/docs/guide/en/chap-exinst.html.*

NOTE *At this point you have to be careful not to overwrite your boot device. For example, prgmr.com gives you only a single physical block device, from which you'll need to carve a /boot partition in addition to the normal filesystem layout.*

The only sticky point is that you have to be careful to set up a boot device that PyGRUB can read, in the place where PyGRUB expects it. (If you have multiple physical devices, PyGRUB will try to boot from the first one.) Since we're installing within the standard prgmr.com domU setup, we only have a single physical block device to work with, which we'll carve into separate */boot* and */* partitions. Our disklabel, with a *32 MB FFS /boot* partition, looks like this:

```
We now have your BSD-disklabel partitions as:
 This is your last chance to change them.

     Start MB   End MB  Size MB FS type     Newfs Mount Mount point
     --------- --------- --------- ---------- ----- ----- -----------
 a:        31      2912     2882 FFSv1        Yes   Yes   /
 b:      2913      3040      128 swap
 c;         0      3071     3072 NetBSD partition
 d:         0      3071     3072 Whole disk
 e:         0        30       31 Linux Ext2
 f:         0         0        0 unused
 g: Show all unused partitions
 h: Change input units (sectors/cylinders/MB)
>x: Partition sizes ok
```

Once the install's done, reboot. Select the regular kernel in PyGRUB, and your domU should be ready to go.

After NetBSD's booted, if you want to change the bootloader configuration, you can mount the *ext2* partition thus:

```
# mount_ext2fs /dev/xbd0d /mnt
```

This will allow you upgrade the domU kernel. Just remember that, whenever you want to upgrade the kernel, you need to mount the partition that PyGRUB loads the kernel from and make sure to update that kernel and *menu.lst*. It would also be a good idea to install the NetBSD kernel in the usual place, in the root of the domU filesystem, but it isn't strictly necessary.

And there you have it—a complete, fully functional NetBSD domU, without any intervention from the dom0 at all. (If you have dom0 access, you can specify the install kernel on the kernel= line of the domain config file in the usual way—but what would be the fun of that?)

Beyond Paravirtualization: HVM

In this chapter, we have outlined the general steps necessary to use Solaris and NetBSD as both dom0 and domU operating systems. This isn't meant to exhaustively list the operating systems that work with Xen—in particular, we haven't mentioned Plan9 or FreeBSD at all—but it does give you a good idea of the sort of differences that you might encounter and easy recipes for using at least two systems other than Linux.

Furthermore, they each have their own advantages: NetBSD is a very lightweight operating system, much better than Linux at handling low-memory conditions. This comes in handy with Xen. Solaris isn't as light, but it is extremely robust and has interesting technologies, such as ZFS. Both of these OSs can support any OS as domU, as long as it's been modified to work with Xen. That's virtualization in action, if you like.

NOTE   *The new Linux paravirt_ops functionality that is included in the kernel.org kernels requires Xen hypervisor version 3.3 or later, so it works with NetBSD but not OpenSolaris.*

Finally, the addition of hardware virtualization extensions to recent processors means that virtually any OS can be used as a domU, even if it hasn't been modified specifically to work with Xen. We discuss Xen's support for these extensions in Chapter 12 and then describe using HVM to run Windows under Xen in Chapter 13. Stay tuned.

9

XEN MIGRATION

*In these situations the combination of virtualization and
migration significantly improves manageability.
—Clark et al., "Live Migration of Virtual Machines"*

So let's review: Xen, in poetic terms, is an abstraction, built atop other abstractions, wrapped around still further abstractions. The goal of all this abstraction is to ensure that you, in your snug and secure domU, never even have to think about the messy, noisy, fallible hardware that actually sends electrical pulses out the network ports.

Of course, once in a while the hardware becomes, for reasons of its own, unable to run Xen. Perhaps it's overloaded, or maybe it needs some preventive maintenance. So long as you have advance warning, even this need not interrupt your virtual machine. One benefit of the sort of *total hardware independence* offered by Xen is the ability to move an entire virtual machine instance to another machine and transparently resume operation—a process referred to as *migration*.

Xen migration transfers the entire virtual machine—the in-memory state of the kernel, all processes, and all application states. From the user's perspective, a live migration isn't even noticeable—at most, a few packets are dropped. This has the potential to make scheduled downtime a thing of the past. (Unscheduled downtime, like death and taxes, shows every sign of being inescapable.[1])

Migration may be either *live* or *cold*,[2] with the distinction based on whether the instance is running at the time of migration. In a live migration, the domain continues to run during transfer, and downtime is kept to a minimum. In a cold migration, the virtual machine is paused, saved, and sent to another physical machine.

In either of these cases, the saved machine will expect its IP address and ARP cache to work on the new subnet. This is no surprise, considering that the in-memory state of the network stack persists unchanged. Attempts to initiate live migration between different layer 2 subnets will fail outright. Cold migration between different subnets will work, in that the VM will successfully transfer but will most likely need to have its networking reconfigured. We'll mention these characteristics again later in our discussion of live migration.

First, though, let's examine a basic, manual method for moving a domain from one host to another.

Migration for Troglodytes

The most basic, least elegant way to move a Xen instance from one physical machine to another is to stop it completely, move its backing storage, and re-create the domain on the remote host. This requires a full shutdown and reboot cycle for the VM. It isn't even "migration" in the formal Xen sense, but you may find it necessary if, for example, you need to change out the underlying block device or if certain machine-specific attributes change, for example, if you're moving a VM between different CPU architectures or from a machine that uses PAE to one that doesn't.[3]

Begin by shutting down the virtual machine normally, either from within the operating system or by doing an xm shutdown from the dom0. Copy its backing store, kernel image (if necessary), and config file over, and finally xm create the machine as usual on the new host.

It's primitive, but at least it's almost certain to work and doesn't require any sort of complex infrastructure. We mention it mostly for completeness; this is a way to move a Xen domain from one physical machine to another.

---

[1] Maybe not; see Project Kemari or Project Remus at *http://www.osrg.net/kemari/* and *http://dsg.cs.ubc.ca/remus/* for work being done on adding hardware redundancy to Xen.

[2] We also like the terms *hot* and *dead*, which are the less-commonly used parallels of the more common terms.

[3] For example, NetBurst (Pentium 4 and friends) to Core (Core 2 et al.). Xen offers no ability to move a VM from, say, x86 to PPC.

Migration with xm save and xm restore

This "cowboy" method aside, all forms of migration are based on the basic idea of saving the domain on one machine and restoring it on another. You can do this manually using the xm save and xm restore commands, simulating the automatic process.

The Xen documentation likens the xm save and restore cycle to hibernation on a physical machine. When a machine hibernates, it enters a power-saving mode that saves the memory image to disk and physically powers off the machine. When the machine turns on again, the operating system loads the saved memory image from the disk and picks up where it left off. xm save behaves exactly the same way. Just like with physical hibernation, the saved domain drops its network connections, takes some time to pause and resume, and consumes no CPU or memory until it is restored.

Even if you're not planning to do anything fancy involving migration, you may still find yourself saving machines when the physical Xen server reboots. Xen includes an init script to save domains automatically when the system shuts down and restore them on boot. To accommodate this, we suggest making sure that */var* is large enough to hold the complete contents of the server's memory (in addition to logs, DNS databases, etc.).

To save the machine, issue:

```
# xm save <domain name or id> <savefile>
```

This command tells the domain to suspend itself; the domain releases its resources back to domain 0, detaches its interrupt handlers, and converts its physical memory mappings back to domain-virtual mappings (because the physical memory mappings will almost certainly change when the domain is restored).

NOTE   *Those of you who maintain a constant burning focus on implementation will notice that this implies domU OS-level support for Xen. HVM save and restore—that is, when the guest can't be counted on to be Xen-aware—are done slightly differently. See Chapter 12 for details.*

At this point, domain 0 takes over, stops the domU, and checkpoints the domain state to a file. During this process it makes sure that all memory page references are canonical (that is, domain virtual, because references to machine memory pages will almost certainly be invalid on restore). Then it writes the contents of pages to disk, reclaiming pages as it goes.

After this process is complete, the domain has stopped running. The entire contents of its memory are in a savefile approximately the size of its memory allocation, which you can restore at will. In the meantime, you can run other domains, reboot the physical machine, back up the domain's virtual disks, or do whatever else required you to take the domain offline in the first place.

NOTE *Although xm save ordinarily stops the domain while saving it, you can also invoke it with the -c option, for checkpoint. This tells xm to leave the domain running. It's a bit complex to set up, though, because you also need some way to snapshot the domain's storage during the save. This usually involves an external device migration script.*

When that's done, restoring the domain is easy:

```
# xm restore <savefile>
```

Restoration operates much like saving in reverse; the hypervisor allocates memory for the domain, writes out pages from the savefile to the newly allocated memory, and translates shadow page table entries to point at the new physical addresses. When this is accomplished, the domain resumes execution, reinstates everything it removed when it suspended, and begins functioning as if nothing happened.

NOTE *The savefile remains intact; if something goes wrong with the restarted machine, you can restore the savefile and try again.*

This ability to save and restore on the local machine works as the backbone of the more complex forms of migration supported by Xen.

Cold Migration

Before we get into Xen's automated migration, we'll give an outline of a manual *cold migration* process that approximates the flow of live migration to get an idea of the steps involved.

In this case, migration begins by saving the domain. The administrator manually moves the save file and the domain's underlying storage over to the new machine and restores the domain state. Because the underlying block device is moved over manually, there's no need to have the same filesystem accessible from both machines, as would be necessary for live migration. All that matters is transporting the content of the Xen virtual disk.

Here are some steps to cold migrate a Xen domain:

```
# xm save <domain id> <savefile>
# scp <savefile> <target.domain.tld:/path/>
```

Perform the appropriate steps to copy the domain's storage to the target computer—rsync, scp, dd piped into ssh, whatever floats your boat. Whatever method you choose, ensure that it copies the disk in such a way that is bit-for-bit the same and has the same path on both physical machines. In particular, do not mount the domU filesystem on machine A and copy its files over to the new domU filesystem on machine B. This will cause the VM to crash upon restoration.

Finally, restart the domain on the new machine:

```
# xm restore <savefile>
```

There's no need to copy the domain config file over to the new machine; the savefile contains all the configuration information necessary to start the machine. Conversely, this also means that you can't change the parameters of the machine between save and restore and expect that to have any effect at all.[4]

Live Migration

Cold migration has its place, but one of the absolute neatest features of Xen is the ability to move a domain from one physical machine to another transparently, that is, imperceptibly to the outside world. This feature is *live migration.*

As with cold migration, live migration transfers the domain's configuration as part of its state; it doesn't require the administrator to manually copy over a config file. Manual copying is, in fact, not required at all. Of course, you will still need the config file if you want to recreate the domain from scratch on the new machine.

Live migration has some extra prerequisites. It relies on the domain's storage being accessible from both machines and on the machines being on the same subnet. Finally, because the copy phase occurs automatically over the network, the machines must run a network service.

How It Works

We would really like to say that live migration works by magic. In reality, however, it works by the application of sufficiently advanced technology.

Live migration is based on the basic idea of *save and restore* only in the most general sense. The machine doesn't hibernate until the very last phase of the migration, and it comes back out of its virtual hibernation almost immediately.

As shown in Figure 9-1, Xen live migration begins by sending a request, or *reservation*, to the target specifying the resources the migrating domain will need. If the target accepts the request, the source begins the *iterative precopy* phase of migration. During this step, Xen copies pages of memory over a TCP connection to the destination host. While this is happening, pages that change are marked as dirty and then recopied. The machine iterates this until only very frequently changed pages remain, at which point it begins the *stop and copy* phase. Now Xen stops the VM and copies over any pages that change too frequently to efficiently copy during the previous phase. In practice, our testing suggests that Xen usually reaches this point after four to eight iterations. Finally the VM starts executing on the new machine.

By default, Xen will iterate up to 29 times and stop if the number of dirty pages falls below a certain threshold. You can specify this threshold and the number of iterations at compile time, but the defaults should work fine.

---

[4] To forestall the inevitable question, we did try using a hex editor on the savefile. The result was an immediate crash.

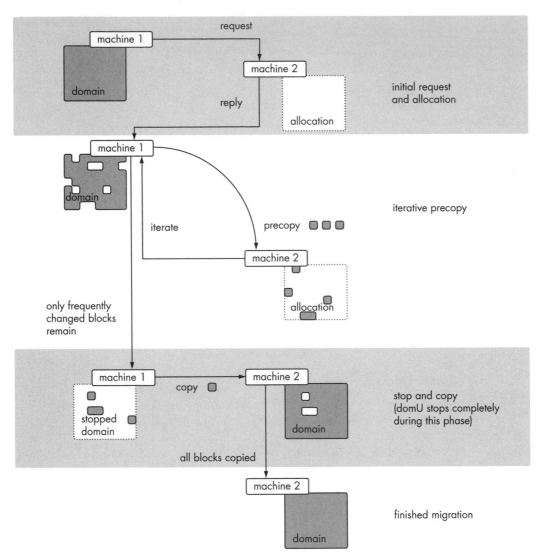

Figure 9-1: Overview of live migration

Making Xen Migration Work

First, note that migration won't work unless the domain is using some kind of network-accessible storage, as described later in this chapter. If you haven't got such a thing, set that up first and come back when it's done.

Second, xend has to be set up to listen for migration requests on both physical machines. Note that both machines need to listen; if only the target machine has the relocation server running, the source machine won't be able to shut down its Xen instance at the correct time, and the restarted domain will reboot as if it hadn't shut down cleanly.

Enable the migration server by uncommenting the following in */etc/ xend-config.sxp*:

```
(xend-relocation-server yes)
```

This will cause xend to listen for migration requests on port 8002, which can be changed with the (xend-relocation-port) directive. Note that this is somewhat of a security risk. You can mitigate this to some extent by adding lines like the following:

```
(xend-relocation-address 192.168.1.1)
(xend-relocation-hosts-allow '^localhost$' '^host.example.org$')
```

The xend-relocation-address line confines xend to listen for migration requests on that address so that you can restrict migration to, for example, an internal subnet or a VPN. The second line specifies a list of hosts to allow migration from as a space-separated list of quoted regular expressions. Although the idea of migrating from the localhost seems odd, it does have some value for testing. Xen migration to and from *other* hosts will operate fine without localhost in the allowed-hosts list, so feel free to remove it if desired.

On distributions that include a firewall, you'll have to open port 8002 (or another port that you've specified using the xend-relocation-port directive). Refer to your distro's documentation if necessary.

With live migration, Xen can maintain network connections while migrating so that clients don't have to reconnect. The domain, after migration, sends an unsolicited ARP (address request protocol) reply to advertise its new location. (Usually this will work. In some network configurations, depending on your switch configuration, it'll fail horribly. Test it first.) The migrating instance can only maintain its network connections if it's migrating to a machine on the same physical subnet because its IP address remains the same.

The commands are simple:

```
# xm migrate --live <domain id> <destination machine>
```

The domain's name in xm list changes to migrating-[domain] while the VM copies itself over to the remote host. At this time it also shows up in the xm list output on the target machine. On our configuration, this copy and run phase took around 1 second per 10MB of domU memory, followed by about 6 seconds of service interruption.

NOTE *If you, for whatever reason, want the migration to take less total time (at the expense of greater downtime), you can eliminate the repeated incremental copies by simply removing the --live option.*

```
# xm migrate <domain id> <destination machine>
```

This automatically stops the domain, saves it as normal, sends it to the destination machine, and restores it. Just as with --live, the final product is a migrated domain.

Here's a domain list on the target machine while the migration is in process. Note that the memory usage goes up as the migrating domain transfers more data:

Name	ID	Mem(MiB)	VCPUs	State	Time(s)
Domain-0	0	1024	8	r-----	169.2
orlando	3	307	0	-bp---	0.0

About 30 seconds later, the domain's transferred a few hundred more MB:

Name	ID	Mem(MiB)	VCPUs	State	Time(s)
Domain-0	0	1024	8	r-----	184.8
orlando	3	615	0	-bp---	0.0

Another 30 seconds further on, the domain's completely transferred and running:

Name	ID	Mem(MiB)	VCPUs	State	Time(s)
Domain-0	0	1024	8	r-----	216.0
orlando	3	1023	1	-b----	0.0

We also pinged the domain as it was migrating. Note that response times go up dramatically while the domain moves its data:

```
PING  (69.12.128.195) 56(84) bytes of data.
64 bytes from 69.12.128.195: icmp_seq=1 ttl=56 time=15.8 ms
64 bytes from 69.12.128.195: icmp_seq=2 ttl=56 time=13.8 ms
64 bytes from 69.12.128.195: icmp_seq=3 ttl=56 time=53.0 ms
64 bytes from 69.12.128.195: icmp_seq=4 ttl=56 time=179 ms
64 bytes from 69.12.128.195: icmp_seq=5 ttl=56 time=155 ms
64 bytes from 69.12.128.195: icmp_seq=6 ttl=56 time=247 ms
64 bytes from 69.12.128.195: icmp_seq=7 ttl=56 time=239 ms
```

After most of the domain's memory has been moved over, there's a brief hiccup as the domain stops, copies over its last few pages, and restarts on the destination host:

```
64 bytes from 69.12.128.195: icmp_seq=107 ttl=56 time=14.2 ms
64 bytes from 69.12.128.195: icmp_seq=108 ttl=56 time=13.0 ms
64 bytes from 69.12.128.195: icmp_seq=109 ttl=56 time=98.0 ms
64 bytes from 69.12.128.195: icmp_seq=110 ttl=56 time=15.4 ms
64 bytes from 69.12.128.195: icmp_seq=111 ttl=56 time=14.2 ms
--- 69.12.128.195 ping statistics ---
111 packets transmitted, 110 received, 0% packet loss, time 110197ms
rtt min/avg/max/mdev = 13.001/226.999/382.360/101.826 ms
```

At this point the domain is completely migrated.

However, the migration tools don't make any guarantees that the migrated domain will actually run on the target machine. One common problem occurs when migrating from a newer CPU to an older one. Because instructions are enabled at boot time, it's quite possible for the migrated kernel to attempt to execute instructions that simply no longer exist.

For example, the sfence instruction is used to explicitly serialize out-of-order memory writes; any writes issued before sfence must complete before writes after the fence. This instruction is part of SSE, so it isn't supported on all Xen-capable machines. A domain started on a machine that supports sfence will try to keep using it after migration, and it'll crash in short order. This may change in upcoming versions of Xen, but at present, all production Xen environments that we know of migrate only between homogeneous hardware.

Migrating Storage

Live migration only copies the RAM and processor state; ensuring that the migrated domain can access its disk is up to the administrator. As such, the storage issue boils down to a question of capabilities. The migrated domain will expect its disks to be exactly consistent and to retain the same device names on the new machine as on the old machine. In most cases, that means the domU, to be capable of migration, must pull its backing storage over the network. Two popular ways to attain this in the Xen world are ATA over Ethernet (AoE), and iSCSI. We also discussed NFS in Chapter 4. Finally, you could just throw a suitcase of money at NetApp.

There are a lot of options beyond these; you may also want to consider cLVM (with some kind of network storage enclosure) and DRBD.

With all of these storage methods, we'll discuss an approach that uses a storage server to export a block device to a dom0, which then makes the storage available to a domU.

Note that both iSCSI and AoE limit themselves to providing simple block devices. Neither allows multiple clients to share the same filesystem without filesystem-level support! This an important point. Attempts to export a single ext3 filesystem and run domUs out of file-backed VBDs on that filesystem will cause almost immediate corruption. Instead, configure your network storage technology to export a block device for each domU. However, the exported devices don't have to correspond to physical devices; we can as easily export files or LVM volumes.

ATA over Ethernet

ATA over Ethernet is easy to set up, reasonably fast, and popular. It's not routable, but that doesn't really matter in the context of live migration because live migration always occurs within a layer 2 broadcast domain.

People use AoE to fill the same niche as a basic SAN setup: to make centralized storage available over the network. It exports block devices that can then be used like locally attached disks. For the purposes of this example, we'll export one block device via AoE for each domU.

Let's start by setting up the AoE server. This is the machine that exports disk devices to dom0s, which in their turn host domUs that rely on the devices for backing storage. The first thing you'll need to do is make sure that you've got the kernel AoE driver, which is located in the kernel configuration at:

```
Device drivers --->
  Block Devices --->
    <*> ATA over Ethernet support
```

You can also make it a module (*m*). If you go that route, load the module:

```
# modprobe aoe
```

Either way, make sure that you can access the device nodes under */dev/ etherd*. They should be created by udev. If they aren't, try installing the kernel source and running the *Documentation/aoe/udev-install.sh* script that comes in the kernel source tree. This script will generate rules and place them in an appropriate location—in our case */etc/udev/rules.d/50-udev.rules*. You may need to tune these rules for your udev version. The configurations that we used on CentOS 5.3 were:

```
SUBSYSTEM=="aoe", KERNEL=="discover",   NAME="etherd/%k", GROUP="disk", MODE="0220"
SUBSYSTEM=="aoe", KERNEL=="err",        NAME="etherd/%k", GROUP="disk", MODE="0440"
SUBSYSTEM=="aoe", KERNEL=="interfaces", NAME="etherd/%k", GROUP="disk", MODE="0220"
SUBSYSTEM=="aoe", KERNEL=="revalidate", NAME="etherd/%k", GROUP="disk", MODE="0220"

# aoe block devices
KERNEL=="etherd*",        NAME="%k", GROUP="disk"
```

AoE also requires some support software. The server package is called vblade and can be obtained from *http://aoetools.sourceforge.net/*. You'll also need the client tools aoetools on both the server and client machines, so make sure to get those.

First, run the `aoe-interfaces` command on the storage server to tell vblade what interfaces to export on:

```
# aoe-interfaces <ifname>
```

vblade can export most forms of storage, including SCSI, MD, or LVM. Despite the name ATA over Ethernet, it's not limited to exporting ATA devices; it can export any seekable device file or any ordinary filesystem image. Just specify the filename on the command line. (This is yet another instance where UNIX's *everything is a file* philosophy comes in handy.)

Although vblade has a configuration file, it's simple enough to specify the options on the command line. The syntax is:

```
# vblade <shelf id> <slot id> <interface> <file to export>
```

So, for example, to export a file:

```
# dd if=/dev/zero of=/path/file.img bs=1024M count=1
# vblade 0 0 <ifname> </path/file.img> &
```

This exports */path/file.img* as */dev/etherd/e0.0.*

NOTE *For whatever reason, the new export is not visible from the server. The AoE maintainers note that this is not actually a bug because it was never a design goal.*

AoE may expect the device to have a partition table, or at least a valid partition signature. If necessary, you can partition it locally by making a partition that spans the entire disk:

```
# losetup /dev/loop0 test.img
# fdisk /dev/loop0
```

When you've done that, make a filesystem and detach the loop:

```
# mkfs /dev/loop0
# losetup -d /dev/loop0
```

Alternately, if you want multiple partitions on the device, fdisk the device and create multiple partitions as normal. The new partitions will show up on the client with names like */dev/etherd/e0.0p1*. To access the devices from the AoE server, performing kpartx -a on an appropriately set up loop device should work.

Now that we've got a functional server, let's set up the client. Large chunks of the AoE client are implemented as a part of the kernel, so you'll need to make sure that AoE's included in the dom0 kernel just as with the storage server. If it's a module, you'll mostly likely want to ensure it loads on boot. If you're using CentOS, you'll probably also need to fix your udev rules, again just as with the server.

Since we're using the dom0 to arbitrate the network storage, we don't need to include the AoE driver in the domU kernel. All Xen virtual disk devices are accessed via the domU xenblk driver, regardless of what technology they're using for storage.[5]

Download aoetools from your distro's package management system or *http://aoetools.sourceforge.net/*. If necessary, build and install the package.

Once the aoetools package is installed, you can test the exported AoE device on the client by doing:

```
# aoe-discover
# aoe-stat
     e0.0          1.073GB    eth0 up
# mount /dev/etherd/e0.0 /mnt/aoe
```

---

[5] A natural extension would be to have the domU mount the network storage directly by including the driver and support software in the initrd. In that case, no local disk configuration would be necessary.

In this case, the device is 1GB (or thereabouts) in size, has been exported as slot 0 of shelf 0, and has been found on the client's eth0. If it mounts successfully, you're ready to go. You can unmount */mnt/aoe* and use */dev/etherd/e0.0* as an ordinary phy: device for domU storage. An appropriate domU config disk= line might be:

```
disk = [ phy:/dev/etherd/e0.0, xvda, w ]
```

If you run into any problems, check */var/log/xen/xend.log*. The most common problems relate to the machine's inability to find devices—block devices or network devices. In that case, errors will show up in the log file. Make sure that the correct virtual disks and interfaces are configured.

iSCSI

AoE and iSCSI share a lot of similarities from the administrator's perspective; they're both ways of exporting storage over a network without requiring special hardware. They both export block devices, rather than filesystems, meaning that only one machine can access an exported device at a time. ISCSI differs from AoE in that it's a routable protocol, based on TCP/IP. This makes it less efficient in both CPU and bandwidth, but more versatile, since iSCSI exports can traverse layer 2 networks.

iSCSI divides the world into *targets* and *initiators*. You might be more familiar with these as *servers* and *clients*, respectively. The servers function as targets for SCSI commands, which are initiated by the client machines. In most installations, the iSCSI targets will be dedicated devices, but if you need to set up an iSCSI server for testing on a general-purpose server, here's how.

Setting Up the iSCSI Server

For the target we recommend the *iSCSI Enterprise Target* implementation (*http://sourceforge.net/projects/iscsitarget/*). Other software exists, but we're less familiar with it.

Your distro vendor most likely provides a package. On Debian it's iscsitarget. Red Hat and friends use the related tgt package, which has somewhat different configuration. Although we don't cover the details of setting up tgt, there is an informative page at *http://www.cyberciti.biz/tips/howto-setup-linux-iscsi-target-sanwith-tgt.html*. For the rest of this section, we'll assume that you're using the iSCSI Enterprise Target.

If necessary, you can download and build the iSCSI target software manually. Download the target software from the website and save it somewhere appropriate (we dropped it onto our GNOME desktop for this example). Unpack it:

```
# tar xzvf Desktop/iscsitarget-0.4.16.tar.gz
# cd iscsitarget-0.4.16
```

Most likely you'll be able to build all of the components—both the kernel module and userspace tools—via the usual make process. Ensure that you've installed the openSSL headers, probably as part of the openssl-devel package or similar:

```
# make
# make install
```

make install will also copy the default config files into */etc*. Our next step is to edit them appropriately.

The main config file is */etc/ietd.conf*. It's liberally commented, and most of the values can safely be left at their defaults (for now). The bit that we're mostly concerned with is the Target section:

```
Target iqn.2001-04.com.prgmr:domU.orlando
      Lun 0 Path=/opt/xen/orlando.img,Type=fileio
```

There are many other variables that we could tweak here, but the basic target definition is simple: the word **Target** followed by a conforming *iSCSI Qualified Name* with a logical unit definition. Note the Type=fileio. In this example we're using plain files, but you'll most likely also want to use this value with whole disk exports and LVM volumes too.

The init script *etc/iscsi_target* should have also been copied to the appropriate place. If you want iSCSI to be enabled on boot, create appropriate start and kill links as well.

Now we can export our iSCSI devices:

```
# /etc/init.d/iscsi_target start
```

To check that it's working:

```
# cat /proc/net/iet/volume
tid:1 name:iqn.2001-04.com.prgmr:domU.orlando
      lun:0 state:0 iotype:fileio iomode:wt path:/opt/xen/orlando
```

You should see the export(s) that you've defined, along with some status information.

iSCSI Client Setup

For the initiator, a variety of clients exist. However, the best-supported package seems to be Open-iSCSI, available at *http://www.open-iscsi.org/*. Both Red Hat and Debian make a version available through their package manager, as iscsi-initiator-utils and open-iscsi, respectively. You can also download the package from the website and work through the very easy installation process.

When you have the iSCSI initiator installed, however you choose to do it, the next step is to say the appropriate incantations to instruct the machine to mount your iSCSI devices at boot.

The iSCSI daemon, iscsid, uses a database to specify its devices. You can interact with this database with the iscsiadm command. iscsiadm also allows you to perform target discovery and login (here we've used the long option forms for clarity):

```
# iscsiadm --mode discovery --type sendtargets --portal 192.168.1.123
192.168.1.123:3260,1 iqn.2001-04.com.prgmr:domU.orlando
```

Note that *portal*, in iSCSI jargon, refers to the IP address via which the resource can be accessed. In this case it's the exporting host. iscsiadm tells us that there's one device being exported, *iqn.2001-04.com.prgmr:domU.odin*. Now that we know about the node, we can update the iSCSI database:

```
# iscsiadm -m node -T iqn.2001-04.com.prgmr:domU.orlando
-p 192.168.1.123:3260 -o update -n node.conn[0].startup -v automatic
```

Here we use iscsiadm to update a node in the iSCSI database. We specify a target, a portal, and the operation we want to perform on the database node: update. We specify a node to update with the -n option and a new value with the -v option. Other operations we can perform via the -o option are new, delete, and show. See the Open-iSCSI documentation for more details.

Restart iscsid to propagate your changes. (This step may vary depending on your distro. Under Debian the script is open-iscsi; under Red Hat it's iscsid.)

```
# /etc/init.d/open-iscsi restart
```

Note the new device in dmesg:

```
iscsi: registered transport (iser)
scsi3 : iSCSI Initiator over TCP/IP
Vendor: IET       Model: VIRTUAL-DISK      Rev: 0
Type:   Direct-Access                      ANSI SCSI revision: 04
SCSI device sda: 8192000 512-byte hdwr sectors (4194 MB)
sda: Write Protect is off
sda: Mode Sense: 77 00 00 08
SCSI device sda: drive cache: write through
SCSI device sda: 8192000 512-byte hdwr sectors (4194 MB)
```

Note that this is the first SCSI device on the dom0, and thus becomes */dev/sda*. Further iSCSI exports become *sdb*, and so on. Of course, using local SCSI device nodes for network storage presents obvious management problems. We suggest mitigating this by using the devices under */dev/disk/by-path*. Here */dev/sda* becomes */dev/disk/by-path/ip-192.168.1.123:3260-iscsi-larry:domU.orlando*. Your device names, of course, will depend on the specifics of your setup.

Now that you're equipped with the device, you can install a Xen instance on it, most likely with a disk= line similar to the following:

```
disk = [ 'phy:/dev/disk/by-path/ip-192.168.1.123:3260-iscsi-larry:domU.orlando ,xvda,rw' ]
```

Since the domain is backed by shared iSCSI storage, you can then migrate the domain to any connected Xen dom0.

Quo Peregrinatur Grex

So that's migration. In this chapter we've described:

- How to manually move a domain from one host to another
- Cold migration of a domain between hosts
- Live migration between hosts on the same subnet
- Shared storage for live migration

Apply these suggestions, and find your manageability significantly improved!

10

PROFILING AND BENCHMARKING UNDER XEN

*Disraeli was pretty close: actually, there are Lies, Damn lies,
Statistics, Benchmarks, and Delivery dates.*
—Anonymous, attributed to Usenet

We've made a great fuss over how Xen,
as a virtualization technology, offers better
performance than competing technologies.
However, when it comes to proofs and signs, we
have been waving our hands and citing authorities. We
apologize! In this chapter we will discuss how to measure Xen's performance for yourself, using a variety of
tools.

We'll look closely at three general classes of performance monitoring,
each of which you might use for a different reason. First, we have benchmarking Xen domU performance. If you are running a hosting service (or
buying service from a hosting service), you need to see how the Xen image
you are providing (or renting) stacks up to the competition. In this category,
we have general-purpose *synthetic benchmarks*.

Second, we want to be able to benchmark Xen versus other virtualization solutions (or bare hardware) *for your workload* because Xen has both strengths and weaknesses compared to other virtualization packages. These *application benchmarks* will help to determine whether Xen is the best match for your application.

Third, sometimes you have a performance problem in your Xen-related or kernel-related program, and you want to pinpoint the bits of code that are moving slowly. This category includes *profiling tools*, such as OProfile. (Xen developers may also ask you for OProfile output when you ask about performance issues on the *xen-devel* list.)

Although some of these techniques might come in handy while troubleshooting, we haven't really aimed our discussion here at solving problems—rather, we try to present an overview of the tools for various forms of speed measurement. See Chapter 15 for more specific troubleshooting suggestions.

A Benchmarking Overview

We've seen that the performance of a paravirtualized Xen domain running most workloads approximates that of the native machine. However, there are cases where this isn't true or where this fuzzy simulacrum of the truth isn't precise enough. In these cases, we move from prescientific assertion to direct experimentation—that is, using benchmarking tools and simulators to find actual, rather than theoretical, performance numbers.

As we're sure you know, generalized benchmarking is, if not a "hard problem,"[1] at least quite difficult. If your load is I/O bound, testing the CPU will tell you nothing you need to know. If your load is IPC-bound or blocking on certain threads, testing the disk and the CPU will tell you little. Ultimately, the best results come from benchmarks that use as close to real-world load as possible.

The very best way to test, for example, the performance of a server that serves an HTTP web application would be to sniff live traffic hitting your current HTTP server, and then replay that data against the new server, speeding up or slowing down the replay to see if you have more or less capacity than before.

This, of course, is rather difficult both to do and to generalize. Most people go at least one step into "easier" and "more general." In the previous example, you might pick a particularly heavy page (or a random sampling of pages) and test the server with a generalized HTTP tester, such as Siege. This usually still gives you pretty good results, is a lot easier, and has fewer privacy concerns than running the aforementioned live data.

There are times, however, when a general benchmark, for all its inadequacies, is the best tool. For example, if you are trying to compare two virtual private server providers, a standard, generalized test might be more readily available than a real-world, specific test. Let's start by examining a few of the synthetic benchmarks that we've used.

---

[1] The phrase "hard problem" is usually used as dry and bleak humor. Classic "hard problems" include natural language and strong AI. See also: "interesting."

UnixBench

One classic benchmarking tool is the public domain UnixBench released by *BYTE* magazine in 1990, available from *http://www.tux.org/pub/tux/niemi/unixbench/*. The tool was last updated in 1999, so it is rather old. However, it seems to be quite popular for benchmarking VPS providers—by comparing one provider's UnixBench number to another, you can get a rough idea of the capacity of VM they're providing.

UnixBench is easy to install—download the source, untar it, build it, and run it.

```
# tar zxvf unixbench-4.1.0.tgz
# cd unixbench-4.1.0
# make
# ./Run
```

(That last command is a literal "Run"—it's a script that cycles through the various tests, in order, and outputs results.)

You may get some warnings, or even errors, about the -fforce-mem option that UnixBench uses, depending on your compiler version. If you edit the Makefile to remove all instances of -fforce-mem, UnixBench should build successfully.

We recommend benchmarking the Xen instance in single user mode if possible. Here's some example output:

TEST	BASELINE	RESULT	INDEX
INDEX VALUES			
Dhrystone 2 using register variables	116700.0	1988287.6	170.4
Double-Precision Whetstone	55.0	641.4	116.6
Execl Throughput	43.0	1619.6	376.7
File Copy 1024 bufsize 2000 maxblocks	3960.0	169784.0	428.7
File Copy 256 bufsize 500 maxblocks	1655.0	53117.0	320.9
File Copy 4096 bufsize 8000 maxblocks	5800.0	397207.0	684.8
Pipe Throughput	12440.0	233517.3	187.7
Pipe-based Context Switching	4000.0	75988.8	190.0
Process Creation	126.0	6241.4	495.3
Shell Scripts (8 concurrent)	6.0	173.6	289.3
System Call Overhead	15000.0	184753.6	123.2
FINAL SCORE..............................		264.5	

Armed with a UnixBench number, you at least have some basis for comparison between different VPS providers. It's not going to tell you much about the specific performance you're going to get, but it has the advantage that it is a widely published, readily available benchmark.

Other tools, such as netperf and Bonnie++, can give you more detailed performance information.

Analyzing Network Performance

One popular tool for measuring low-level network performance is netperf. This tool supports a variety of performance measurements, with a focus on measuring the efficiency of the network implementation. It's also been used in Xen-related papers. For one example, see "The Price of Safety: Evaluating IOMMU Performance" by Muli Ben-Yehuda et al.[2]

First, download netperf from *http://netperf.org/netperf/DownloadNetperf.html*. We picked up version 2.4.4.

```
# wget ftp://ftp.netperf.org/netperf/netperf-2.4.4.tar.bz2
```

Untar it and enter the netperf directory.

```
# tar xjvf netperf-2.4.4.tar.bz2
# cd netperf-2.4.
```

Configure, build, and install netperf. (Note that these directions are a bit at variance with the documentation; the documentation claims that */opt/netperf* is the hard-coded install prefix, whereas it seems to install in */usr/local* for me. Also, the manual seems to predate netperf's use of Autoconf.)

```
# ./configure
# make
# su
# make install
```

netperf works by running the client, netperf, on the machine being benchmarked. netperf connects to a netserver daemon and tests the rate at which it can send and receive data. So, to use netperf, we first need to set up netserver.

In the standard service configuration, netserver would run under inetd; however, inetd is obsolete. Many distros don't even include it by default. Besides, you probably don't want to leave the benchmark server running all the time. Instead of configuring inetd, therefore, run netserver in standalone mode:

```
# /usr/local/bin/netserver
Starting netserver at port 12865
Starting netserver at hostname 0.0.0.0 port 12865 and family AF_UNSPEC
```

Now we can run the netperf client with no arguments to perform a 10-second test with the local daemon.

```
# netperf
TCP STREAM TEST from 0.0.0.0 (0.0.0.0) port 0 AF_INET to localhost (127.0.0.1)
port 0 AF_INET
```

---

[2] See *http://ols.108.redhat.com/2007/Reprints/ben-yehuda-Reprint.pdf*.

```
Recv    Send    Send
Socket  Socket  Message  Elapsed
Size    Size    Size     Time     Throughput
bytes   bytes   bytes    secs.    10^6bits/sec
87380   16384   16384    10.01    10516.33
```

Okay, looks good. Now we'll test from the dom0 to this domU. To do that, we install the netperf binaries as described previously and run `netperf` with the -H option to specify a target host (in this case, .74 is the domU we're testing against):

```
# netperf -H 216.218.223.74,ipv4
TCP STREAM TEST from 0.0.0.0 (0.0.0.0) port 0 AF_INET to 192.0.2.74
(192.0.2.74) port 0 AF_INET
Recv    Send    Send
Socket  Socket  Message  Elapsed
Size    Size    Size     Time     Throughput
bytes   bytes   bytes    secs.    10^6bits/sec
 87380  16384   16384    10.00    638.59
```

Cool. Not as fast, obviously, but we expected that. Now from another physical machine to our test domU:

```
# netperf -H 192.0.2.66
TCP STREAM TEST from 0.0.0.0 (0.0.0.0) port 0 AF_INET to 192.0.2.66
(192.0.2.66) port 0 AF_INET
Recv    Send    Send
Socket  Socket  Message  Elapsed
Size    Size    Size     Time     Throughput
bytes   bytes   bytes    secs.    10^6bits/sec
 87380  16384   16384    10.25    87.72
```

Ouch. Well, so how much of that is Xen, and how much is the network we're going through? To find out, we'll run the `netserver` daemon on the dom0 hosting the test domU and connect to that:

```
# netperf -H 192.0.2.74
TCP STREAM TEST from 0.0.0.0 (0.0.0.0) port 0 AF_INET to 192.0.2.74
(192.0.2.74) port 0 AF_INET
Recv    Send    Send
Socket  Socket  Message  Elapsed
Size    Size    Size     Time     Throughput
bytes   bytes   bytes    secs.    10^6bits/sec
 87380  16384   16384    10.12    93.66
```

It could be worse, I guess. The moral of the story? xennet introduces a noticeable but reasonable overhead. Also, netperf can be a useful tool for discovering the actual bandwidth you've got available. In this case the machines are connected via a 100Mbit connection, and netperf lists an actual throughput of 93.66Mbits/second.

Measuring Disk Performance with Bonnie++

One of the major factors in a machine's overall performance is its disk subsystem. By exercising its hard drives, we can get a useful metric to compare Xen providers or Xen instances with, say, VMware guests.

We, like virtually everyone else on the planet, use Bonnie++ to measure disk performance. Bonnie++ attempts to measure both random and sequential disk performance and does a good job simulating real-world loads. This is especially important in the Xen context because of the degree to which domains are partitioned—although domains share resources, there's no way for them to coordinate resource use.

One illustration of this point is that if multiple domains are trying to access a platter simultaneously, what looks like sequential access from the viewpoint of one VM becomes random accesses to the disk. This makes things like seek time and the robustness of your tagged queuing system much more important. To test the effect of these optimizations on domU performance, you'll probably want a tool like Bonnie++.

The Bonnie++ author maintains a home page at *http://www.coker.com.au/ bonnie++/*. Download the source package, build it, and install it:

```
# wget http://www.coker.com.au/bonnie++/bonnie++-1.03c.tgz
# cd bonnie++-1.03c
# make
# make install
```

At this point you can simply invoke Bonnie++ with a command such as:

```
# /usr/local/sbin/bonnie++
```

This command will run some tests, printing status information as it goes along, and eventually generate output like this:

```
Version  1.03       ------Sequential Output------ --Sequential Input- --Random-
                    -Per Chr- --Block-- -Rewrite- -Per Chr- --Block-- --Seeks--
Machine        Size K/sec %CP K/sec %CP K/sec %CP K/sec %CP K/sec %CP  /sec %CP
alastor       2512M 20736  76 55093  14 21112   5 26385  87 55658   6 194.9   0
...........        ------Sequential Create------ --------Random Create-------
                  -Create-- --Read--- -Delete-- -Create-- --Read--- -Delete--
              files /sec %CP /sec %CP /sec %CP /sec %CP /sec %CP /sec %CP
                256 35990  89 227885  85 16877  28 34146  84 334227  99  5716  10
```

Note that some tests may simply output a row of pluses. This indicates that the machine finished them in less than 500 ms. Make the workload more difficult. For example, you might specify something like:

```
# /usr/local/sbin/bonnie++ -d . -s 2512 -n 256
```

This specifies writing 2512MB files for I/O performance tests. (This is the default file size, which is twice the RAM size on this particular machine. This is important to ensure that we're not just exercising RAM rather than disk.) It also tells Bonnie++ to create 256*1024 files in its file creation tests.

We also recommend reading Bonnie++'s online manual, which includes a fair amount of pithy benchmarking wisdom, detailing why the author chose to include the tests that he did, and what meanings the different numbers have.

Application Benchmarks

Of course, the purpose of a server is to run applications—we're not really interested in how many times per second the VM can do absolutely nothing. For testing application performance, we use the applications that we're planning to put on the machine, and then throw load at them.

Since this is necessarily application-specific, we can't give you too many pointers on specifics. There are good test suites available for many popular libraries. For example, we've had customers benchmark their Xen instances with the popular web framework Django.[3]

httperf: A Load Generator for HTTP Servers

Having tested the effectiveness of your domain's network interface, you may want to discover how well the domain performs when serving applications through that interface. Because of Xen's server-oriented heritage, one popular means of testing its performance in HTTP-based real-world applications is httperf. The tool generates HTTP requests and summarizes performance statistics. It supports HTTP/1.1 and SSL protocols and offers a variety of workload generators. You may find httperf useful if, for example, you're trying to figure out how many users your web server can handle before it goes casters-up.

First, install httperf on a machine other than the one you're testing—it can be another domU, but we usually prefer to install it on something completely separate. This "load" machine should also be as close to the target machine as possible—preferably connected to the same Ethernet switch.

You can get httperf through your distro's package-management mechanism or from *http://www.hpl.hp.com/research/linux/httperf/*.

If you've downloaded the source code, build it using the standard method. httperf's documentation recommends using a separate build directory rather than building directly in the source tree. Thus, from the httperf source directory:

```
# mkdir build
# cd build
```

---

[3] *http://journal.uggedal.com/vps-comparison-between-slicehost-and-prgmr* uses Django among other tools.

```
# ../configure
# make
# make install
```

Next, run appropriate tests. What we usually do is run httperf with a command similar to this:

```
# httperf --server 192.168.1.80 --uri /index.html --num-conns 6000
--rate 1500
```

In this case we're just demanding a static HTML page, so the request rate is obscenely high; usually we would use a much smaller number in tests of real-world database-backed websites.

httperf will then give you some statistics. The important numbers, in our experience, are the connection rate, the request rate, and the reply rate. All of these should be close to the rate specified on the command line. If they start to decline from that number, that indicates that the server has reached its capacity.

However, httperf isn't limited to repeated requests for a single file. We prefer to use httperf in session mode by specifying the --wsesslog workload generator. This gives a closer approximation to the actual load on the web server. You can create a session file from your web server logs with a bit of Perl, winding up with a simple formatted list of URLs:

```
/newsv3/
......./style/crimson.css
......./style/ash.css
......./style/azure.css
......./images/news.feeds.anime/sites/ann-xs.gif
......./images/news.feeds.anime/sites/annpr-xs.gif
......./images/news.feeds.anime/sites/aod-xs.gif
......./images/news.feeds.anime/sites/an-xs.gif
......./images/news.feeds.anime/header-lite.gif
/index.shtml
......./style/sable.css
......./images/banners/igloo.gif
......./images/temp_banner.gif
......./images/faye_header2.jpg
......./images/faye-birthday.jpg
......./images/giant_arrow.gif
......./images/faye_header.jpg
/news/
/events/
......./events/events.css
......./events/summergathering2007/coverimage.jpg
```

(and so forth.)

This session file lists files for `httperf` to request, with indentations to define bursts; a group of lines that begin with whitespace is a burst. When run, `httperf` will request the first burst, wait a certain amount of time, then move to the next burst. Equipped with this session file, we can use `httperf` to simulate a user:

```
# httperf --hog --server 192.168.1.80 --wsesslog=40,10,urls.txt --rate=1
```

This will start 40 sessions at the rate of one per second. The new parameter, `--wsesslog`, takes the input of *urls.txt* and runs through it in bursts, pausing 10 seconds between bursts to simulate the user thinking.

Again, throw this at your server, increasing the rate until the server can't meet demand. When the server fails, congratulations! You've got a benchmark.

Another Application Benchmark: POV-Ray

Of course, depending on your application, `httperf` may not be a suitable workload. Let's say that you've decided to use Xen to render scenes with popular open source raytracer POV-Ray. (If nothing else, it's a good way to soak up spare CPU cycles.)

The POV-Ray benchmark is easy to run. Just give the `-benchmark` option on the command line:

```
# povray -benchmark
```

This renders a standard scene and gives a large number of statistics, ending with an overall summary and rendering time. A domU with a 2.8 GHz Pentium 4 and 256MB of memory gave us the following output:

```
Smallest Alloc:                 9 bytes
Largest  Alloc:           1440008 bytes
Peak memory used:         5516100 bytes
Total Scene Processing Times
  Parse Time:    0 hours  0 minutes  2 seconds (2 seconds)
  Photon Time:   0 hours  0 minutes 53 seconds (53 seconds)
  Render Time:   0 hours 43 minutes 26 seconds (2606 seconds)
  Total Time:    0 hours 44 minutes 21 seconds (2661 seconds)
```

Now you've got a single number that you can easily compare between various setups running POV-Ray, be they Xen instances, VMware boxes, or physical servers.

Tuning Xen for Optimum Benchmarking

Most system administration work involves comparing results at the machine level—analyzing the performance of a Xen VM relative to another machine, virtual or not. However, with virtualization, there are some performance knobs that aren't obvious but can make a huge difference in the final benchmark results.

First, Xen allocates CPU dynamically and attempts to keep the CPU busy as much as possible. That is, if dom2 isn't using all of its allocated CPU, dom3 can pick up the extra. Although this is usually a good thing, it can make CPU benchmark data misleading. While testing, you can avoid this problem by specifying the cap parameter to the scheduler. For example, to ensure that domain ID 1 can get no more than 50 percent of one CPU:

```
# xm sched-credit -d 1 -c 50
```

Second, guests in HVM mode absolutely must use paravirtualized drivers for acceptable performance. This point is driven home in a XenSource analysis of benchmark results published by VMware, in which XenSource points out that, in VMware's benchmarks, "XenSource's Xen Tools for Windows, which optimize the I/O path, were not installed. The VMware benchmarks should thus be disregarded in their entirety."

Also, shared resources (like disk I/O) are difficult to account, can interact with dom0 CPU demand, and can be affected by other domUs. For example, although paravirtualized Xen can deliver excellent network performance, it requires more CPU cycles to do so than a nonvirtualized machine. This may affect the capacity of your machine.

This is a difficult issue to address, and we can't really offer a magic bullet. One point to note is that the dom0 will likely use more CPU than an intuitive estimate would suggest; it's very important to weight the dom0's CPU allocation heavily, or perhaps even devote a core exclusively to the dom0 on boxes with four or more cores.

For benchmarking, we also recommend minimizing error by benchmarking with a reasonably loaded machine. If you're expecting to run a dozen domUs, then they should all be performing some reasonable synthetic task while benchmarking to get an appreciation for the real-world performance of the VM.

Profiling with Xen

Of course, there is one way of seeing shared resource use more precisely. We can *profile* the VM as it runs our application workload to get a clear idea of what it's doing and—with a Xen-aware profiler—how other domains are interfering with us.

Profiling refers to the practice of examining a specific application to see what it spends time doing. In particular, it can tell you whether an app is CPU or I/O limited, whether particular functions are inefficient, or whether performance problems are occurring outside of the app entirely, perhaps in the kernel.

Here, we'll discuss a sample setup with Xen and OProfile, using the kernel compile as a standard workload (and one that most Xen admins are likely to be familiar with).

Xenoprof

OProfile is probably the most popular profiling package for Linux.[4] The kernel includes OProfile support, and the user-space tools come with virtually every distro we know. If you have a performance problem with a particular program and want to see precisely what's causing it, OProfile is the tool for the job.

OProfile works by incrementing a counter whenever the program being profiled performs a particular action. For example, it can keep count of the number of cache misses or the number of instructions executed. When the counter reaches a certain value, it instructs the OProfile daemon to sample the counter, using a non-maskable interrupt to ensure prompt handling of the sampling request.

Xenoprofile, or Xenoprof, is a version of OProfile that has been extended to work as a system-wide profiling tool under Xen, using hypercalls to enable domains to access hardware performance counters. It supports analysis of complete Xen instances and accounts for time spent in the hypervisor or within another domU.

Getting OProfile

As of recent versions, Xen includes support for OProfile versions up to 0.9.2 (0.9.3 will require you to apply a patch to the Xen kernel). For now, it would probably be best to use the packaged version to minimize the tedious effort of recompilation.

If you're using a recent version of Debian, Ubuntu, CentOS, or Red Hat, you're in luck; the version of OProfile that they ship is already set up to work with Xen. Other distro kernels, if they ship with Xen, will likely also incorporate OProfile's Xen support.

Building OProfile

If you're not so lucky as to have Xen profiling support already, you'll have to download and build OProfile, for which we'll give very brief directions just for completeness.

The first thing to do is to download the OProfile source from *http://oprofile.sourceforge.net/*. We used version 0.9.4.

First, untar OProfile, like so:

```
# wget http://prdownloads.sourceforge.net/oprofile/oprofile-0.9.4.tar.gz
# tar xzvf oprofile-0.9.4.tar.gz
# cd oprofile-0.9.4
```

---

[4] Excluding top(1), of course.

Then configure and build OProfile:

```
# ./configure --with-kernel-support
# make
# make install
```

Finally, do a bit of Linux kernel configuration if your kernel isn't correctly configured already. (You can check by issuing gzip -d -i /proc/config.gz | grep PROFILE.) In our case that returns:

```
CONFIG_PROFILING=y
CONFIG_OPROFILE=m
```

NOTE   */proc/config.gz is an optional feature that may not exist. If it doesn't, you'll have to find your configuration some other way. On Fedora 8, for example, you can check for profiling support by looking at the kernel config file shipped with the distro:*

```
# cat  /boot/config-2.6.23.1-42.fc8 | grep PROFILE
```

If your kernel isn't set up for profiling, rebuild it with profiling support. Then install and boot from the new kernel (a step that we won't detail at length here).

OProfile Quickstart

To make sure OProfile works, you can profile a standard workload in domain 0. (We chose the kernel compile because it's a familiar task to most sysadmins, although we're compiling it out of the Xen source tree.)

Begin by telling OProfile to clear its sample buffers:

```
# opcontrol --reset
```

Now configure OProfile.

```
# opcontrol --setup --vmlinux=/usr/lib/debug/lib/modules/vmlinux
--separate=library --event=CPU_CLK_UNHALTED:750000:0x1:1:1
```

The first three arguments are the command (setup for profiling), kernel image, and an option to create separate output files for libraries used. The final switch, event, describes the event that we're instructing OProfile to monitor.

The precise event that you'll want to sample varies depending on your processor type (and on what you're trying to measure). For this run, to get an overall approximation of CPU usage, we used CPU_CLK_UNHALTED on an Intel Core 2 machine. On a Pentium 4, the equivalent measure would be GLOBAL_POWER_EVENTS. The remaining arguments indicate the size of the counter, the unit mask (in this case, 0x1), and that we want both the kernel and userspace code.

To start collecting samples, run:

```
# opcontrol --start
```

Then run the experiment that you want to profile, in this case a kernel compile.

```
# /usr/bin/time -v make bzImage
```

Then stop the profiler.

```
# opcontrol --shutdown
```

Now that we have samples, we can extract meaningful and useful information from the mass of raw data via the standard postprofiling tools. The main analysis command is opreport. To get a basic overview of the processes that consumed CPU, we could run:

```
# opreport -t 2
CPU: Core 2, speed 2400.08 MHz (estimated)
Counted CPU_CLK_UNHALTED events (Clock cycles when not halted) with a unit mask
of 0x01 (Unhalted bus cycles) count 750000
CPU_CLK_UNHALT...|
  samples|      %|
------------------
  370812 90.0945 cc1
        CPU_CLK_UNHALT...|
          samples|      %|
```

```
   ------------------
      332713 89.7255 cc1
       37858 10.2095 libc-2.5.so
         241  0.0650 ld-2.5.so
11364   2.7611 genksyms
      CPU_CLK_UNHALT...|
         samples|      %|
   ------------------
        8159 71.7969 genksyms
        3178 27.9655 libc-2.5.so
          27  0.2376 ld-2.5.so
```

This tells us which processes accounted for CPU usage during the compile, with a threshold of 2 percent (indicated by the -t 2 option.) This isn't terribly interesting, however. We can get more granularity using the --symbols option with opreport, which gives a best guess as to what functions accounted for the CPU usage. Try it.

You might be interested in other events, such as cache misses. To get a list of possible counters customized for your hardware, issue:

```
# ophelp
```

Profiling Multiple Domains in Concert

So far, all this has covered standard use of OProfile, without touching on the Xen-specific features. But one of the most useful features of OProfile, in the Xen context, is the ability to profile entire domains against each other, analyzing how different scheduling parameters, disk allocations, drivers, and code paths interact to affect performance.

When profiling multiple domains, dom0 still coordinates the session. It's not currently possible to simply profile in a domU without dom0's involvement—domUs don't have direct access to the CPU performance counters.

Active vs. Passive Profiling

Xenoprofile supports both active and passive modes for domain profiling.

When profiling in passive mode, the results indicate which domain is running at sample time but don't delve more deeply into what's being executed. It's useful to get a quick look at which domains are using the system.

In active mode, each domU runs its own instance of OProfile, which samples events within its virtual machine. Active mode allows better granularity than passive mode, but is more inconvenient. Only paravirtualized domains can run in active mode.

Active Profiling

Active profiling is substantially more interesting. For this example, we'll use three domains: dom0, to control the profiler, and domUs 1 and 3 as active domains.

```
0 # opcontrol --reset
1 # opcontrol --reset
3 # opcontrol --reset
```

First, set up the daemon in dom0 with some initial parameters:

```
0 # opcontrol --start-daemon --event=GLOBAL_POWER_EVENTS:1000000:1:1
   --xen=/boot/xen-syms-3.0-unstable
   --vmlinux=/boot/vmlinux-syms-2.6.18-xen0 --active-domains=1,3
```

This introduces the --xen option, which gives the path to the uncompressed Xen kernel image, and the --active-domains option, which lists the domains to profile in active mode. The :1 s at the end of the event option tells OProfile to count events in both userspace and kernel space.

NOTE   *Specify domains by numeric ID. OProfile won't interpret names.*

Next, start OProfile in the active domUs. The daemon must already be running in dom0, otherwise the domU won't have permission to access the performance counters.

```
1 # opcontrol --reset
1 # opcontrol --start
```

Run the same commands in domain 3. Finally, begin sampling in domain 0:

```
0 # opcontrol --start
```

Now we can run commands in the domains of interest. Let's continue to use the kernel compile as our test workload, but this time complicate matters by running a disk-intensive benchmark in another domain.

```
1 # time make bzImage
3 # time bonnie++
```

When the kernel compile and Bonnie++ have finished, we stop OProfile:

```
0 # opcontrol --stop

0 # opcontrol --shutdown
1 # opcontrol --shutdown
3 # opcontrol --shutdown
```

Now each domU will have its own set of samples, which we can view with opreport. Taken together, these reports form a complete picture of the various domains' activity. We might suggest playing with the CPU allocations and seeing how that influences OProfile's results.

An OProfile Example

Now let's try applying OProfile to an actual problem. Here's the scenario: We've moved to a setup that uses LVM mirroring on a pair of 1 TB SATA disks. The hardware is a quad-core Intel QX6600, with 8GB memory and an ICH7 SATA controller, using the AHCI driver. We've devoted 512MB of memory to the dom0.

We noted that the performance of mirrored logical volumes accessed through xenblk was about one-tenth that of nonmirrored LVs, or of LVs mirrored with the --corelog option. Mirrored LVs with and without –corelog performed fine when accessed normally within the dom0, but performance dropped when accessed via xm block-attach. This was, to our minds, ridiculous.

First, we created two logical volumes in the volume group *test*: one with mirroring and a mirror log, and one with the --corelog option.

```
# lvcreate -m 1 -L 2G -n test_mirror test
# lvcreate -m 1 --corelog -L 2G -n test_core test
```

Then we made filesystems and mounted them:

```
# mke2fs -j /dev/test/test*
# mkdir -p /mnt/test/mirror
# mkdir -p /mnt/test/core
# mount /dev/test/test_mirror /mnt/test/mirror
```

Next we started OProfile, using the --xen option to give the path to our uncompessed Xen kernel image. After a few test runs profiling various events, it became clear that our problem related to excessive amounts of time spent waiting for I/O. Thus, we instruct the profiler to count BUS_IO_WAIT events, which indicate when the processor is stuck waiting for input:

```
# opcontrol --start --event=BUS_IO_WAIT:500:0xc0
--xen=/usr/lib/debug/boot/xen-syms-2.6.18-53.1.14.el5.debug
--vmlinux=/usr/lib/debug/lib/modules/2.6.18-53.1.14.el5xen/vmlinux
--separate=all
```

Then we ran Bonnie++ on each device in sequence, stopping OProfile and saving the output each time.

```
# bonnie++ -d /mnt/test/mirror
# opcontrol --stop
# opcontrol --save=mirrorlog
# opcontrol --reset
```

The LV with the corelog displayed negligible iowait, as expected. However, the other experienced quite a bit, as you can see in this output from our test of the LV in question:

```
# opreport -t 1 --symbols session:iowait_mirror
warning: /ahci could not be found.
CPU: Core 2, speed 2400.08 MHz (estimated)
Counted BUS_IO_WAIT events (IO requests waiting in the bus queue) with a unit mask of 0xc0 (All
cores) count 500
Processes with a thread ID of 0
Processes with a thread ID of 463
Processes with a thread ID of 14185
```

samples	%	samples	%	samples	%	app name	symbol name
32	91.4286	15	93.7500	0	0	xen-syms-2.6.18-53.1.14.el5.debug	pit_read_counter
1	2.8571	0	0	0	0	ahci	(no symbols)
1	2.8571	0	0	0	0	vmlinux	bio_put
1	2.8571	0	0	0	0	vmlinux	hypercall_page

Here we see that the Xen kernel is experiencing a large number of BUS_IO_WAIT events in the pit_read_counter function, suggesting that this function is probably our culprit. A bit of searching for that function name reveals that it's been taken out of recent versions of Xen, so we decide to take the easy way out and upgrade. Problem solved—but now we have some idea why.

Used properly, profiling can be an excellent way to track down performance bottlenecks. However, it's not any sort of magic bullet. The sheer amount of data that profiling generates can be seductive, and sorting through the profiler's output may take far more time than it's worth.

Conclusion

So that's a sysadmin's primer on performance measurement with Xen. In this chapter, we've described tools to measure performance, ranging from the general to the specific, from the hardware focused to the application oriented. We've also briefly discussed the Xen-oriented features of OProfile, which aim to extend the profiler to multiple domUs and the hypervisor itself.

11

CITRIX XENSERVER: XEN FOR THE ENTERPRISE

Until now, we've focused exclusively on the open source version of Xen. However, that's not the only choice available. The Xen guys have also released a packaged version of Xen that's aimed at turning Xen into a product that is suitable for the enterprise.[1]

One implication that you may have gotten reading between the lines of this book is that Xen is still in a state of development. It is, in a word, hacker-ware. It's good 'ware—obviously we think it's stable enough for real people to use every day—but it's still a lot of work to set up and get going.

There are a couple of reasonable explanations for this state of affairs. Partly this is because hackers are not, as a group, very good at finishing things. The work to take a product from 90 percent finished to 100 percent finished isn't usually difficult, just tedious. Open source is wonderful, but it's

---

[1] Sorry, we know, marketing speak. But it is the easiest way for us to convey the aim of the product.

not great at producing full-on commercial *products*.[2] Another issue is that Xen, by nature, is invasive and fundamental. One hesitates to use words like *paradigm*, but there you have it—virtualization is a different way of computing, a different way of thinking about computers, and it requires a lot of very polished software support.

Citrix (who acquired XenSource, the company founded by the original Xen team) works to ease the transition by providing this software—creating a software stack, developing a certification process, and establishing best practices so that administrators can roll out Xen with a minimum of fuss and uncertainty. They work on the open source version of Xen and contribute changes to it, but they also do an additional level of QA aimed at turning Xen into a product that you can feel comfortable trusting with your business.

You may ask how this is possible, considering that Xen is still under the GPL. Citrix can do this while obeying the terms of Xen's license because Xen's client/server architecture and modular design allow them to extend the basic hypervisor, adding new features as modules and userspace processes that work in conjunction with the GPL software. Citrix uses the open source hypervisor with open source Linux, plus added modules and proprietary control software to provide an integrated distribution of Xen, much like a traditional Linux distro but with a strong emphasis on virtualization.

Citrix's Xen Products

The Citrix product consists of two components, XenServer and XenEssentials. XenServer is the hypervisor and basic management tools, and it is available for free.[3] XenEssentials is a suite of utilities that cost money.

The basic free product is simply called XenServer. XenServer supports most of the features of the paid Citrix products, with the same management interface. It's aimed at development, test, and noncritical production deployments, as well as people who want to test or play with Xen.

Citrix's pay product is called Citrix Essentials for XenServer, with various levels of licensing. It doesn't have all the features of open source Xen, but it has all the features Citrix feels comfortable supporting and some commercial product exclusives. Citrix, as far as we can tell, charges as much as the market will bear for this version.[4] This is, of course, subject to change at any time. Negotiate with your Citrix representative, preferably in some form of gladiatorial combat.[5]

By and large, we're going to focus exclusively on the base product and components that are available for free.

---

[2] This is not to disparage the fine work of the people behind polished products we use daily, such as Linux, Mozilla, and Vim. We're just saying that the last 10 percent is the most difficult, not that it never gets done.

[3] That's free as in beer, as the greybeards say.

[4] We were unable to find coherent pricing information.

[5] After spending weeks trying to get prices for colocation out of salespeople, Luke suspects gladiatorial combat would be more pleasant than the traditional methods for negotiating price. prgmr.com favors the "the price on the website is the price you pay" model.

The Benefits of Using Citrix XenServer

The XenServer product improves on open source Xen primarily in the area of manageability. They've streamlined and automated common tasks while retaining most of the transparency of open source Xen.

Ten Minutes to Xen

> Our model is one where the CD enters the drive and the computer is a better machine as a result (in ten minutes or less). That is what XenExpress[6] is all about.
>
> —Frank Artale, XenSource

One of the best demonstrations of this is in what Citrix calls *Xen in ten minutes* or *Ten to Xen.* They've dramatically simplified the bootstrap aspect of Xen, where you have to install a dom0 OS and modify it to work nicely with Xen's control software and the hypervisor.

Citrix reasons that you shouldn't actually be *doing* anything with the dom0, other than controlling domUs. Therefore, the product installs a basic Linux OS that includes only the components needed to run Xen: a kernel, a shell, some libraries, a text editor, Python, syslog, SSH (and so forth), and the Xen software. In this approach, software that's not needed to control Xen, such as the daemons that provide a server's *raison d'etre*, should be installed in a domU. Of course, it's still Linux—based on CentOS, in fact— and there's nothing to stop you from installing other software. However, we recommend sticking with Citrix's approach and keeping your core virtualization server uncluttered.

The basic package does, in fact, take about 10 minutes to install, as advertised. Be sure to get the supplementary Linux pack, which includes Debian templates and supporting tools for Linux VMs. When that's done, it's a simple matter to create domUs from the included Debian template or from install media.

Citrix XenServer has other advantages. Perhaps most important, it feels much more centralized than the open source Xen. All of the decisions that we've been writing about—storage, networking, and so forth—are handled in a centralized way, using a consistent interface. Where possible, they've made sensible default decisions for you. They're not necessarily going to be the best for all situations, but at least they'll be reasonable for Xen's purposes.

Take storage, for example. Citrix uses the same architecture as open source Xen, using unmodified Linux drivers in the dom0 to access physical devices. They layer LVM on top of this to abstract physical storage and increase flexibility, as we've outlined elsewhere. Citrix builds on these open source tools by offering a way of administering storage through the same GUI as the more Xen-specific aspects of the system, allowing you to focus on virtual machines rather than obscure disk-administration commands. If you

---

[6] XenExpress was the name of the free product when XenSource was XenSource, before Citrix bought them.

like, you can still use the familiar commands. Citrix's Xen product isn't out to reinvent the wheel or obfuscate the basic workings of the system; they've just provided an alternative to make common tasks a little easier.

The Disadvantages of Using Citrix XenServer

Even with the high-end Essentials product, there's a trade-off between stability and features. Citrix exposes only those hypervisor features that they feel are mature enough to use in a production environment. For example, migration was added a couple of years after it had been introduced in the open source version.

There's also no easy way of moving VMs between open source and commercial Xen at the moment. (You can, of course, move VMs manually by using the lower-level methods outlined in Chapter 9.) If you standardize on open source or commercial Xen, it may be difficult to reverse that decision later, although the Open Virtualization Format (OVF), which has some support from open source tools,[7] promises to improve the situation.

Beyond that, open source is still an ideological issue. Some people use it whenever possible; some avoid it as a pestilence. We use the open source product because it's good enough for us and because apparently our time is worthless. Citrix offers a straightforward transaction: Give them money and they'll give you Xen as a product, rather than Xen as heavily customizable hackerware. Step on board and take your chances.

Getting Started

Having said all that, the best way to get started with Citrix's XenServer is probably just to try the product and see if you like it. The entry-level version is available for free. You can download it at *http://www.citrix.com/xenserver/getitfree/* and upgrade it at any time simply by entering a license key. Besides, they're telling the truth when they say it takes about 10 minutes to install, so why not?

Prerequisites

First, check to make sure that you meet the minimum system requirements:

- 64-bit CPU, that is, AMD Opteron, Athlon 64, Phenom, or whatever else AMD's marketing department has come up with, or most Intel Xeons of the last few years, as well as the Core 2 (but not Core).
- A certain amount of memory, depending on how many virtual machines you want. Citrix's minimum is 1GB, which sounds reasonable to us.
- Sufficient disk space. The XenServer backend will take 8GB, leaving the rest available for domUs. Of course, you can also use network storage for VMs.

---

[7] *http://open-ovf.wiki.sourceforge.net/* is a good place to start.

- HVM support is required if you want to run Windows domUs, but otherwise it's optional.

Installing Citrix XenServer

As we've mentioned, Citrix's product is a complete system; install it like any other OS. For us, that meant downloading the ISO, burning it to a CD, and booting our target machine from the CD. We also grabbed the *Linux Guest Support disc*, which includes support for Linux guests.

The machine goes through a nongraphical install and asks some standard questions about keyboard, time, and network setup—the usual. Compared to a normal Linux install, it's incredibly spare and streamlined because the product itself has the single focus of virtualization. For example, there's no opportunity to set up partitioning. At the end, it prompted us to insert supplementary CDs, so we put in the Linux support disc.

Ten minutes and one reboot later, we're staring at a screen that advises us to log in via the administration frontend, XenCenter.

USING A SERIAL CONSOLE WITH XENSERVER

We would never consider using a server without serial console access. Citrix's Xen product, although it doesn't support a serial console out of the box, can support a serial console with a little configuration.

It's a little more difficult than you'd expect because Citrix uses Extlinux to boot rather than GRUB. However, Extlinux's configuration is similar. The only file we need to adjust is */boot/extlinux.cfg*. Note that we specify the options to Xen and the Linux kernel on the same long line:

```
SERIAL 0 115200

default xe

prompt 1

timeout 50


label xe

  # XenServer

  kernel mboot.c32

  append /boot/xen.gz dom0_mem=752M lowmem_emergency_pool=16M \
    crashkernel=64M@32M com1=115200,8n1 console=com1 --- \
    /boot/vmlinuz-2.6-xen root=LABEL=root-jhawazvh ro \
    console=ttyS0,115200n8 --- /boot/initrd-2.6-xen.img
```

Because this is basically CentOS, it already has ttyS0 listed in */etc/inittab* with a getty. Reboot and enjoy the serial console.

Citrix's Xen GUI: XenCenter

We are, of course, fond of following advice.

Citrix's system, like the open source version of Xen, uses a client/server architecture to control the virtual machines. Unlike the open source version, they include a graphical Xen console that can automate many of the boring details of running Xen.[8]

In fact, the package includes both a GUI and a command-line utility. As of version 5, the GUI is a Windows application called XenCenter, and the command-line tool is called xe. They offer roughly the same functionality, but the XenCenter GUI has more features, and xe supports certain more arcane operations. Citrix suggests using xe for scripted (or otherwise automated) operation and the XenCenter for interactive administration. There's also a character-based menu system called xsconsole that normally runs on the Xen server's physical console, but which can be run in any shell session in dom0. It provides access to many common operations.

You'll need a Windows machine for the GUI client. Although version 3.2 and previous versions were written in Java, and are therefore cross-platform, versions 4.0 and above require the .NET-based XenCenter. Previous versions of the client will not be able to connect to the XenServer host. The requirement that the client runs under Windows, of course, also means that you can't run the client directly on the machine that's running Citrix's product.[9]

Unlike the open source version of Xen, communication between the tools and hypervisor doesn't go through xend. Instead, both the command-line and graphical tools connect to the xapi service on the Xen server via TCP/IP, using SSL to encrypt traffic.

Administering VMs with the XenCenter

Having successfully installed both the Citrix server and the XenCenter client, we started our nice, shiny GUI frontend, told it about our XenServer, and logged in. The login process is straightforward and immediately drops you into a comprehensive two-panel interface, as shown in Figure 11-1.

The left panel displays hosts, both physical and virtual, in a tree view. On the right side, we can interact with the selected VM or change its parameters via the tabs at the top. Most tasks are broken out into a wizard-based interface.

These tasks are based on a concept of *lifecycle management*; you can create VMs, edit them, and destroy them, all by clicking through a series of dialog boxes. The user interface aims to make these steps, especially creation, as easy as possible; after all, part of the attraction of virtual computing appliances is that it's easy to add more machines or scale back as necessary.

---

[8] The XenCenter cannot connect to open source Xen. We tried.

[9] Although you could run the client inside of a Windows install under the XenSource product it does raise an interesting chicken-and-egg problem.

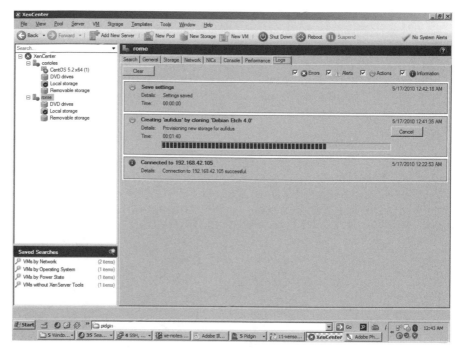

Figure 11-1: XenCenter console

Installing DomU Images

XenServer offers several install methods: First, you can install from the included Debian Etch template. Second, you can install a supported distro using a template and distro-specific installer. Third, there is the HVM install using emulated devices. Finally, we have physical-to-virtual conversion using the P2V tool.

The Debian install is the fastest and easiest, but it's the least flexible. Templated installation is a good option, allowing PV installs of a good variety of Linux distros, though not all of them. The HVM install works well for everything but requires a machine that supports HVM and results in a domain running in HVM mode (which may be suboptimal, depending on your application). P2V allows you to clone an existing hardware-based Linux installation and to create templates based on that existing system, but it is inconvenient and works with only a few older distros.

Installing from the Debian Templates

The easiest way to install a VM is to use the prepopulated Debian Etch template. This template is a preconfigured basic install, designed to make starting a Xen instance almost a one-click affair. (There is also a Debian Lenny template, but it is an installer, not a fully populated instance.)

To install from a template, log in to the Xen host using the graphical interface, select the XenServer from the list in the left panel of the screen (it should be the first entry), right-click it, and select **New VM**. It will pop up a wizard interface that allows you to configure the machine. Select the Debian Etch template. Answer the questions about RAM and disk space (the defaults should be fine), click **Finish**, and it'll create a guest.

After the guest boots, it performs some first-boot configuration, then starts as a normal paravirtualized Xen instance, with the text console and graphical console already set up and ready to work with, as shown in Figure 11-2.

Figure 11-2: The graphical console of a freshly installed domU

Templated Linux VM

To ensure that the VM kernels are compatible with both Xen and the domU operating environment, the XenServer product supports installation of only a few RPM-based distros and, of course, the already-mentioned Debian VM templates. This support is implemented through templates, which are essentially canned VM configurations.

Installing a supported distro is almost as easy as installing the Debian templates. Go to the **Install** dialog, select your distro and an install source (physical media, ISO, or network), enter a name, tweak the parameters if desired, and click **Install**.

It's a bit harder to install an unsupported distro. However, the hardware emulation mode allows you to install any Linux distro by selecting the **Other Install Media** template and booting from the OS CD. From that point, proceed as with a normal install on hardware.

When you have the domain installed, you can configure it for paravirtualization and then convert it to a template.

Windows Install

Install Windows by selecting the **XenServer** server, selecting **Install VM** from the context menu, and then filling in the resulting dialog. Select the template that corresponds to the version of Windows that you want to install, and change the CD-ROM/DVD setting so that it points to the install media.

Click **Install**. Xen will create a new VM. When the machine comes up, it'll be in HVM mode, with the HVM BIOS configured to boot from the emulated CD-ROM. From that point, you can install Windows in the ordinary way. It's really quite a turnkey process; Citrix has put a lot of work into making Windows installation easy.

Creating DomU Images with P2V

The final way of installing is with the P2V install tool, short for *physical to virtual*. The tool creates domU images from physical Linux boxes, allowing you to install domUs on hardware that doesn't support HVM. Unfortunately, the P2V tool only supports a small number of Red Hat–like systems. Any other systems will cause it to quit with an error.

The tool comes as part of the XenServer install CD. To use it, boot the source machine from the XenServer CD. Interrupt the boot and enter **p2v-legacy** at the prompt if you're virtualizing a 32-bit system, or boot to the installer and select the **P2V** option if you're virtualizing a 64-bit system. A series of prompts will guide you through network setup and selecting a destination.

Existing filesystems on the machine will be copied and sent to the remote Citrix Xen server, which automatically creates configuration files and uses an appropriate kernel. Note that the P2V tool will conflate partitions in the copy process. In this way it's similar to the tar(1) process that we describe in Chapter 3, with added autoconfiguration magic.

Converting Pre-existing Virtual or Physical Machines with XenConvert

If you have virtual machines in the VMware VMDK, Microsoft VHD, or cross-platform OVF formats, you can convert them to Xen virtual machines using Citrix's Windows-based XenConvert utility. XenConvert will also work on physical Windows machines, similarly to the P2V utility.

XenConvert is quite simple to use. First, download the Windows installer from Citrix's site, at *http://www.citrix.com/xenserver_xenconvert_free*. Install the package, run the program, and follow the prompts.

XenServer Tools in the DomU

When you have a domain installed, you will almost certainly want to install the XenServer tools, which improve integration between the domain and the management interface. In particular, the tools allow the XenCenter to collect performance data from the domU. Under Windows, the Citrix tools also include paravirtualized drivers, which bypass the (slow) emulated drivers in favor of Xen-style ring buffers and so forth.

To install the tools, select the virtual machine in XenCenter, right-click it, and choose the **Install XenServer Tools** option from the context menu to switch the emulated CD. An alert box will pop up, advising you of the proper steps to perform.

Under Windows, the installer will autorun. Answer the prompts and let it go ahead with the install.[10] Reboot, selecting the **PV** option at the bootloader. Windows will detect and configure your new PV devices.

With Linux VMs, as the prompt says, perform these commands:

```
# mount /dev/xvdd /mnt
# /mnt/Linux/install.sh
```

The *install.sh* script will select an appropriate package and install it. Reboot and enjoy the utilization graphs.

xe: Citrix XenServer's Command-Line Tool

Citrix also ships a command-line interface alongside the graphical console. This command-line tool is called xe, and it's recommended for backups and similar automated tasks. In our opinion, it's definitely less pleasant than the XenCenter for everyday use. It's probably just our bias, but it also seems more cumbersome than the open source equivalent, xm.

You can use xe either from a separate management host (which can run either Windows or Linux) or in local mode directly on the XenServer host.[11]

Citrix includes xe as an RPM on the Linux supplement CD in the *client_install* directory. Make sure you have the required stunnel package. In our case, to install it on Slackware, we did:

```
# cd /media/XenServer-5.0.0 Linux Pack/client_install
# rpm -ivh --nodeps xe-cli-5.0.0-13192p.i386.rpm
```

When the client is installed on a remote machine, you can run it. Make sure to specify -s, otherwise it'll assume that you want to connect to the local host and fail.

```
# xe help -s corioles.prgmr.com
```

Whether you're using xe locally or remotely, the commands and parameters are the same. xe is actually a very thin wrapper around the Xen API. It exposes almost all the functionality offered by the API, with a corresponding difficulty of use. If you run it with the help --all command, it outputs a daunting usage message, detailing a huge variety of possible actions.

Fortunately, we can break these commands into groups. In general, there are commands to interact with the host and with virtual machines.

---

[10] By the way, Citrix is, in fact, serious about the drivers not supporting pre-SP2 Windows XP. We tried.

[11] We are told that you can even use xe on Windows. Not that we would dirty our hands using an OS like Windows to administer a Linux/Xen server.

There are commands to get logging information. There are pool commands. We have commands to administer virtual devices such as vifs and vbds.

Although some of the xe commands are similar to xm commands, the xe syntax is a bit more elaborate. The first argument must be a command name, followed by any switches, followed by any command parameters, in name=value syntax. It looks cumbersome, but Citrix has shipped a very nice bash completion setup to make autocomplete work well for the xe-specific parameters. It even fills in UUIDs. Thus:

```
# xm network-list 1
Idx BE    MAC Addr.      handle state evt-ch tx-/rx-ring-ref BE-path
0   0  00:16:3E:B9:B0:53    0    4     8      522 /523    /local/domain/0/backend/vif/1/0
```

becomes, with xe:

```
# xe vm-vif-list vm-name=aufidius

name: eth0
        mac: 00:16:3E:B9:B0:53
         ip: 192.168.1.64
    vbridge: xenbr0
       rate: 0
```

The documentation and the various recipes that are offered on Citrix's website have more advice on using xe.

XenServer's Disk Management

The XenServer software reserves a pair of 4GB partitions for itself, leaving the rest of the disk available for domUs. The first partition has the active XenServer install. The second partition is ordinarily left blank; however, if the server is upgraded, that partition is formatted and used as a complete backup of the previous install.

WARNING   *Note that this backup only applies to the dom0 data; the installer will wipe domU storage repositories on the disk. The moral? Back up domUs manually before upgrading XenSource.*

The rest of the space is put into a volume group, or, as Citrix calls it, a *storage repository*. As domUs are created, the server divides the space using LVM. The storage setup, for a single disk, can be seen in Figure 11-3. Each additional disk becomes a single PV, which is added to the storage pool.

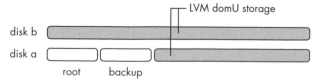

Figure 11-3: XenSource disk layout

Each LV gets a very long name that uses a UUID (universally unique identifier) to associate it with a VM.

Xen Storage Repositories

If you log in to the XenServer on the console or via SSH using the root password that you entered during the install, you can use standard Linux commands to examine the installed environment. To continue our example, you can use the LVM tools:

```
# vgs
  VG                                                    #PV #LV #SN Attr   VSize   VFree
  VG_XenStorage-03461f18-1189-e775-16f9-88d5b0db543f      1   0   0 wz--n- 458.10G 458.10G
```

However, you'll usually want to use the Citrix-provided higher-level commands because those also update the storage metadata. Equivalently, to list storage repositories using xe:

```
# xe sr-list
uuid ( RO)                    : 03461f18-1189-e775-16f9-88d5b0db543f
          name-label ( RW): Local storage
    name-description ( RW):
                host ( RO): localhost.localdomain
                type ( RO): lvm
        content-type ( RO): user
```

Note that the SR UUID matches the name of the volume group.

A complete description of xe's capabilities with regard to storage is best left to Citrix's documentation. However, we'll describe a brief session to illustrate the relationship between LVM, Xen's storage pools, and the hypervisor.

Let's say that you've added a new SATA disk to your XenServer, */dev/sdb*. To extend the default XenServer storage pool to the new disk, you can treat the storage pool as a normal LVM volume group:

```
# pvcreate /dev/sdb1
  Physical volume "/dev/sdb1" successfully created
# vgextend VG_XenStorage-9c186713-1457-6edb-a6aa-cbabb48c1e88 /dev/sdb1
  Volume group "VG_XenStorage-9c186713-1457-6edb-a6aa-cbabb48c1e88" successfully extended
# vgs
  VG                                                    #PV #LV #SN Attr   VSize   VFree
  VG_XenStorage-9c186713-1457-6edb-a6aa-cbabb48c1e88      2   2   0 wz--n- 923.86G 919.36G
# service xapi restart
```

The only unusual thing that we've done here is to restart the xapi service so that the various administration tools can use the new storage.

However, Citrix recommends that you perform these operations through their management stack. If you want to do anything more complex, like create a new storage repository, it's better to use the appropriate xe commands rather than work with LVM directly. Here's an example of the same operation, using xe:

```
# xe sr-create name-label="Supplementary Xen Storage" type=lvm device-config-device=/dev/sdb1
a154498a-897c-3f85-a82f-325e612d551d
```

That's all there is to it. Now the GUI should immediately show a new storage repository under the XenServer machine. We can confirm its status using xe sr-list:

```
# xe sr-list
uuid ( RO)                    : 9c186713-1457-6edb-a6aa-cbabb48c1e88
          name-label ( RW): Local storage on corioles
    name-description ( RW):
                type ( RO): lvm
        content-type ( RO): user
uuid ( RO)                    : a154498a-897c-3f85-a82f-325e612d551d
          name-label ( RW): Supplementary Xen Storage
    name-description ( RW):
                type ( RO): lvm
        content-type ( RO): disk
```

Citrix's website has more information on adding storage with xe, including the options of using file-backed storage, iSCSI, or NFS. They also cover such topics as removing storage repositories and setting QoS controls on VM storage. We defer to them for further details.

Emulated CD-ROM Access

One of the slickest things about Citrix's product is their CD-ROM emulation.[12] In addition to giving VMs the option of mounting the physical drives attached to the machine, it presents ISO images as possible CDs. When you change the CD, the domU immediately registers that a new disc has been inserted.

XenServer looks for local ISO images in */opt/xensource/packages/iso*, and it looks for shared ISO images in */var/opt/xen/iso_import*. Both of these paths are on the server, not the admin host. Note that the XenServer host has a very limited root filesystem and devotes most of its disk space to virtual machines; thus, we recommend using shared NFS or CIFS storage for ISOs. However, local ISO storage is still possible. For example, to make a Windows 2003 ISO conveniently accessible to the XenServer VM installer, we can:

```
# dd if=/dev/cdrom of=/opt/xensource/packages/iso/win2003.iso
```

---

[12] After years of being too lazy to set up an automounter, we are easily impressed.

Then restart the xapi service as before, and select the new ISO from the drop-down menu in XenCenter's graphical console tab. You can also use this ISO as an install source when creating virtual machines.

XenServer VM Templates

The templates are one of the nicest features of XenCenter. They allow you to create a virtual machine with predefined specifications with a couple of clicks. Although Citrix includes some templates, you'll probably want to add your own.

The easiest way to create VM templates is to create a VM with the desired setup and then convert it to a template using the XenSource management software. Right-click the machine in the GUI and select **Convert to Template**. Conceptually, this is like the *golden client* concept used by, say, SystemImager; you first tailor a client to meet your needs and then export it as the model for future installs.

```
# xe vm-param-set uuid=<UUID OF VM BEING CONVERTED TO TEMPLATE> is-a-template=true
```

Another option is to use the P2V tool. To create a template from a physical machine, boot the machine from the XenServer CD as you would to create a VM, but direct the output of the P2V tool at an NFS share rather than a XenServer host. The template will show up in the XenCenter client's list of available templates.

XenServer Resource Pools

One of the most compelling features of Citrix's product is their integration of resource pools. These pools are the manifestation of the utility computing model for Xen, in which a program is decoupled from a physical machine and run in a virtual machine on any member of a cluster of physical machines.

To create a resource pool, just select a XenServer virtualization host in the XenCenter client and create a pool from it.[13] When that's done, you can add more machines to the pool through the interface. (Up to 16 hosts are supported in a pool, although we've heard of people using more.) Furthermore, you can add storage to the pool, rather than to an individual machine, and create VMs that use shared storage. When you have domains based on shared storage, you can easily migrate them to other machines in the pool through the XenCenter GUI, as shown in Figure 11-4.

As you can see, Citrix has made migration basically a point-and-click operation.

We're not going to discuss pool administration at length; we mention it here mostly to emphasize that the feature exists.

---

[13] Some of the documentation claims that this feature is only available to paying customers, but we were able to manage fine. Consult Citrix for further clarification.

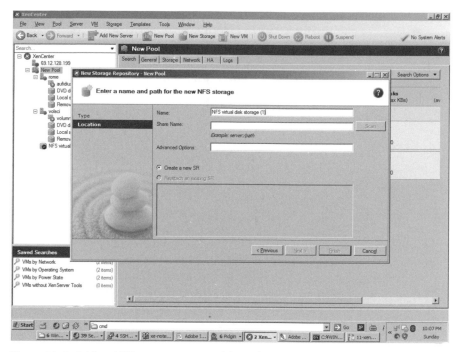

Figure 11-4: Adding NFS storage to a pool through XenCenter

Citrix XenServer: A Brief Review

Overall, we're quite pleased with Citrix's product. They have a polished tool that takes the drudgery out of Xen administration, and they've made a stable product. In our opinion, it's considerably better than using any of the frontends that are available from the open source version, and it's at least as reliable.

Along with the XenCenter frontend (the most obvious difference), XenServer does well in ease of installation and manageability. The combination of templates and streamlined domU creation is particularly nice.

Another advantage of the XenServer product is its inclusion of paravirtualized drivers for Windows. Although GPL PV drivers are in development and available (see Chapter 13 for more information), they aren't as mature as the Citrix implementation. The drivers make a huge difference and aren't available with the open source product. They may be the single most compelling reason to run XenServer.

Finally, virtually all of the interesting features of open source Xen are supported. Storage and network options are pared down somewhat, but the available options should be enough for most purposes.

It isn't all roses, however. The biggest problem that we ran into while testing it was its narrow support for obscure platforms, or even less-popular Linux distros like Gentoo or Slackware. Although it's possible to get other distros running, it's inconvenient, and convenience is one of XenServer's key selling points. Another annoyance is the need for a Windows machine to administer the Xen server—previous versions used a cross-platform Java client. However, because the frontend is apparently written in C#, perhaps we'll see a Mono port at some point.

Can Citrix's product replace the open source Xen? As always, the answer is maybe. It offers significant improvements in management and some interesting new capabilities, but that's balanced against the substantial cost and annoying limitations. We're sticking with the free version, but, then, our time is worthless.

12

HVM: BEYOND PARAVIRTUALIZATION

Throughout this book, we've described the standard Xen virtualization technique, *paravirtualization*. Paravirtualization is a wonderful thing—as we've already outlined, it allows excellent performance and strong isolation, two goals that are difficult to achieve simultaneously. (See Chapter 1 for more on this topic.)

However, paravirtualization requires a modified operating system. Although porting an OS to Xen is relatively painless, by the standards of such things, it's not a trivial task, and it has the obvious limitation of being impossible with closed source operating systems. (While the Xen team did port Windows to Xen during the development process, no *released* version of Windows can run under Xen in paravirtualized mode.)

One way around this is to add extensions to the processor so that it supports virtualization in hardware, allowing unmodified operating systems to run on the "bare metal," yet in a virtualized environment. Both Intel and AMD have done precisely that by extending the x86 architecture.

Intel uses the term *VT-x* to refer to the virtualization extensions for x86.[1] (*VT-i* is Itanium's hardware virtualization. For our purposes, it's basically identical to VT-x. We will not discuss VT-i separately.[2]) AMD likewise has a set of virtualization extensions.[3] Most of the Xen-related documentation that you might find refers to the extensions by their internal code name, *Pacifica*, but you'll also see the AMD marketing term *SVM*, for *secure virtual machine.*

Although VT-x and Pacifica are implemented slightly differently, we can gloss over the low-level implementation details and focus on capabilities. Both of these are supported by Xen. Both will allow you to run an unmodified operating system as a domU. Both of these will suffer a significant perform- ance penalty on I/O. Although there are differences between the two, the differences are hidden behind an abstraction layer.

Properly speaking, it's this abstraction layer that we refer to as HVM (hardware virtual machine)—a cross-platform way of hiding tedious imple- mentation details from the system administrator. So, in this chapter, we'll focus on the HVM interface and how to use it rather than on the specifics of either Intel's or AMD's technologies.

Principles of HVM

If you think back to the "concentric ring" security model that we introduced in Chapter 1, you can characterize the HVM extensions as adding a *ring −1* inside (that is, with superior privileges to) ring 0. New processor opcodes, invisible to the virtual machine, are used to switch between the superprivileged mode and normal mode. The unmodified operating system runs in ring 0 and operates as usual, without knowing that there's another layer between it and the hardware. When it makes a privileged system call, the call actually goes to ring −1 rather than the actual hardware, where the hypervisor will intercept it, pause the virtual machine, perform the call, and then resume the domU when the call is done.

Xen also has to handle memory a bit differently to accommodate unmodified guests. Because these unmodified guests aren't aware of Xen's memory structure, the hypervisor needs to use shadow page tables that present the illusion of contiguous physical memory starting at address 0, rather than the discontiguous physical page tables supported by Xen-aware operating systems. These shadows are in-memory copies of the page tables used by the hardware, as shown in Figure 12-1. Attempts to read and write to the page tables are intercepted and redirected to the shadow. While the guest runs, it reads its shadow page tables directly, while the hardware uses the pretranslated version supplied to it by the hypervisor.

---

[1] Intel has a nice introduction to their virtualization extensions at *http://www.intel.com/technology/ itj/2006/v10i3/3-xen/1-abstract.htm* and a promotional overview page at *http://www.intel.com/ technology/platform-technology/virtualization/index.htm.* They're worth reading.

[2] Also, Gentle Reader, your humble authors lack a recent Itanium to play with. Please forward offers of hardware to *lsc@prgmr.com.*

[3] AMD has a light introduction to their extensions at *http://developer.amd.com/TechnicalArticles/ Articles/Pages/630200615.aspx.*

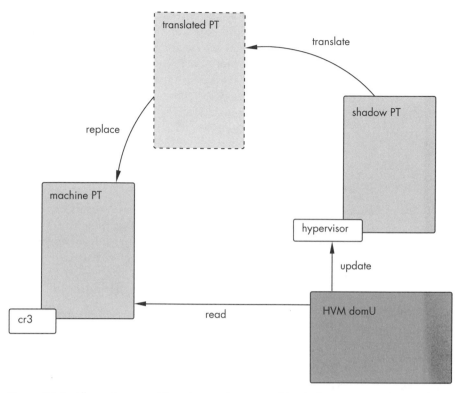

Figure 12-1: All guest page table writes are intercepted by the hypervisor and go to the shadow page tables. When the execution context switches to the guest, the hypervisor translates pseudophysical addresses found in the shadow page tables to machine physical addresses and updates the hardware to use the translated page tables, which the guest then accesses directly.

Device Access with HVM

Of course, if you've been paying attention thus far, you're probably asking how the HVM domain can access devices if it hasn't been modified to use the Xen virtual block and network devices. Excellent question!

The answer is twofold: First, during boot, Xen uses an emulated BIOS to provide simulations of standard PC devices, including disk, network, and framebuffer. This BIOS comes from the open source Bochs emulator at *http://bochs.sourceforge.net/*. Second, after the system has booted, when the domU expects to access SCSI, IDE, or Ethernet devices using native drivers, those devices are emulated using code originally found in the QEMU emulator. A userspace program, qemu-dm, handles translations between the native and emulated models of device access.

HVM Device Performance

This sort of translation, where we have to mediate hardware access by breaking out of virtualized mode using a software device emulation and then reentering the virtualized OS, is one of the trade-offs involved in running unmodified operating systems.[4] Rather than simply querying the host machine for information using a lightweight page-flipping system, HVM domains access devices precisely as if they were physical hardware. This is quite slow.

Both AMD and Intel have done work aimed at letting guests use hardware directly, using an IOMMU (I/O Memory Management Unit) to translate domain-virtual addresses into the real PCI address space, just as the processor's MMU handles the translations for virtual memory.[5] However, this isn't likely to replace the emulated devices any time soon.

HVM and SMP

SMP (symmetric multiprocessing) works with HVM just as with paravirtualized domains. Each virtual processor has its own control structure, which can in turn be serviced by any of the machine's physical processors. In this case, by *physical processors* we mean logical processors as seen by the machine, including the virtual processors presented by SMT (simultaneous multithreading or hyperthreading).

To turn on SMP, include the following in the config file:

```
acpi=1
vcpus=<n>
```

(Where *n* is an integer greater than one. A single CPU does not imply SMP. Quite the opposite, in fact.)

NOTE   *Although you can specify more CPUs than actually exist in the box, performance will . . . suffer. We strongly advise against it.*

Just as in paravirtualized domains, SMP works by providing a VCPU abstraction for each virtual CPU in the domain, as shown in Figure 12-2. Each VCPU can run on any physical CPU in the machine. Xen's CPU-pinning mechanisms also work in the usual fashion.

Unfortunately, SMP support isn't perfect. In particular, time is a difficult problem with HVM and SMP. Clock synchronization seems to be entirely unhandled, leading to constant complaints from the kernel with one of our test systems (CentOS 5, Xen version 3.0.3-rc5.el5, kernel 2.6.18-8.el5xen). Here's an example:

```
Timer ISR/0: Time went backwards: delta=-118088543 delta_cpu=25911457 shadow=157034917204
off=452853530 processed=157605639580 cpu_processed=157461639580
```

---

[4] As Intel points out, the actual implementation of HVM drivers is much better than this naïve model. For example, device access is asynchronous, meaning that the VM can do other things while waiting for I/O to complete.

[5] There's an interesting paper on the topic at *http://developer.amd.com/assets/IOMMU-ben-yehuda.pdf.*

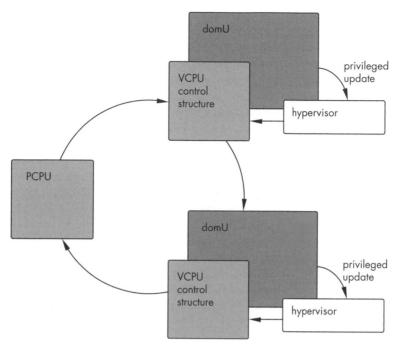

Figure 12-2: As each domain's time allocation comes up, its VCPU's processor state is loaded onto the PCPU for further execution. Privileged updates to the VCPU control structure are handled by the hypervisor.

One other symptom of the problem is in bogomips values reported by */proc/cpuinfo*—on a 2.4GHz core 2 duo system, we saw values ranging from 13.44 to 73400.32. In the dom0, each core showed 5996.61—an expected value.

Don't worry, this might be unsettling, but it's also harmless.

HVM and Migration

HVM migration works as of Xen 3.1. The migration support in HVM domains is based on that for paravirtualized domains but is extended to account for the fact that it takes place without the connivance of the guest OS. Instead, Xen itself pauses the VCPUs, while xc_save handles memory and CPU context. qemu-dm also takes a more active role, saving the state of emulated devices.

The point of all this is that you can migrate HVM domains just like paravirtualized domains, using the same commands, with the same caveats. (In particular, remember that attempts to migrate an HVM domain to a physical machine that doesn't support HVM will fail ungracefully.)

Xen HVM vs. KVM

Of course, if your machine supports virtualization in hardware, you might be inclined to wonder what the point of Xen is, rather than, say, KVM or lguest.

There are some excellent reasons to consider the idea. KVM and lguest are both easier to install and less invasive than Xen. They support strong virtualization with good performance.

However, KVM is, at the moment, less mature than Xen. It's not (yet) as fast, even with the kernel accelerator. Xen also supports paravirtualization, whereas KVM does not. Xen PV offers a handy way of migrating domUs and a good way of multiplexing virtual machines—that is, expanding to a two-level VM hierarchy. But honestly, we haven't got much experience with KVM, and we've got quite a lot with Xen.

Similarly, lguest is smaller, lighter, and easier to install than Xen, but it doesn't support features like SMP or PAE (though 64-bit kernels are in development). Lguest also doesn't yet support suspend, resume, or migration.

Nonetheless, right now it's difficult to say which is better—all of these technologies are out there being actively developed. If you are truly silly, you might even decide to use some combination, running Xen hypervisors under KVM, with paravirtualized domains under that. Or you might use Xen for now but keep your options open for future deployments, perhaps when HVM-capable hardware becomes more common. These technologies are interesting and worth watching, but we'll stick to our usual "wait and see" policy.

Indeed, Red Hat has opted to do exactly that, focusing its development efforts on a platform-independent interface layer, libvirt, allowing (we hope) for easy migration between virtualization options. See Chapter 6 for more on libvirt and its associated suite of management tools.

Working with HVM

Regardless of what sort of hardware virtualization you want to use, the first thing to do is check whether your machine supports HVM. To find out if you've got a supported processor, check */proc/cpuinfo*. Processors that support VT-x will report vmx in the flags field, while Pacifica-enabled processors report svm.

Even if you have a supported processor, many manufacturers have HVM turned off in the BIOS by default. Check xm dmesg to ensure that the hypervisor has found and enabled HVM support correctly—it should report "(XEN) VMXON is done" for each CPU in the machine. If it doesn't, poke about in the BIOS for an option to turn on hardware virtualization. On our boards, it's under *chipset features* and called *VT Technology*. Your machine may vary.

The hypervisor will also report capabilities under */sys*:

```
# cat /sys/hypervisor/properties/capabilities
xen-3.0-x86_32p hvm-3.0-x86_32 hvm-3.0-x86_32p
```

In this case, the two "hvm" entries show that HVM is supported in both PAE and non-PAE modes.

NOTE   *One of the minor advantages of HVM is that it sidesteps the PAE-matching problem
that we've been prone to harp on. You can run any mix of PAE and non-PAE kernels
and hypervisors in HVM mode, although paravirtualized domains will still need to
match PAE-ness, even on HVM-capable machines.*

Creating an HVM Domain

When you've got the hypervisor and domain 0 running on an HVM-capable
machine, creating an HVM domain is much like creating any Xen guest.

Here's a sample HVM config file. (It's got a snippet of Python at the
beginning to set the appropriate library directory, borrowed from the sample
configs distributed with Xen.)

```
import os, re
arch = os.uname()[4]
if re.search('64', arch):
arch_libdir = 'lib64'
else:
arch_libdir = 'lib'

device_model = '/usr/' + arch_libdir + '/xen/bin/qemu-dm'

kernel = "/usr/lib/xen/boot/hvmloader" builder='hvm'
memory = 384
shadow_memory = 16
name = "florizel"
vcpus = 1
vif = [ 'type=ioemu, bridge=xenbr0' ]
disk = [ 'file:/opt/florizel.img,hda,w', 'file:/root/slackware-12.0-install-dvd.iso,hdc:cdrom,r' ]

boot="cda"

sdl=0
vnc=1
stdvga=0
serial='pty'
```

Most of this is pretty standard stuff. It starts with a snippet of Python to
choose the correct version of qemu-dm, then it launches into a standard domU
config. The config file changes for HVM guests are approximately as follows:

```
builder = "HVM"
device_model = "/usr/lib/xen/bin/qemu-dm" kernel = "/usr/lib/xen/boot/hvmloader"
```

NOTE   *There are other directives you can put in, but these are the ones that you can't leave out.*

Breaking this down, the domain builder changes from the default to
HVM, while the devices change from the standard Xen paravirtualized devices
to the QEMU emulated devices. Finally, the kernel line specifies an HVM
loader that loads a kernel from within the HVM domain's filesystem, rather
than the Linux kernel that would be specified in a PV configuration.

We're already familiar with the kernel line, of course. The device_model line, however, is new. This option defines a userspace program that handles mediation between real and virtual devices. As far as we know, qemu-dm is the only option, but there's no reason that other device emulators couldn't be written.

There are some other directives that are only used by HVM domains.

```
shadow_memory = 16
boot="dca"
```

The shadow_memory directive specifies the amount of memory to use for shadow page tables. (Shadow page tables, of course, are the aforementioned copies of the tables that map process-virtual memory to physical memory.) Xen advises allocating at least 2KB per MB of domain memory, and "a few" MB per virtual CPU. Note that this memory is *in addition* to the domU's allocation specified in the memory line.

Finally we have the boot directive. The entire concept of boot order, of course, doesn't apply to standard Xen paravirtualized domains because the domain config file specifies either a kernel or a bootloader. However, because HVM emulates legacy BIOS functions, including the traditional bootstrap, Xen provides a mechanism to configure the boot order.

In that vein, it's worth noting that one advantage of HVM is that it can effectively duplicate the QEMU install procedure we've already described, with Xen instead of QEMU. To recap, this allows you to install in a strongly partitioned virtual machine, using the distro's own install tools, and end with a ready-to-run VM. We'll leave the details as an exercise to the reader, of course (we wouldn't want to take all the fun out of it).

Now that you've got the config file written, create the domain as usual:

```
# xm create florizel
Using config file "./florizel".
Started domain florizel
# xm list
Name                                  ID Mem(MiB) VCPUs State Time(s)
Domain-0                               0    3458     2 r----- 5020.8
florizel                               6     396     1 r----- 14.6
```

Interacting with an HVM Domain

One of the first changes you might notice is that connecting to the console using xm -c doesn't work. The Xen console requires some infrastructure support to get working, which a PV-oblivious standard distro naturally doesn't have.

So, while the machine is booting, let's chat for a bit about how you actually log in to your shiny new domain.

As you're no doubt sick of us mentioning, HVM is founded on an idea of *total hardware simulation*. This means that when the machine boots, it loads an emulated VGA BIOS, which gets drawn into a graphics window.

Xen knows about two targets for its emulated VGA graphics: VNC and SDL. VNC is the familiar and well-beloved network windowing system from AT&T, while *SDL, Simple DirectMedia Layer,* is better known as a lightweight hardware-accelerated graphics option.

We opted to stick with the VNC console for most of our Linux domUs to reap the benefits of network-centric computing.[6]

Now that the domain is created, use VNC to access its console:

```
# vncviewer 127.0.0.1
```

(Or use whatever the IP address of the Xen machine is.) If you have more than one domU using the VNC console, append a display number—for example, to access the console of the second domU:

```
# vncviewer 127.0.0.1:1
```

If the vncunused= option in the config file is set, the domain will take the first available display number. If not, it'll take the display number that corresponds to its domain number. We tend to leave it set, but unset is fine too.

---

[6] By which I mean, we didn't want to have to stand up and walk over to a test machine to access the console.

Somewhat to our surprise, X11 worked quite well out of the box with the vesa driver, taking over the VNC framebuffer console and providing a usable display without further configuration.

Getting the Standard Xen Console to Work

Now, logging in via the graphical console is an irritating bit of overhead and, we would argue, overkill for a server. Fortunately, you can circumvent this by using the standard Xen emulated serial console. First, make sure that your domU config file (e.g., */etc/xen/leontes*) contains the following:

```
serial='pty'
```

This directive tells QEMU (and therefore Xen) to pass serial output to the Xen console.

Now the bootloader needs to be told to pass its messages to the serial line. Add the following to */boot/grub.conf* in the domU:

```
serial --unit=0 --speed=115200 --word=8 --parity=no --stop=1 serial console
```

These two lines give GRUB some settings for the serial port and tell it to actually use the serial port as its console.

Next, set up the kernel to output its boot information via serial:

```
title CentOS (2.6.18-8.el5)
root (hd0,0)
kernel /vmlinuz-2.6.18-8.el5 ro root=/dev/VolGroup00/LogVol00 rhgb quiet console=ttyS0
module /initrd-2.6.18-8.el5.img
```

(If you're loading the Xen hypervisor in HVM mode—which is a perfectly reasonable thing to do—your *menu.lst* file will look a bit different, of course.)

Finally, edit inittab to start a getty on the emulated serial line by adding a line like this:

```
s1:12345:respawn:/sbin/agetty -L ttyS0 9600 vt100
```

Boot the machine, and you should be able to see messages and log in via both xm console and VNC.

HVM Devices

If you poke around in your new HVM domain, you'll see devices like "QEMU harddisk," or "RealTek Ethernet controller." These take the place of the corresponding Xen devices, like xenblock or xennet. Examine this dmesg output, for example:

```
PIIX3: IDE controller at PCI slot 0000:00:01.1 PIIX3: chipset revision 0
PIIX3: not 100% native mode: will probe IRQs later PCI: Setting latency timer
of device 0000:00:01.1 to 64
```

```
ide0: BM-DMA at 0xc000-0xc007, BIOS settings: hda:pio, hdb:pio ide0: BM-DMA at
0xc008-0xc00f, BIOS settings: hdc:pio, hdd:pio
Probing IDE interface ide0...
hda: QEMU HARDDISK, ATA DISK drive
```

This shows the QEMU emulated hard drive. Further on, we see:

```
eth0: RealTek RTL8139 at 0xc200, 00:16:3e:0b:7c:f0, IRQ 11 eth0:  Identified
8139 chip type 'RTL-8139'
```

The difference between PV and HVM domains doesn't end in the domU, either. With HVM domains, you'll see *tap* devices in the dom0.

Think of the tap devices as QEMU analogues to the vifs discussed earlier—bits shoved into them come out on the virtual network devices in the domU. You can manage them just like vifs—adding them to bridges, configuring them down or up, and so on.

Paravirtualized Drivers

The best solution to the problem of slow emulated HVM devices, in the context of Xen, is to use paravirtualized drivers that work on the same split-driver model as non-HVM domains—backend drivers in domain 0, with a small frontend driver in domU that communicates with the backend via event channels, using ring buffers and page flipping. (See Chapter 1 for boring details on Xen's split driver model.)

XenSource includes such drivers for Windows, of course. For users of open source Xen, Novell distributes an expensive driver package that performs the same function—paravirtualized device support for Windows. GPL drivers also exist for Windows on open source Xen (we discuss those in more detail in Chapter 13).

However, you can also build PV drivers for Linux HVM domains. These drivers are included with the Xen source tree in the *unmodified_drivers* directory. Unfortunately, the kernel API keeps changing, so the PV drivers might not compile against your kernel version (the drivers with Xen 3.1 refused to compile with kernel versions 2.6.20 and above).

Compiling PV Drivers for HVM Linux

Nonetheless, the best way to figure out if the drivers will work is to try it. Here's how we compiled our drivers out of a standard Xen source tree.

```
# cd unmodified_drivers/linux-2.6 # ./mkbuildtree
# make -C /usr/src/linux M=$PWD modules
```

This builds standard Xen devices as modules—install them into your modules tree and load them like any other driver, with insmod or modprobe. You'll wind up with four modules, one each for block and network devices, one for xenbus, and one for PCI emulation. Load xen-platform-pci first, then xenbus, then block and network.

```
# insmod xen-platform-pci
# insmod xenbus
# insmod xenblk
# insmod xennet
```

Because we were using Slackware as our domU, we then built a minimal kernel—without drivers for the emulated IDE or Realtek network card—and built an initrd with the Xen devices included.

We also needed to modify */etc/fstab* to refer to the Xen backend devices.

Finally (this is starting to seem like a lot of trouble, isn't it?) we edited the domain's configuration to specify netfront and blkfront instead of the ioemu devices. We did this by changing the device lines:

```
vif = [ 'type=ioemu, bridge=xenbr0' ]
disk = [ 'file:/opt/florizel.img,ioemu:hda,w', 'file:/root/slackware-12.0-
install-dvd.iso,ioemu:hdc:cdrom,r' ]
```

to:

```
vif = [ 'bridge=xenbr0' ]
disk = [ 'file:/opt/florizel.img,hda,w', 'file:/root/slackware-12.0-install-
dvd.iso,hdc:cdrom,r' ]
```

and removing the device_model= line.

Modify these directions to work with your setup, of course.

And, for Our Next Trick . . .

As always, there are some areas of ongoing work. Both Intel and AMD have announced successor techniques for dealing with guest page tables by adding a new level to the page table structure. AMD terms the concept *nested paging*, while Intel calls it *Extended Page Tables*. IOMMU development is another exciting area of research.

HVM is nice in general, but of course all of this is a prelude to Chapter 13, where we'll apply all of this stuff to getting a virtual Windows machine up and running in HVM mode. Stay tuned!

13

XEN AND WINDOWS

In the last chapter we described Xen's hardware virtualization support and how to use it. Now that we have Xen operating with hardware virtualization, we can run unmodified operating systems, including Windows, that 800-pound gorilla of the computing world.

Why Run Windows Under Xen?

Now, why exactly would you want to do this terrible thing? We could say, "because you can," and that's reason enough to do many things. But it might not be entirely satisfying—it sounds like a lot of work, after all.

Fortunately, reasons abound. Probably the best of these is the software—especially the server software, considering that Xen's strengths are in the server field.[1] Much of the Windows server software, like Exchange Server, has a giant installed base and would be difficult to replace. The same holds for

---

[1] At least in light of the ongoing commodification of the operating system, which really is at least part of what Xen is all about, isn't it?

the client software. Take, for example, Office, Outlook, Visual Studio—Microsoft continues to be a fact of life. Xen with VNC, SDL, or rdesktop allows you to run productivity software at acceptable speeds, with full, albeit unaccelerated, graphics support, all while retaining your comfortable Linux computing environment.

Xen also gives you a way out from the old worry that the next security fix or driver update will leave the machine completely unbootable—it provides an equivalent to Microsoft's "system restore points" but under your own control, rather than the OS's. By running Windows in a virtual machine with an effective storage backend, you can snapshot it, roll back updates, and protect yourself from malware—all without involving the domU.

Security furnishes another reason to run Windows under Xen. Although it's cliche to say that Windows is insecure, the fact remains that virtualization, when properly used, can be an effective layer of isolation for any server, Windows, *nix, or otherwise. The fact that Windows is a popular target makes this reasoning even more compelling.

It's also worth noting that Xen's design, which partitions drivers in isolated domains, at least contributes to security. An intrusion in the Windows domain, even if it manages to exploit driver code to interact with physical hardware, is unlikely to compromise other domains on the same hardware. This doesn't mean that Xen is inherently secure, but it does suggest that it might be possible to secure it. Work remains to be done, of course—indeed, a lot of the present work in QEMU is in precisely the area of validating emulated device access to improve security. But even as things are, Xen can help to reduce the exposure of Windows machines.

Besides, it's easier to run Windows in a domU than you might suppose.

Windows on Xen: Prerequisites

Before stepping into the brave new world of virtualized Windows, make sure that you've got a few things.

First, you're going to need a box that does HVM. (See Chapter 12 for details on what that is, how it works, and how to tell if you have it.) The box will also need enough free memory and storage for a Windows install—Xen can help to use resources more efficiently, but it's not magic. For example, we suggest that a Xen box running Windows Server 2003 domUs have 512MB of memory and about 10GB of hard drive space for each domU, plus 512MB and another 10GB for dom0. You might want to consult Microsoft's website for more specific system requirements or requirements for other Windows versions.

It might sound obvious, but you're also going to need a copy of Windows, with a license that allows virtualization. This copy of Windows should be reasonably new. We're going to focus on Windows XP Service Pack 2 and Windows Server 2003 in this chapter—Vista's just too much hassle at this point. Windows NT and 9x, while they should in theory work, seem to crash during the install step. No one (us included) seems too interested in figuring out why this happens. Life is full of mysteries.

Windows on Xen: Installation

Windows is actually quite easy to get installed and running. The basic steps are exactly like any other Xen install, with some extra configuration:

1. Get Windows install media and put it somewhere that Xen can find it.
2. Make a config file.
3. Boot from the install media.
4. Install using the Windows installer.
5. Reboot from the emulated hard drive.
6. Install paravirtualized drivers.
7. Use Windows.

Easy, right? Let's get started.

Installing Windows Manually

The first thing to do is get a copy of Windows. In our case, we used a physical CD-ROM, which we put in the Xen server's CD-ROM drive. For convenience, you can of course create an image from the CD and use it just like the physical disc:

```
# dd if=/dev/cdrom of=/var/tmp/windows2k3.iso
```

(If you go that route, specify file:/var/tmp/windows2k3.iso instead of phy:/dev/cdrom in the following steps.)

While you're at it, create the backing store in the usual way. Here we'll use a file-backed device, but you can use any storage backend that Xen knows about.

```
# dd if=/dev/zero of=/opt/xen/falstaff/falstaff.img bs=1M count=8192
```

Next, create a config file. Here's a sample (pulled from Chapter 12 with minor changes). We'll save this as */etc/xen/falstaff*:

```
import os, re
arch = os.uname()[4]
if re.search('64', arch):
    arch_libdir = 'lib64'
else:
    arch_libdir = 'lib'

device_model = '/usr/' + arch_libdir + '/xen/bin/qemu-dm'

kernel = '/usr/lib/xen/boot/hvmloader'
builder = 'hvm'
memory = 512
name = 'falstaff'
vif = [ 'type=ioemu, bridge=xenbr0' ]
```

```
disk = [ 'file:/opt/xen/falstaff/falstaff.img,ioemu:hda,w',
    'phy:/dev/cdrom,ioemu:hdc:cdrom,r' ]
boot = 'd'

vnc = 1
```

This should be pretty familiar by now. Note that we're leaving ACPI and APIC at their default "off" values to avoid confusing the Windows installer. You'll want to point the entries in the disk= lines to the appropriate locations for your install, of course. You might also want to diverge from our configuration by setting sdl=1 rather than vnc—SDL works only on the local X display but has the virtue of popping up automatically.

Then create the machine as usual:

```
# xm create falstaff
```

Start a VNC session so that you can talk to it, assuming you decided against SDL. Insert the correct host and display number—in this case we're on the local machine, and this is the first VNC session running:

```
# vncviewer localhost:1
```

Now Windows Setup will start in its accustomed fashion. Install Windows as usual.

A Discussion of HALs

One problem that occasionally pops up at this stage involves the Windows HAL (hardware abstraction layer). Windows ships with a selection of possible DLLs to implement the abstraction layer, picking one of six choices during the install process. The correct HAL to use with the system is affected by the acpi, apic, and vcpus configuration directives, as indicated in Table 13-1.

Table 13-1: HALs Available with Windows

OPTIONS	HAL	COMMENTS
acpi=0,apic=0	HAL.DLL	Standard PC Non-ACPI Programmable Interrupt Controller (PIC) Works with everything
acpi=0,apic=1	HALAPIC.DLL	MPS (Multiprocessor Specification) Uniprocessor PC Non-ACPI APIC uniprocessor HAL Uniprocessor only Doesn't work with PIC machines
acpi=0,apic=1	HALMPS.DLL	Non-ACPI APIC multiprocessor HAL Does not work with ACPI machines
acpi=1,apic=0	HALACPI.DLL	Advanced Configuration and Power Interface (ACPI) ACPI PIC (not APIC) HAL Do these even exist in hardware?

Table 13-1: HALs Available with Windows (continued)

OPTIONS	HAL	COMMENTS
acpi=1,apic=1	HALAACPI.DLL	ACPI Uniprocessor PC
		ACPI APIC uniprocessor HAL
		ACPI only
		APIC only
		Uniprocessor only
acpi=1,apic=1	HALMACPI.DLL	ACPI Multiprocessor PC
		ACPI APIC multiprocessor HAL

The lucky winner becomes *$SYSTEMROOT\system32\HAL.DLL*.

The easy answer, therefore, is to use *HAL.DLL*, regardless of the values of ACPI and APIC. This should always work, but it might reduce performance. Microsoft also warns that such a configuration is unsupported.[2] We generally turn ACPI and APIC on so that Windows will install the ACPI APIC HAL, and it hasn't caused the machine to burst into flames yet.

With Windows XP, however, this sometimes doesn't work. Setting ACPI can cause the install process to fail, usually by hanging at Setup is Starting Windows. The easiest way to install Windows XP is to leave ACPI and APIC off during the initial boot from the CD-ROM and then turn them on before the first boot into graphical mode.

```
acpi=0
apic=0
on_reboot = 'destroy'
```

Then go through the initial format, copy, and so on. When the first phase of Windows Setup completes and the VM turns off, change the config file to read:

```
acpi=1
apic=1
on_reboot = 'restart'
```

This will cause Windows to install the correct HAL during its second-phase installation.

If you need to change the HAL later on—for example, if you decide to move from a uniprocessor to a multiprocessor configuration—we recommend reinstalling Windows. It's possible to change the HAL manually by overwriting the various driver files, but it's probably not a great idea.

Installing Windows the Red Hat Way

Red Hat's virt-manager app can handle most of the trouble of setting up Windows for you. Just create a machine from the virt-manager GUI, select **Fully Virtualized** rather than Paravirtualized in the appropriate dialog, and indicate the location of Windows install media (either an ISO file or physical

---

[2] So is everything else about running Windows under Xen, as far as we can tell.

CD-ROM). Indicate whether you'd like to connect to the network using a virtual network or shared physical device (corresponding to networking via virbr and xenbr, respectively). Install Windows as normal, using Microsoft's install program.

The configuration generated by virt-manager will look something like this:

```
name = "hal"
uuid = "5b001f4d-7891-90d8-2f55-96a56e8d07df"
maxmem = 512
memory = 512
vcpus = 1
builder = "hvm"
kernel = "/usr/lib/xen/boot/hvmloader"
boot = "c"
pae = 1
acpi = 0
apic = 0
on_poweroff = "destroy"
on_reboot = "restart"
on_crash = "restart"
device-model = "/usr/lib/xen/bin/qemu-dm"
sdl = 0
vnc = 1
vncunused = 1
keymap = "en-us"
disk = [ "file:/var/lib/xen/images/falstaff.img,hda,w" ]
vif = [ "mac=00:16:3e:7e:f3:15,bridge=virbr0,type=ioemu" ]
serial = "pty"
```

Unfortunately, this doesn't get you quite to the end of the Windows install. For whatever reason, the emulated CD-ROM isn't presented to Windows after the first reboot in the install process, so Windows will complain that it can't find its files.

Red Hat's documentation will tell you that Windows needs to format its virtual disk as a FAT or FAT32 partition so that you can copy the install files to it. While this approach will work, we prefer to avoid FAT32 in favor of NTFS. To get around this problem, we use the I/O emulator. Modify the disk= line to use QEMU's I/O emulation as follows:

```
disk = ['<hda>','file:/mnt/winxp.iso,ioemu:hdc:cdrom,r']
```

(Put your definition for the first hard drive in the appropriate place, of course.) The second stanza specifies an ISO to use as a virtual CD-ROM drive, with hardware emulation provided by Xen's hardware emulation layer (inherited from QEMU). When you've made this change, the CD will appear to the domU as a QEMU emulated device, and you can proceed with the installation.

Windows with the Virtual Framebuffer

"What's the best remote administration tool for Windows NT?"
"A car."

—Anonymous, Usenet

However you've gone about installing Windows, you'll almost certainly want to log in and use the system when it's running. That's where the virtual framebuffer comes in.

Xen's virtual framebuffer allows you to interact with the domU at all stages—from BIOS load, through the bootloader, to postsystem boot. It can be accessed through SDL on the local console or via VNC over the network. It's one of the neater features of HVM domUs, and it really helps to cement the illusion of a real machine.

Wonderful though the virtual framebuffer is, however, it's got some annoyances. Mouse tracking, for example, can be kind of iffy out of the box. Here are some ways to fix the most common problems that we've had with the VNC framebuffer.

First, by default Xen's built-in VNC server won't listen on interfaces other than the loopback. To change this behavior, set vnc-listen in */etc/xen/xend-config.sxp* to listen on all interfaces:

```
(vnc-listen '0.0.0.0')
```

You can also specify the IP address of the interface that you want the VNC server to listen on. Note that this will expose the machine's console over the network and should probably only be done on trusted networks.

One useful trick when working with the VNC framebuffer under Windows is to specify a tablet as the pointing device, rather than a mouse. This improves the mouse tracking by using absolute positioning.

```
usb=1
usbdevice="tablet"
```

(The usb=1 line isn't strictly necessary—it's turned on implicitly by usbdevice=. However, it's a useful reminder that Xen's USB emulation has been turned on.)

One last minor annoyance: Sometimes the VNC mouse and keyboard interface just stops working (or else the display stops updating). Nine times out of ten, if you close and reopen the VNC session, it'll come back.

In addition to Xen's virtual framebuffer, you can handle access at the OS level—for example, by installing the VNC server under Windows or using Microsoft's built-in RDP (Remote Desktop Protocol). These have the advantage of allowing the virtual machine to handle its own graphics tasks rather than involving an emulator in dom0. RDP is also a higher-level, more efficient protocol than VNC, analogous to X in its handling of widgets and graphics primitives. We recommend using it if possible. As Figure 13-1 shows, VNC, RDP, and SDL can coexist, with multiple independent sessions on the same VM.

To enable RDP in administration mode, access **System Properties**, click the **Remote** tab, and check the box marked **Enable Remote Desktop**.

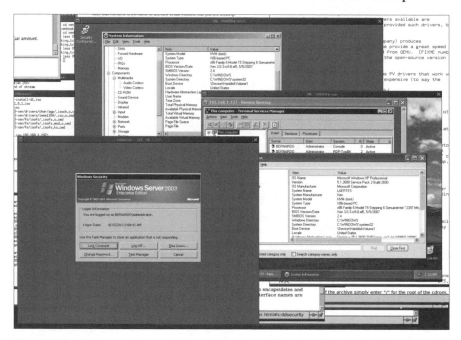

Figure 13-1: Here we see two domains: one running Windows XP and being accessed through VNC; and one Windows Server 2003 domU being accessed through VNC, RDP from the Windows XP domain, and rdesktop from a Linux machine.

Windows XP and Windows Server 2003 include RDP clients. On other platforms, the open source rdesktop client allows you to access Windows machines from Unix-like operating systems (including Mac OS X). Simply run the following:

```
# rdesktop <destination address>
```

Et Voilà!

Now you have Windows running. This would be a good time to make a backup of your clean Windows install so that you can conveniently reimage it when something goes wrong. Just create an LVM snapshot or file-based CoW device, as we outline in the Chapter 4. It'll be good for your peace of mind.

When you've got a backup, you can do whatever it is you are accustomed to do with Windows. We would not presume to instruct you in this regard.

There are, however, some things to keep in mind about this new Windows install.

Windows Activation

Windows licenses and activations are tied to hardware unless you've got a volume license. Thus, it would be a good idea to decide on a hardware configuration ahead of time and keep it constant to avoid the computer demanding reactivation.

In particular, specify a MAC address so that Xen doesn't randomly generate a new one on every reboot—this is the single most important value in Windows XP's hardware hash calculation. Other things to keep in mind are the memory amount and virtual CD-ROM.

Graphics Cards

Another of the big caveats about Windows under Xen is that it still won't allow you to use 3D hardware—so the scenario of a desktop Linux box that runs games in a Windows domU is still purely in the realm of fantasy for now. As our discussion above has shown, the virtual Windows machine uses an emulated framebuffer via SDL or VNC. Neither of these modes supports any sort of acceleration.

The problem with hardware access in HVM mode (this applies to any PCI device, not just graphics cards) is that there's no way to map the hardware's memory space into the memory of the guest—the guest has an additional layer of abstraction, translating a discontiguous block of physical memory into something that the unmodified domU operating system can use. Recently, chipsets have been incorporating an *IOMMU*, which is hardware that can do this translation job in a manner analogous to the processor's memory management unit (hence the name). Xen's support for Intel's IOMMU implementation, under the name of VT-d, is progressing, but it hasn't gotten to the point where it can make a graphics card usable by a Windows domU.

> **VT-D SUPPORT**
>
> If you're curious about whether your machine supports VT-d, you can run xm dmesg | grep -i vt-d in the dom0 to find out. A machine with VT-d will say something like *Intel VT-d has been enabled.* If you see this, congratulations! The next Xen version will likely include facilities to enable you to use this advanced feature.

Another approach to graphics—one that wouldn't require replacement of all existing hardware—would be for the the graphics driver authors to implement the translation from domU addresses to machine addresses in driver software. Rumor has it that NVIDIA has a Xen-aware driver that could be assigned to an HVM domU and used for 3D acceleration; however, it hasn't yet been released, so there's a good chance it doesn't actually exist.

One other promising direction uses a virtual 3D graphics driver to forward OpenGL calls to the actual graphics hardware. There are a couple of Xen-based projects that use this principle, but they are Linux only at the moment.

VMware has also done some work on a driver architecture that allows for 3D, which appears to take the same tack.

No finished products exist, that we know of, to allow hardware 3D support under Windows. Nonetheless, it's a much-requested feature, and it is being worked on. We wouldn't make it an essential part of any Xen deployment just yet, however.

Paravirtualized Drivers for Windows

As we've already mentioned (several times), HVM is somewhat slower than paravirtualization. Partially this is because of the need to virtualize memory access; however, this overhead is minimal compared with emulated I/O and its attendant context switches. (See Chapter 12 for mind-numbing detail.)

You can address many of the speed issues related to HVM by swapping the emulated devices for paravirtualized devices after the install process completes. These devices will improve I/O speeds dramatically; however, Windows driver support is lacking. There are two options: proprietary and expensive drivers, or free and unfinished ones.

Proprietary Windows PVM Drivers

Three companies have so far provided Windows drivers that take advantage of paravirtualization: XenSource, Virtual Iron, and Novell. All of these drivers are signed by Microsoft for trouble-free installation on Windows.

Citrix, wearing its XenSource hat, produces paravirtualized drivers for Windows as part of its Xen-based virtualization suite. These drivers work well, and you can test them for yourself by downloading the free version of the XenSource product. Unfortunately, these drivers don't work with the open source version of Xen.

Virtual Iron (*http://virtualiron.com/*) also provides paravirtualized drivers for Windows as part of its product. These drivers work with open source Xen, and Virtual Iron has been working on contributing changes to the Xen community. However, the drivers themselves are still closed source.

Finally, Novell offers Windows PV drivers that work with open source Xen as an independent product. These drivers are quite expensive (to say the least)—they are so expensive that we haven't actually tried them. More information is at *http://www.novell.com/products/vmdriverpack/* if you're curious.

At this point, while all of these drivers (in our experience) function as advertised, none of them seem especially compelling to us. We're content to use Windows, with the HVM drivers, solely in light productivity tasks.

GPL Windows Paravirtualized Drivers

There is one thing that you can try if you're sufficiently adventurous. GPL Windows PV drivers do exist. They are under active development, which is developer-speak for "don't use these for anything important." They work pretty well for us, but occasionally they do something surprising (usually unpleasant). These drivers try to improve performance by avoiding some of the inefficient device emulation and by using advanced techniques such as TCP Segmentation Offload, or TSO.

The GPL PV drivers are easy to install. First, we recommend checking the *xen-devel* archives to figure out which version is the latest. As of this writing, 0.8.8 is the most current version, and it's available at *http://www.meadowcourt .org/WindowsXenPV-0.8.8.zip.* Unfortunately, there's no web page that lists releases, so you'll want to search the archives of the *xen-devel* mailing list to find out the most recent version. (Alternatively, you can check the current version using Mercurial—check the repository at *http://xenbits.xensource.com/ ext/win-pvdrivers.hg.*)

We opted to download the binary driver package directly within an HVM Windows XP Professional instance. It includes a fairly comprehensive set of installation instructions, but we'll go over what we did anyway, just for convenience.

First, unpack the drivers. We just dragged the appropriate folder to the desktop.

Next, run *install.bat.* Windows will complain several times about the drivers not being signed. Just click **OK.**

When the install finishes, reboot to make sure that everything still works.

Assuming you rebooted successfully, you should now be able to access PV devices from Windows. Try creating a scratch device in the dom0, then running an xm block-attach command like the following (with appropriate names, as always):

```
# xm block-attach falstaff phy:/dev/mapper/falstaff_sdb sdb w
```

This should cause Windows to notice a new device, use the correct driver, and present a blank disk, which we can then format, as shown in Figure 13-2. Similarly, you can attach a network device with the xm network-attach command.

Finally, you'll need to edit the *boot.ini* file to tell the GPL PV drivers to activate. (You might need to turn on Show Hidden Files and Folders and uncheck Hide Protected Operating System Files in Tools ▶ Folder Options to make *boot.ini* accessible.)

```
[boot loader]
timeout=30
default=multi(0)disk(0)rdisk(0)partition(1)\WINDOWS

[operating systems]
multi(0)disk(0)rdisk(0)partition(1)\WINDOWS="Windows XP Professional" /noexecute=optin /fastdetect
multi(0)disk(0)rdisk(0)partition(1)\WINDOWS="Windows XP Professional (PV drivers)"
/noexecute=optin /fastdetect /gplpv
```

Here we've modified the boot entry by putting /gplpv on the end to tell the GPL PV drivers to activate.

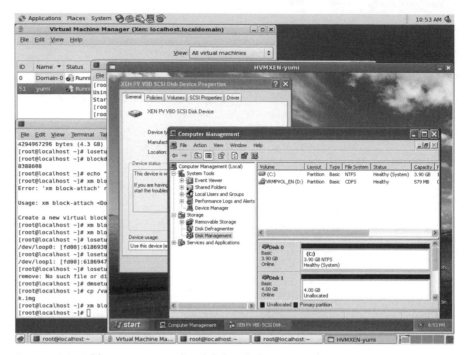

Figure 13-2: Adding a paravirtualized disk with the GPL PV drivers

Now shut down the Windows install.

Reboot, select the **Windows XP Professional (PV Drivers)** entry from the boot menu, and you should have a full set of PV devices.

Ongoing Development

Windows under Xen is still immature, but it's already developed far enough to be useful. Using Xen, you can consolidate Windows servers in a robust, manageable platform and run client software in a native environment on the desktop. You have a reasonable way of accessing the machine via the framebuffer or rdesktop, and finally you have PV drivers for reasonable speed.

All in all, Xen is quite a good platform for Windows. Not perfect, but certainly usable.

14

TIPS

By now you're some kind of Xen expert, we imagine.[1] As such, now we'd like to devote a chapter to the more esoteric aspects of working with Xen. Here are some things that didn't seem to fit anywhere else—stuff like the frame-buffer, forwarding PCI devices, or building added functionality into the XenStore. Tips, in other words.

A number of the topics in Chapter 15 might also come in handy when you work through our examples here. Some of the software discussed here is even more bleeding edge than the rest of Xen, which is itself some kind of *heavenly sword*, ravening and incarnadine. What we're trying to get at is that the material in this chapter might not work straight off.

---

[1] Or at least, anyone who hasn't thrown this book out the window must be extremely good at filling in vague directions.

Compiling Xen

Although we've relied, for the most part, on Xen packages provided by distro maintainers, we think it's generally worthwhile to compile Xen from scratch. This will allow you to use a much more up-to-date version of Xen than versions that come with the distros. It also lets you enable options that the distro maintainers may have disabled.

If you're feeling adventurous, it's also nice to be able to play with the code—change it around a bit, perhaps, or add some printk messages to help with debugging.

The easiest way to compile is to check out the latest source from the Mercurial repository. Start by making sure you have Mercurial and a bunch of build dependencies. On CentOS 5, we installed these packages with yum:[2]

- mercurial
- zlib-devel
- gcc
- libX11-devel
- openssl-devel
- ncurses-devel
- bridge-utils
- python-devel
- git
- dev86
- glibc-devel

If you want the docs to build successfully, you should also install the following packages:

- texinfo
- tetex-latex
- pstoedit
- transfig

Given the large amount of Xen documentation available online and from other sources, the included docs are fairly optional.

When these packages are installed, clone the development repository. We're using *xen-unstable* here, but if you'd like to use a less unstable repo, you might want to try something like *xen-3.3-testing.hg*. As of early 2009, prgmr.com runs *xen-3.3-testing.hg*. It has been pretty stable.

```
# hg clone http://xenbits.xen.org/xen-unstable.hg
```

---

[2] We've also included a more Debian-centric set of compilation instructions in "paravirt_ops Dom0" on page 203 and "paravirt_ops DomU" on page 205.

This will download the repo to a local directory (*xen-unstable.hg* in this case). Next, cd into that directory and run make world:

```
# cd xen-unstable.hg
# make world && make install
```

This will build and install the Xen hypervisor, its supporting tools, and a Linux kernel for dom0. DomUs can use it as well. Often, this will be all you need. However, if you want to change your kernel configuration, you can. To configure the Linux kernel, run:

```
# make linux-2.6-xen-config configmode=MENUCONFIG
```

This will open the standard Linux kernel configurator. Configure the kernel as usual.

NOTE   *You probably want to leave the dom0 8250 serial driver disabled because it conflicts with the Xen serial console. As usual, don't forget the drivers for your boot device.*

Then run:

```
# make linux-2.6-build
# make linux-2.6-install
```

This builds and installs the kernel. Now, if you are on CentOS, you probably want to make an initrd:

```
# mkinitrd /boot/initrd-2.6.18.8-xen.img 2.6.18.8-xen
```

NOTE *There is a bug in early releases of RHEL 5.3 that causes problems with this. See https://bugzilla.redhat.com/show_bug.cgi?id=488991 for details. The solution is to add --allow-missing to the* mkinitrd *command line, thus:* # mkinitrd /boot/ initrd-2.6.18.8-xen.img 2.6.18.8-xen --allow-missing.

Now, you need to fix */boot/grub/menu.lst*. Add a stanza like this, but remember to use appropriate devices, paths, and possibly filenames:

```
title Xen.org 2.6.18.8-xen-3.3
       root (hd0,0)
       kernel /boot/xen-3.3.gz
       module /boot/vmlinuz-2.6.18.8-xen ro root=/dev/md0
       module /boot/initrd-2.6.18.8-xen.img
```

Reboot and enjoy your new Xen installation.

Compile-Time Tuning

That's the quick and easy way to build Xen, but the basic compilation with make world is just the beginning. Compilation represents the first opportunity we have to configure Xen, and there's a lot more that we can do with it now that we've had some practice.

Most of the compile-time tuning can be done by twiddling variables in *Config.mk*, at the top level of the Xen source tree. This file is fairly extensively commented and amenable to editing—take a look. You'll find that there's a brief section where you can decide which optional Xen bits to build.

We usually turn on all of the optional components except for the Virtual Trusted Platform Module (VTPM) tools, leading to a section like this:

```
XENSTAT_XENTOP     ?= y
VTPM_TOOLS         ?= n
LIBXENAPI_BINDINGS ?= y
XENFB_TOOLS        ?= y
PYTHON_TOOLS       ?= y
```

NOTE *Xen's VTPM tools are interesting. They've been a subject of heavy development, they have some interesting implications for signed code, and there's the looming specter of DRM, but we just haven't gotten into them. If you decide to build them, you can add virtual TPMs to domains via the* vtpm= *option in the domain configuration.*

If you're having trouble (trust us, you probably will at some point), it would be a good idea to make a debug build. To do that, set the DEBUG variable at the top of the file:

```
DEBUG               ?= y
```

Don't worry: Xen will not run in debug mode unless you specifically instruct it to do so at runtime.

These optional Xen components have a bunch of undocumented dependencies, some of which aren't checked for by the Makefiles. In particular, the LIBXENAPI_BINDINGS demand libxml2 and curl or the -devel versions of these packages, if you're using a Red Hat derivative.

Also, if something doesn't work when you build the tools, it would probably be a good idea to avoid running make world again because that takes a while. Most likely, you can get by with just make tools.

Alternate Kernels (Dom0 and DomU)

The default Xen Makefile will build a single kernel that can be used in both the dom0 and domU. If saving memory is a high priority, you can build a separate kernel for each. These kernels will each have a reasonable set of configuration options: minimal for the domU, modular for the dom0. Specify the KERNELS variable on your make command line:

```
# make KERNELS="linux-2.6-dom0 linux-2.6-domU"
```

The primary reason to do this, of course, is so that you can strip all the non-Xen device drivers out of the domU kernel. This saves memory and—if you happen to be testing a lot of kernels—compile time.

paravirt_ops Dom0

To understand why paravirt_ops gets treated as a separate piece, we have to recall that a lot of the early Xen development took place before virtualization went mainstream. The Xen developers, to paravirtualize the Linux kernel, made sweeping changes that proved to be difficult to merge with mainline kernel development.

paravirt_ops is a generic solution to this problem. It's a kernel-level framework for adding code to enable Linux to run under various hypervisors, including Xen. The idea is that, by making these interfaces part of the official kernel, we can make Xen less invasive and easier to maintain.

Xen has supported paravirt_ops domUs since version 3.1, and the official Linux kernel has had domU support since version 2.6.23 for i386 and since version 2.6.26 for x86_64. Unfortunately, the kernel.org kernel, as of this writing, only has guest support.

But there is light at the end of the tunnel. With the latest patches from Jeremy Fitzhardinge's paravirt_ops dom0 work and a Xen 3.4 hypervisor, it is, in fact, possible to run a paravirt_ops dom0 based on Linux kernel version 2.6.30.

These directions represent a snapshot from a very long development process. They work for us today. URLs may change. The status of the software certainly will. With that in mind, though, here's how we set up a functioning paravirt_ops dom0.

First, you're going to need some development packages. This time we're using the Debian package names:

- mercurial
- build-essential
- libncurses5-dev
- gawk
- openssl
- xorg-dev
- gettext
- python-dev
- gitk
- libcurl4-openssl-dev
- bcc
- libz-dev
- libxml2-dev

Next, check out Xen-unstable with Mercurial. We warned you that this stuff is still in development.

```
# hg clone http://xenbits.xensource.com/xen-unstable.hg
# cd xen-unstable.hg
# make xen
# make install-xen
# make tools
# make install-tools
```

Then check out the current Linux patches from Jeremy Fitzhardinge's git repo:

```
# git clone git://git.kernel.org/pub/scm/linux/kernel/git/jeremy/xen.git linux-2.6-xen
# cd linux-2.6-xen
# git checkout origin/push2/xen/dom0/master -b push2/xen/dom0/master
```

Configure the kernel. We copied the Ubuntu configuration to *.config* and used that as a base.

```
# cp /boot/config-2.6.26-11-server .config
# make menuconfig
```

Since we're building a paravirt_ops dom0, make sure to turn on the appropriate support:

```
Processor type and features
    -> Paravirtualized guest support
........-> Enable Xen privileged domain support
```

Be sure to turn on the Xen block device frontend support, under:

```
Device Drivers
    -> Block devices
```

Next, build the kernel.

```
# make
# make modules_install install
# depmod 2.6.30-tip
# mkinitramfs -o /boot/initrd-2.6.30-tip.img 2.6.30-tip
```

Add */proc/xen* to fstab and mount it so that tools like xend will be able to communicate with the hypervisor:

```
none /proc/xen xenfs defaults 0 0
```

Create a GRUB entry to boot your new Xen paravirt_ops dom0:

```
title Xen 3.4 / Ubuntu 8.10, kernel 2.6.30-tip
kernel /boot/xen-3.4.gz
module /boot/vmlinuz-2.6.30-tip root=/dev/sdb2 ro console=tty0
module /boot/initrd-2.6.30-tip.img
```

Make sure that these are appropriate values for your setup, of course. That's all there is to it.

paravirt_ops DomU

"But what," you ask, "is all this about using a kernel.org kernel in a domU?" If you just want to make your own domU kernel, this is a much less involved process, supported without out-of-tree patches since version 2.6.23. All of these directions are presented from within a domU that boots using PV-GRUB or PyGRUB—no intervention from the dom0 administrator should be necessary.

First, download the kernel source you prefer:

```
# wget http://kernel.org/pub/linux/kernel/v2.6/linux-2.6.29.3.tar.bz2
```

Next, install the packages normally required to build the kernel. This example is for Debian, but it should be easy enough to find out what packages your favorite distro needs to build the kernel.

```
# apt-get install build-essential libncurses5-dev
```

Untar and configure the kernel. Personally, we like menuconfig, but that's just a matter of taste:

```
# tar -jxf linux-2.6.29.3.tar.bz2
# cd linux-2.6.29.3
# make menuconfig
```

Don't forget to enable Xen support:

```
-> Processor type and features
  -> Paravirtualized guest support
    -> XEN
```

Don't forget your network driver:

```
-> Device Drivers
  -> Network device support
    -> XEN_NETDEV_FRONTEND
```

or your disk driver:

```
-> Device Drivers
  -> Block devices
    -> XEN_BLKDEV_FRONTEND
```

Xenfs, which allows you to access the XenBus, is sometimes useful:

```
-> Device Drivers
  -> XENFS
```

Then customize to your heart's content. Remember, you can remove support for just about all hardware now. We also leave out the balloon driver. RAM is cheap, and we like having definite memory allocations.

Now, make the kernel as usual:

```
make -j4 ; make install modules_install
```

Make your initrd as per the usual kernel build. Since we're using Debian for this example, that means using mkinitramfs. If you compiled xenblk as a module, make sure to include it.

```
mkinitramfs -o /boot/initrd-2.6.29.3.img 2.6.29.3
```

Set up GRUB as you normally would:

```
title kernel.org paravirt DomU
  root (hd0,0)
  kernel /boot/vmlinuz-2.6.29.3  root=LABEL=DISK1 ro
  initrd /boot/initrd-2.6.29.3.img
```

One last thing before you reboot: Note that the device name for your console will be hvc0, for *hypervisor console*. This takes the place of the Xen-specific xvc0. If your distro doesn't do so already, you probably want to set up the domain to start a getty on hvc0. Now, simply restart your domain (halt it and start it up if you are using PyGRUB) and enjoy your modern kernel.

```
# uname -a
Linux sebastian.xen.prgmr.com 2.6.29.3 #1 SMP Tue May 12 06:32:52 UTC 2009 x86_64 GNU/Linux 2009
```

The Xen API: The Way of the Future

The Xen API is an XML-RPC interface to Xen that replaces the old interface used for communication with the hypervisor. It promises to provide a standard, stable interface so that people can build Xen frontends without worrying about the interface changing out from under them. It also extends the previous Xen command set so that more of Xen's functionality can be harnessed in a standardized tool.

In current versions of Xen, the API is an optional component, but that shouldn't deter you from using it; the most recent Citrix Xen Server product, for example, relies on the API exclusively for communication between the administration frontend and the virtualization host.

The Xen API is enabled by setting the LIBXENAPI_BINDINGS flag at the top of *Config.mk*:

```
LIBXENAPI_BINDINGS ?= y
```

When you've built Xen with support for the Xen API, the use of the API is controlled by the (xen-api-server) directive in */etc/xen/xend-config.sxp*.

```
(xen-api-server ((9363 none) (unix none)))
```

This directive turns on the API server and specifies how to connect to it. Each list in parentheses is a connection method. In this case, we're using TCP port 9363 and a local Unix socket, each with no authentication whatsoever.

To specify that we want to authenticate using PAM, we can modify this configuration a bit:

```
(xen-api-server ((9363 pam '192.0.2.*')))
```

Ordinarily, even when developing a Xen client, you won't need to interact with the Xen API at a low level. Bindings exist for most of the popular languages, including C and, of course, Python. The Xen.org API documentation, accessible from *http://wiki.xensource.com/xenwiki/XenApi/*, is the last word on the subject.

Managing Memory with the Balloon Driver

Moving on from compile time and installation issues to the serious day-to-day business of running Xen, we encounter the problem of memory. As we've mentioned, most Xen installations are limited in practice by physical memory.

Xen expends a great deal of effort on virtualizing memory; its approach is one of the defining features of paravirtualization, and it usually "just works," on a level low enough to ignore completely. However, it sometimes can benefit from a bit of attention by the administrator.

We've been dancing around the subject of memory oversubscription for a long time, and we'd better come clean: It is possible to assign a dynamic amount of memory to a domU, but we don't do it because it's not suitable for our *virtual private server* model. Also, the developers have historically been leery about recommending it for production. However, it does exist, and there are some good reasons to use it, which we're sure you can imagine.

Xen's control over reallocating memory to virtual machines is somewhat indirect. First, the value in the domU config file for memory is a *maximum*—conceptually, the amount of memory that's physically accessible to the virtual machine. The amount of memory in the config file is what the kernel sees at boot. Adding more would require a reboot. This is being worked on, mostly from the direction of Linux's memory hotplug. We confidently expect someone to provide a patch soon.

Within this inflexible maximum, Xen can reduce this memory using the *balloon driver*, which is nothing but a module that sits in the domU and *inflates* to consume memory, which it then hands back to the hypervisor.

Because the dom0 is also a Xen domain, it also can have a memory balloon, which Xen uses to reclaim dom0 memory for allocation to domUs.

NOTE   *We favor setting the dom0 memory directly with the* dom0_mem *boot option, which actively hides memory from the dom0. By setting* (dom0-min-mem 0) *and* (enable-dom0-ballooning no) *in* xend-config.sxp, *we can ensure that dom0 doesn't balloon out, and thus has a consistent memory reservation.[3]*

You can use xm to manually adjust the amount of memory used by the balloon:

```
# xm mem-set sebastian 112
```

---

[3] In newer versions of Xen, you really only need (enable-dom0-ballooning no), but that has no effect on older versions. Before the enable-dom0-ballooning option was enabled, setting dom0-min-mem to 0 would disable ballooning. Really, you could get away with just setting dom0-min-mem to 0; I tested it after embarrassing myself on the xen-devel list, and it works, but (enable-dom0-ballooning no) is nice and clear, and this sort of thing is important enough to specify twice.

The domain treats this as a target, giving memory to the balloon as it becomes free.[4] Thus, it's possible that a heavily loaded domain will take a while to give up memory to the balloon.

You can see the effect of the balloon in the list of VMs:

```
# xm list sebastian
Name                             ID Mem(MiB) VCPUs State   Time(s)
sebastian                        71     111     1 -b----    38.4
```

You can also see balloon-related information from within the domU via */proc/xen/balloon*:

```
# cat /proc/xen/balloon
Current allocation:    114688 kB
Requested target:      114688 kB
Low-mem balloon:        24576 kB
High-mem balloon:           0 kB
Driver pages:             136 kB
Xen hard limit:           ??? kB
```

NOTE *The balloon is pretty aggressive; it can cause an out-of-memory condition in the domU. Use it with caution.*

PCI Forwarding

You can allow a domU to access arbitrary PCI devices and use them with full privileges. Of course, there's no such thing as a free lunch; Xen can't miraculously duplicate PCI hardware. For a domU to use a PCI device, it has to be hidden from the dom0 and not forwarded to any other domUs.

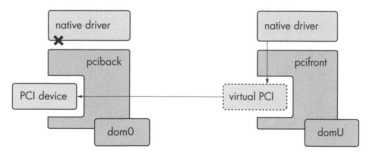

Figure 14-1: Xen PCI device forwarding

As Figure 14-1 shows, PCI forwarding uses a client/server model in which the *pcifront driver* runs in the domU and communicates directly with the *pciback driver*, which binds to the PCI device and hides it from the dom0.

First, consider the device that you want to forward to the domU. The test machine that we're sitting in front of appears to have seven (!) USB controllers, so we'll just take a couple of those.

---

[4] Although Linux does its best to keep memory in use at all times, it'll give memory to the balloon rather than using it for buffers or cache.

Use lspci to determine bus IDs:

```
# lspci

00:1a.0 USB Controller: Intel Corporation 82801H (ICH8 Family) USB
UHCI #4 (rev 02)
00:1a.1 USB Controller: Intel Corporation 82801H (ICH8 Family) USB
UHCI #5 (rev 02)
00:1a.7 USB Controller: Intel Corporation 82801H (ICH8 Family) USB2
EHCI #2 (rev 02)

(&c.)
```

We'll forward 00:1a.1 and 00:1a.7, which are the second of the USB1 controllers listed and the USB2 controller. Your device names will most likely vary from those in this example.

If pciback is compiled into the kernel, you can boot the dom0 with a pciback.hide option on the kernel command line. For these two controllers, the option would look like this:

```
pciback.hide=(00:1a.1)(00:1a.7)
```

If pciback is a module, it's a little more difficult. We need to detach the PCI device from its driver and attach it to the pciback passthrough.

```
# insmod pciback hide=(00:1a.1)(00:1a.7)
# echo -n 00:1a.1 > /sys/bus/pci/drivers/uhci_hcd/unbind
# echo -n 00:1a.1 > /sys/bus/pci/drivers/pciback/new_slot
# echo -n 00:1a.1 > /sys/bus/pci/drivers/pciback/bind
```

Now put these devices into the domU config file:

```
pci = [ '00:1a.1', '00:1a.7' ]
```

On the next domU boot, these USB controllers should appear and be available to the native drivers in the domU. Hardware devices on platforms without an IOMMU can DMA to arbitrary memory regions. This can be a security problem if you're giving PCI access to arbitrary domains. The moral is to treat all domains with access to the PCI bus as privileged. Make sure you can trust them.

GRUB Configuration

Of course, we've dealt with GRUB in passing because it's one of the basic prerequisites for Xen. However, there are a few more aspects of GRUB that are worth mentioning in depth. A fair number of Xen's behavior knobs can be tweaked in GRUB at boot time by adjusting the command-line parameters passed to the hypervisor.

For example, the already-mentioned domO_mem parameter adjusts the amount of memory that Xen allows the dom0 to see:

```
kernel /boot/xen.gz domO_mem=131072
```

To keep the system from rebooting if you have a kernel panic, which happens more often than we would like, especially when trying to get machines initially set up, add noreboot to the kernel line:

```
kernel /boot/xen.gz domO_mem=131072 noreboot
```

as well as panic=0 to the Linux module line:

```
module /boot/vmlinuz-2.6.18-53.1.21.el5xen panic=0
```

This is, of course, in addition to the plethora of options supported by the Linux kernel, which you can then add to vmlinuz's module line as you see fit.

The Serial Console

One other important GRUB-related task is setting up your serial console. As mentioned, we consider the serial console to be the gold standard for console access to any sort of server. It's much simpler than any sort of graphical interface, easy to access with a variety of devices, and is the output most likely to provide useful information when the machine is crashing. Furthermore, because of the client/server architecture inherent in the system, anything that a crashing machine manages to print goes to another, physically separate machine, where it can be analyzed at leisure.

Xen comes with miniterm, a minimal serial client for this sort of thing, in case you don't have access to a serial client. This is unlikely, but the client is tiny, so why not?

Miniterm is in the *tools/misc/miniterm* subdirectory of the Xen source tree. If you've built all the tools with Xen, it'll already be built and possibly even installed; if not, you can simply type **make** in that directory and run the resulting executable.

Enabling Serial Output

There are four components that need to have their output redirected to the serial port: GRUB, Xen, the Linux kernel, and Linux's userland. Each of the first three is a simple matter of adding a directive to GRUB's *menu.lst*.

First, near the top of the file, add these lines:

```
serial --unit=0 --speed=115200 --word=8 --parity=no --stop=1
terminal --timeout 10 serial console
```

Edit the Xen kernel line to tell the hypervisor to use the first serial port for output:

```
kernel /boot/xen.gz-2.6.18-53.1.21.el5 console=com1 com1=115200,8n1
```

Tell the Linux kernel to print its messages on ttyS0:

```
module /boot/vmlinuz-2.6.18-53.1.21.el5xen ro root=/dev/md0
console=ttyS0,115200n8
```

Finally, edit */etc/inittab* and add a line like the following:

```
7:2345:respawn:/sbin/agetty 115200 ttyS0
```

You may also want to add ttyS0 to */etc/securetty* so that root will be able to log in, after the manner of a traditional console.

The Xen Hypervisor Console

Xen adds another layer to the serial console by using it to access extra hypervisor features. First, break into the hypervisor console by pressing CTRL-A three times on the serial console. This won't work on the VGA console. You'll get a (XEN) prompt.

When you're in the hypervisor console, there are several useful (or at least interesting) commands you can give Xen. Try typing h for help or one of the informational commands, like m. You can also crash the machine, reboot it, or dump various pieces of information. Poke around and try it.

To exit the hypervisor console, type CTRL-A three more times.

Xen and LILO

This section only applies to the real dinosaurs out there, but we sympathize. In keeping with the feeling that you have vanished into the mysterious past, we will present this example using Xen 3.0.

If you're dead set on using LILO, rather than GRUB, you will be pleased to learn that it is possible. Although it's generally thought that LILO's lack of an equivalent to GRUB's module directive makes it impossible for it to boot Xen, it's possible to get around that by combining the hypervisor, dom0 kernel, and initrd into one file using mbootpack.

Consider the following entry in *grub.conf*:

```
title slack-xen
      root (hd0,0)
      kernel /boot/xen.gz
      module /vmlinuz-2.6-xen ro root=/dev/hda1 ro
      module /initrd-2.6.18-xen.gz
```

It loads the hypervisor, *xen-3.0.gz*, as the kernel then unpacks *vmlinuz-2.6-xen* and *initrd.gz* into memory. To combine those files, first decompress:

```
# cd /boot
# gzcat xen-3.0.gz > xen-3.0
# gzcat vmlinuz-2.6-xen0 > vmlinux-2.6-xen0
# gzcat initrd.gz > initrd.img
```

Note the change from *vmlinuz* to *vmlinux*. It's not important except that it keeps you from overwriting the kernel at the beginning of the gzcat process. Then combine the three files using `mbootpack`:

```
# mbootpack -o vmlinux-2.6-xen.mpack -m vmlinux-2.6-xen0 -m initrd.gz
  -m initrd.img xen3.0
```

The *grub.conf* entry then becomes a *lilo.conf* entry:

```
image=/boot/vmlinux-2.6-xen.mpack
    label=xen
    root=/dev/ram0
```

Finally, run the `lilo` command.

```
# /sbin/lilo
```

The Virtual Framebuffer

For as much as purists would like to claim that all administration should be done via serial port, there's something to be said for all this newfangled graphical technology that we've been using for, oh, around the last 25 years. Xen makes a concession to these forward-thinking beliefs by including a facility for a *virtual framebuffer*.

You will need to edit your *Config.mk* file to build the VFB:

```
XENFB_TOOLS        ?= y
```

At this point you'll also need libvncserver and libsdl-dev. Install them in your chosen way. We installed CentOS's SDL-devel package and installed libvncserver from source. Then we built Xen and installed it in the usual way.

To actually use the framebuffer within a domain, you'll need to specify it in the config file. Recent versions of Xen have improved the syntax somewhat. The `vfb=` option controls all aspects of the virtual framebuffer, just as the `vif=` and `disk=` lines control virtual interfaces and virtual block devices. For example:

```
vfb = [ 'type=vnc, vncunused=1' ]
```

Here we specify a VNC VFB and tell the VNC server to listen on the first unused port that's over the given number. (We go into more detail on the options available in Appendix B.) Or, if you're feeling adventurous, there's the SDL version:

```
vfb = [ 'type=sdl' ]
```

Simple.

Use of the XenStore for Fun and Profit

The XenStore is the configuration database in which Xen stores information on the running domUs. Although Xen uses the XenStore internally for vital matters like setting up virtual devices, you can also write arbitrary data to it from domUs as well as from dom0. Think of it as some sort of interdomain socket.

This opens up all sorts of possibilities. For example, domains could, in theory, negotiate among themselves for access to shared resources. Or you could have something like the *talk* system on the shared UNIX machines of yore—multiuser chat between people running on the same host. You could use it to propagate host-specific messages, for example, warning people of impending backups or migration. For the most part, though, such applications remain to be written.

It's a little inconvenient to interact with the XenStore manually because no one's gotten around to providing a handy shell-style interface. In the meantime, we have to make do with tools that interrogate single keys.

To look at the XenStore, you can use the xenstore-list command. Here's a shell script from the Xen wiki that dumps keys from the xenstore recursively with xenstore-list:

```
#!/bin/sh

function dumpkey() {
    local param=${1}
    local key
    local result
    result=$(xenstore-list ${param})
    if [ "${result}" != "" ] ; then
      for key in ${result} ; do dumpkey ${param}/${key} ; done
    else
      echo -n ${param}'='
      xenstore-read ${param}
    fi
}

for key in /vm /local/domain /tool ; do dumpkey ${key} ; done
```

You'll see that we have three hard-coded top-level keys: vm, local/domain, and tool. These each have a well-defined purpose to the hypervisor: vm stores domain information by UUID; local/domain stores domain information by ID (one might say that vm exports domain data in a form suitable for migration, and local/domain stores it for local use); and tool stores tool-specific information.

Poke around, look at the keys and how they map the information that you already know about the domain from other sources, like xm list --long. For example, to get the memory usage target for the domain, run:

```
# xenstore-read /local/domain/15/memory/target
1048576
```

Many of the keys in the XenStore are also writable. Although we don't recommend adjusting memory usage by writing to the XenStore, see the next section for an example of interdomain communication via writable XenStore keys.

Automatically Connecting to the VNC Console on Domain Boot

One neat feature of the Xen LiveCD is that Xen domains, when started, will automatically pop up a VNC window when they've finished booting. The infrastructure that makes this possible is a script in the domU, a listener in the dom0, and the XenBus between them.

The script in the domU, *vnc-advertiser*, fires off from the domU startup scripts and waits for an Xvnc session to start. When it finds one, it writes to the XenStore:

```
xenstore-write /tool/vncwatch/${domid} ${local_addr}${screen}
```

In the dom0, a corresponding script watches for writes to the XenStore. On the LiveCD, it's named *vnc-watcher.py*. This script is a good example of general-purpose uses for the XenStore, so we've copied it wholesale here, with verbose annotations:

```python
#!/usr/bin/env python
###
# VNC watch utility
# Copyright (C) 2005 XenSource Ltd
#
# This file is subject to the terms and conditions of the GNU General
# Public License.  See the file "COPYING" in the main directory of
# this archive for more details.
###
# Watches for VNC appearing in guests and fires up a local VNC
# viewer to that guest.
###

# Import libraries necessary to interact with the xenstore.  Xswatch
# watches a xenstore node and activates a script-defined function
# when the node changes, while xstransact supports standard read and
# write operations.

from xen.xend.xenstore import xswatch
from xen.xend.xenstore.xstransact import xstransact
from os import system

def main():
    # first make the node:
    xstransact.Mkdir("/tool/vncwatch")
    xstransact.SetPermissions("/tool/vncwatch",
                            { "dom" : 0,
                              "read" : True,
                              "write" : True })
```

```
    active_connections = {}

# The watchFired method does the actual work of the script.  When the
# watcher notes changes to the path "/tool/vncwatch/", it calls
# watchFired with the path (and arguments, which are unused in this
# script).

    def watchFired(path, *args, **nargs):
        if path == "/tool/vncwatch":
            # not interested:
            return 1

# If we reach this point, something's changed under our path of
# interest.  Let's read the value at the path.

        vncaddr = xstransact.Read(path)
        print vncaddr

# When the vnc-advertiser notices that Xvnc's shut down in the domU,
# it removes the value from the xenstore.  If that happens, the
# watcher than removes the connection from its internal list (because
# presumably the VNC session no longer exists).

        if vncaddr == None:
            # server terminated, remove from connection list:
            if path in active_connections:
                active_connections.remove(path)
        else:
            # server started or changed, find out what happened:
            if (not active_connections.has_key(path)) or
                active_connections[path] != vncaddr:

# Recall that the vnc-advertiser script writes ${domid}
# ${local_addr}${screen}  to the patch /tool/vncwatch/.  The watcher
# takes that information and uses it to execute the vncviewer command
# with appropriate arguments.

        active_connections[path] = vncaddr system("vncviewer
-truecolour " + vncaddr + " &") return 1

# Associate the watchFired event with a watcher on the path
# "tool/vncwatch"

    mywatch = xswatch.xswatch("/tool/vncwatch", watchFired)
    xswatch.watchThread.join()

if __name__ == "__main__":
    main()


===
```

There are a couple of other sections that we would have loved to include here, but that aren't ready as of this writing, for example, the ongoing open source efforts to build an Amazon EC2 clone or the high-availability work being done by Project Kemari.

Anyway, please visit our website (*http://prgmr.com/xen/*) for more on the cool yet frightfully everyday things that we do with Xen.

Also, if you've broken your system trying to upgrade Xen from source, there's no better time than the present to take a look at the next chapter.

15

TROUBLESHOOTING

With any luck, you're just reading this chapter for fun, not because your server has just erupted in a tower of flame. Of course, sysadmins being almost comically lazy, it's most likely the latter, but the former is at least vaguely possible, right?

If the machine is in fact already broken, don't panic. Xen is complex, but the issues discussed here are fixable problems with known solutions. There's a vast arsenal of tools, a great deal of information to work with, and a lot of expertise available.

In this section, we'll outline a number of troubleshooting steps and techniques, with particular reference to Xen's peculiarities. We'll include explanations for some of the vague error messages that you might come across, and we'll make some suggestions about where to get help if all else fails.

Let's start with a general overview of our approach to troubleshooting, which will help to put the specific discussion of Xen-related problems in context.

The most important thing when troubleshooting is to get a clear idea of the machine's state: what it's doing, what problems it's having, what telegraphic errors it's spitting out, and where the errors are coming from. This is doubly important in Xen because its modular, standards-based design brings together diverse and unrelated tools, each with its own methods of logging and error handling.

Our usual troubleshooting technique is to:

- Reproduce the problem.
- If the problem generates an error message, use that as a starting point.
- If the error message doesn't provide enough information to solve the problem, consult the logs.
- If the logs don't help, use set -x to make sure the scripts are firing correctly, and closely examine the control flow of the non–Xen-specific parts of the system.
- Use strace or pdb to track the flow of execution in the more Xen-specific bits and see what's failing.

If you get truly stuck, you might want to think about asking for help. Xen has a couple of excellent mailing lists (*xen-devel* and *xen-users*) and a useful IRC channel, *#xen* on *irc.oftc.net*. For more information about how and where to get help, see the end of the chapter.

Troubleshooting Phase 1: Error Messages

The first sign that something's amiss is likely to be an error message and an abrupt exit. These usually occur in response to some action—booting the machine, perhaps, or creating a domU.

Xen's error messages can be, frankly, infuriating. They're somewhat vague and developer oriented, and they usually come from somewhere deep in the bowels of the code where it's difficult to determine what particular class of user error is responsible, or even if it's user error at all.

Better admins than us have been driven mad, have thrown their machines out the window and vowed to spend the rest of their lives wearing animal skins, killing dinner with fire-hardened spears. And who can say they are wrong?

Regardless, the error messages are a useful diagnostic and often provide enough information to solve the problem.

Errors at Dom0 Boot

The first place to look for information about system-wide problems (if only because there's nothing else to do while the machine boots) is the boot output, both from the hypervisor and the domU kernel.

Many of the Xen-specific problems we've encountered at boot have to do with kernel/hypervisor mismatches. The Xen kernel must match the dom0 kernel in terms of PAE support, and if the hypervisor is 64 bit, the dom0 must be 64 bit or i386-PAE. Of course, if the hypervisor is 32 bit, so must be the dom0.

You can run an i386-PAE dom0 with an x86_64 hypervisor and x86_64 domUs, but only on recent Xen kernels (in fact, this is what some versions of the Citrix Xen product do). In no case can you mismatch the PAE-ness. Modern versions of Xen don't even include the compile-time option to run in i386 non-PAE mode, causing all sorts of problems if you want to run older operating systems, such as NetBSD 4.

Of course, many of the problems that we've had at boot aren't especially Xen-specific; for example, the machine may not boot properly if the initrd isn't correctly matched to the kernel. This often causes people trouble when moving to the Xen.org kernel because it puts the drivers for the root device into an initrd, rather than into the kernel.

If your distro expects an initrd, you probably want to use your distro's initrd creation script after installing the Xen.org kernel. With CentOS, after installing the Xen.org kernel, make sure that */etc/modprobe.conf* correctly describes your root device (with an entry like alias `scsi_hostadapter sata_nv`), then run something like:

```
# mkinitrd  /boot/initrd-2.6.18.8-xen.img 2.6.18.8-xen
```

Replace */boot/initrd-2.6.18.8-xen.img* with the desired filename of your new initrd, and replace *2.6.18.8-xen* with the output of uname -r for the kernel that you're building the initrd for. (Other options, such as --preload, may also come in handy. Refer to the distro manual for more information.)

Assuming you've booted successfully, there are a variety of informative error messages that Xen can give you. Usually these are in response to an attempt to do something, like starting xend or creating a domain.

DomU Preboot Errors

If you're using PyGRUB (or another bootloader, such as pypxeboot), you may see the message `VmError: Boot loader didn't return any data!` This means that PyGRUB, for some reason, wasn't able to find a kernel. Usually this is either because the disks aren't specified properly or because there isn't a valid GRUB configuration in the domU. Check the disk configuration and make sure that */boot/grub/menu.lst* exists in the filesystem on the first domU VBD.

NOTE *There's some leeway; PyGRUB will check a bunch of filenames, including but not limited to /boot/grub/menu.lst, /boot/grub/grub.conf, /grub/menu.lst, and /grub/grub.conf. Remember that PyGRUB is a good emulation of GRUB, but it's not exact.*

You can troubleshoot PyGRUB problems by running PyGRUB manually:

```
# /usr/bin/pygrub type:/path/to/disk/image
```

This should give you a PyGRUB boot menu. When you choose a kernel from the menu, PyGRUB exits with a message like:

```
Linux (kernel /var/lib/xen/boot_kerne.hH9kEk)(args "bootdev=xbd1")
```

This means that PyGRUB successfully loaded a kernel and placed it in the dom0 filesystem. Check the listed location to make sure it's actually there.

PyGRUB is quite picky about the terminal it's connected to. If PyGRUB exits, complaining about libncurses, or if PyGRUB on the same domain works for some people and not for others, you might have a problem with the terminal.

For example, with the version of PyGRUB that comes with CentOS 5.1, you can repeatedly get a failure by executing `xm create -c` from a terminal window less than 19 lines long. If you suspect this may be the problem, resize your console to 80 × 24 and try again.

PyGRUB will also expect to find your terminal type (the value of the `TERM` variable) in the terminfo database. Manually setting `TERM=vt100` before creating the domain is usually sufficient.

Creating Domains in Low-Memory Conditions

This is one of the most informative error messages in Xen's arsenal:

```
XendError: Error creating domain: I need 131072 KiB, but dom0_min_mem
is 262144 and shrinking to 262144 KiB would leave only -16932 KiB
free.
```

The error means that the system doesn't have enough memory to create the domU as requested. (The system in this case had only 384MiB, so the error really isn't surprising.)

The solution is to adjust domo_min_mem to compensate or adjust the domU to require less memory. Or, as in this case, do both (and possibly add more memory).

Configuring Devices in the DomU

Most likely, if the domU fails to start because of missing devices, the problem is tied to storage. (Broken network setups don't usually cause the boot to fail outright, although they can render your VM less than useful after booting.)

Sometimes the domU will load its kernel and get through the first part of its boot sequence but then complain about not being able to access its root device, despite a correctly specified root kernel parameter. Most likely, the problem is that the domU doesn't have the root device node in the /dev directory in the initrd.

This can lead to trouble when attempting to use the semantically more correct xvd* devices. Because many distros don't include the appropriate device nodes, they'll fail to boot. The solution, then, is to use the hd* or sd* devices in the disk= line, thus:

```
disk = ['phy:/dev/tempest/sebastian,sda1,r']
root = "/dev/sda1"
```

After starting the domain successfully, you can create the xvd devices properly or edit your udev configuration.

The Xen block driver may also have trouble attaching to virtual drives that use the sdX naming convention if the domU kernel includes a SCSI driver. In that case, use the xvdX convention, like this:

```
disk = ['phy:/dev/tempest/sebastian,xvda1,r']
```

Troubleshooting Disks

Most disk-related errors will cause the domU creation to fail immediately. This makes them fairly easy to troubleshoot. Here are some examples:

```
Error: DestroyDevice() takes exactly 3 arguments (2 given)
```

These pop up frequently and usually mean that something's wrong in the device specification. Check the config file for typos in the vif= and disk= lines. If the message refers to a block device, the problem is often that you're referring to a nonexistent device or file.

There are a few other errors that have similar causes. For example:

```
Error: Unable to find number for device (cdrom)
```

This, too, is usually caused by a phy: device with an incorrectly specified backing device.

However, this isn't the only possible cause. If you're using file-backed block devices, rather than LVM volumes, the kernel may have run out of block loops on which to mount these devices. (In this case, the message is particularly frustrating because it seems entirely independent of the domain's config.) You can confirm this by looking for an error in the logs like:

```
Error: Device 769 (vbd) could not be connected. Backend device not found.
```

Although this message usually means that you've mistyped the name of the domain's backing storage device, it may instead mean that you've run out of block loops. The default loop driver only creates seven of the things—barely enough for three domains with root and swap devices.

We might suggest that you move to LVM, but that's probably overkill. The more direct answer is to make more loops. If your loop driver is a module, edit */etc/modules.conf* and add:

```
options loop max_loop=64
```

or another number of your choice; each domU file-backed VBD will require one loop device in dom0. (Do this in whatever domain is used as the backend, usually dom0, although Xen's new stub domains promise to make non-dom0 driver domains much more prevalent.) Then reload the module. Shut down all domains that use loop devices (and detach loops from the dom0) and then run:

```
# rmmod loop
# insmod loop
```

If the loop driver is built into the kernel, you can add the max_loop option to the dom0 kernel command line. For example, in */boot/grub/menu.lst*:

```
module linux-2.6-xen0 max_loop=64
```

Reboot and the problem should go away.

VM Restarting Too Fast

Disk problems, if they don't announce themselves through a specific error message, often manifest in log entries like the following:

```
[2007-08-23 16:06:51 xend.XendDomainInfo 2889] ERROR
(XendDomainInfo:1675) VM sebastian restarting too fast (4.260192
seconds since the last restart). Refusing to restart to avoid loops.
```

This one is really just Xen's way of asking for help, the domain is stuck in a reboot cycle. Start the domain with the -c option (for console autoconnect) and look at what's causing it to die on startup. In this case, the domain booted and immediately panicked for lack of a root device.

NOTE *In this case, the VM is restarting every 4.2 seconds, long enough to get console output. If the restarting too fast number is less than 1 or 2 seconds, often* xm create -c *shows no output. If this happens, check the logs for informative messages. See later sections of this chapter for more details on Xen's logging.*

Troubleshooting Xen's Networking

In our experience, troubleshooting Xen's networking is a straightforward process, given some general networking knowledge. Unless you've modified the networking scripts, Xen will fairly reliably create the vif devices. However, if you have problems, here are some general guidelines. (We'll focus on network-bridge here, although similar steps apply to network-route and network-nat.)

To troubleshoot networking, you really need to understand how Xen does networking. There are a number of scripts and systems working together, and it's important to decompose each problem and isolate it to the appropriate components. Check Chapter 5 for a general overview of Xen's network components.

The first thing to do is run the network script with the status argument. For example, if you're using network-bridge, /etc/xen/scripts/network-bridge status will provide a helpful dump of the state of your network as seen in dom0. At this point you can use brctl show to examine the network in more detail, and use the xm vnet-create and vnet-delete commands in conjunction with the rest of the userspace tools to get a properly set up bridge and Xen virtual network devices.

When you've got the backend sorted, you can address the frontend. Check the logs and check dmesg from within the domU to make sure that the domU is initializing its network devices.

If these look normal, we usually attack the problem more systematically, from bottom to top. First, make sure that the relevant devices show up in the domU. Xen creates these pretty reliably. If they aren't there, check the domU config and the logs for relevant-looking error messages.

At the next level (because we know that the dom0's networking works, right?) we want to check that the link is functioning. Our basic tool for that is arping from within the domU, combined with tcpdump -i [interface] on the domU's interface in the dom0.

```
# xm list
Name          ID    Mem    VCPUs    State     Time(s)
Domain-0      0     1024   8        r-----    76770.8
caliban       72    256    1        -b----    4768.3
```

Here we're going to demonstrate connectivity between the domain *caliban* (IP address 192.0.2.86) and the dom0 (at 192.0.2.67).

```
# arping 192.0.2.67
ARPING 192.0.2.67 from 192.168.42.86 eth0
Unicast reply from 192.0.2.67 [00:12:3F:AC:3D:BD]  0.752ms
Unicast reply from 192.0.2.67 [00:12:3F:AC:3D:BD]  0.671ms
Unicast reply from 192.0.2.67 [00:12:3F:AC:3D:BD]  2.561ms
```

Note that the dom0 replies with its MAC address when queried via ARP.

```
# tcpdump -i vif72.0
tcpdump: WARNING: vif72.0: no IPv4 address assigned
tcpdump: verbose output suppressed, use -v or -vv for full protocol decode
listening on vif1.0, link-type EN10MB (Ethernet), capture size 96 bytes
18:59:33.704649 arp who-has caliban (00:12:3f:ac:3d:bd (oui Unknown)) tell
192.168.42.86
18:59:33.707406 arp reply caliban is-at 00:12:3f:ac:3d:bd (oui Unknown)
18:59:34.714986 arp who-has caliban (00:12:3f:ac:3d:bd (oui Unknown)) tell
192.168.42.86
```

The ARP queries show up correctly in the dom0.

Now, most of the time, you will see appropriate output in tcpdump as shown. This tells you that Xen is moving packets from the domU to the dom0. Do you see a response to the ARP who-has? (It should be ARP is-at.) If not, it's possible your bridge in the dom0 isn't set up correctly. One easy way to check the bridge is to run brctl show:

```
# brctl show
bridge name     bridge id               STP enabled     interfaces
eth0            8000.00304867164c       no              caliban
                                                        prospero
                                                        ariel
```

NOTE   *In Xen.org versions before Xen 3.2, the bridge name is, by default, xenbr0 for network-bridge. Xen 3.2 and later, however, named the bridge eth0 (0, in this case, is the number of the related network interface). RHEL/CentOS, by default, creates another bridge, virbr0, which is part of the libvirt stuff. In practical terms, it functions like network-nat, with a DHCP server handing out private addresses on the dom0.*

Now, for troubleshooting purposes, a bridge is like a switch. Make sure the bridge (switch) your domU interface is connected to is also connected to an interface that touches the network you want the domU on, usually a pethX device. (As explained in Chapter 5, network-bridge renames ethX to pethX and creates a fake ethX device from vif0.x when it starts up.)

Check the easy stuff. Can anything else on the bridge see traffic from the outside world? Do tcpdump -n -i peth0. Are the packets flowing properly?

Check your routes. Don't forget higher level stuff, like DNS servers.

The DomU Interface Number Increments with Every Reboot

When Xen creates a domain, it looks at the vif=[] statement. Each string within the [ ] characters (it's a Python array) is another network device. If I just say vif=['',''] it creates two network devices for me, with random MAC addresses. In the domU, they are (ideally) named eth0 and eth1. In the dom0, they are named vifX.0 and vifX.1, where X is the domain number.

Most modern Linux distros, by default, lock ethX to a particular MAC address on the first boot. In RHEL/CentOS, the setting is HWADDR= in */etc/sysconfig/network-scripts/ifcfg-ethX*. Most other distros use udev to handle persistent MAC addresses, as described in Chapter 5. We circumvent the problem by specifying the MAC address on the vif= line in the xm config file:

```
vif=['mac=00:16:3E:AA:AA:AB','mac=00:16:3E:AA:AA:AC']
```

Here we're using the XenSource MAC prefix, 00:16:3E. If you start your MAC with that prefix, you know it won't conflict with any assigned hardware MAC addresses.

If you don't specify the MAC address, it'll be randomly generated every time the domU boots, which causes some inconvenience if your domU OS has locked down ethX to a particular MAC. For more on the possible effects and why it's a good idea to specify a MAC address, see Chapter 5.

iptables

The iptables rules can also be a source of trouble with Xen. As with any iptables setup, it's easy to mess up in subtle ways and break everything. The best way we've found to make sure that iptables rules are working is to send packets through and watch what happens to them. Run iptables -L -v to see counters for how many packets have hit each rule or have been affected by the chain policy.

NOTE *The interface counters for vifs that are examined from the dom0 end will be inverted; outgoing traffic will report as incoming, and vice versa. See Chapter 5 for more information about why that happens.*

You may also have trouble getting antispoof to work. If you enable antispoof but find you can still spoof arbitrary IP addresses in the domU, add the following to your network startup:

```
echo 1 >/proc/sys/net/bridge/bridge-nf-call-iptables
```

This will cause packets sent through the bridges to traverse the forward chain, where Xen puts the antispoof rules. We added the command to the end of */etc/xen/scripts/network-bridge*.

Another problem can occur if you're using vifnames, as we suggest in Chapter 5. Make sure the names are short—eight characters or less. Longer names can get truncated, and different parts of the system truncate at different lengths (at least in CentOS 5.0). In our particular case, we saw problems where the actual vifnames were truncated at one length, and our firewall rules (for antispoof) were truncated at another length, blocking all packets from the domain in question. It is better to avoid the problem and keep the vifnames short.

Memory Issues

Xen (or rather, the Linux driver domain) can act rather strangely when memory is running low. Because Xen and the dom0 require a certain amount of contiguous, unswappable memory, it's surprisingly easy (in our experience) to find the oom-killer snacking on processes like candy. This even happens when there's plenty of swap available.

The best solution we've found—and we freely admit that it's not perfect—is to give dom0 more memory. We also prefer to fix its memory allocation at something like 512MB so that it doesn't have to cope with Xen constantly adjusting its memory size.

The basic way of tuning dom0's memory allocation is by adjusting the dom0_mem kernel parameter, which sets an upper limit, and the dom0-min-mem parameter in */etc/xen/xend-config.sxp*, which sets a lower limit. Again, we usually set both of these to the same value.

To set the maximum amount of memory available to the dom0, edit *menu.lst* and put the option after the kernel line, like this:

```
kernel /xen.gz dom0_mem=512M noreboot
```

In the absence of units, Xen will assume that the value is in KB.

Next, edit */etc/xen/xend-config.sxp* and add a line that says:[1]

```
(dom0-min-mem 512)
```

We do this because we've seen the dom0 have problems with ballooning. Ballooning usually works, but, like taking backups from a nonquiescent filesystem, *usually works* is not good enough for something as important as the dom0.

Other Messages

```
xenconsole: Could not read tty from store: No such file or directory
```

This message usually shows up in response to an attempt to connect to a domain's virtual console (especially when Xen's kernel doesn't match its

---

[1] Recent versions of Xen also support the option (enable-dom0-ballooning no).

userland; for example, if we've upgraded Xen's supporting tools without changing the hypervisor).

If this is a paravirtualized domain, first try killing and restarting the xenconsoled process. Make sure it dies. We have seen cases where xenconsoled hangs and must be killed with a -9.

```
# pkill xenconsoled && /usr/sbin/xenconsoled
```

Then reconnect with xm console.

If the problem persists, you're most likely trying to access a domain that doesn't have the necessary Xen frontend console device configured in. There are several possibilities: If this is a custom kernel, you may have simply forgotten to include it, for example. Check the configuration of the domain's kernel and the initrd for the xvc driver.

If you are accessing an HVM domain running a default (nonenlightened) kernel that doesn't include the console driver, try using the framebuffer or booting a different kernel. You might also be able to set serial=pty in the domain config file and set the domU OS to use com1 as the console. See Chapter 12 for details.

```
VmError: (22, 'Invalid argument')
```

This error can mean a number of things. Often the problem is a version mismatch between the tools and the running Xen hypervisor. Although the binaries installed in */usr/sbin* may be correct, the underlying Python modules may be wrong. Check that they're correct using whatever evidence is available: dates, comments in the files themselves, output of xm info, and so on.

The error can also indicate a PAE mismatch. In this case *xend-debug.log* will give a succinct description of the problem:

```
# tail /var/log/xen/xend-debug.log
ERROR: Non PAE-kernel on PAE host.
ERROR: Error constructing guest OS
```

Incidentally, your dom0—which is, after all, just a special Xen guest domain—can also suffer from this problem. If it happens, the hypervisor will report a PAE mismatch in a large boxed-off error message at boot time and immediately reboot.

```
"no version for struct_module found: kernel tainted"
```

We got this error while trying to install the binary Xen distribution on a Slackware machine. The binary distro comes with a very minimal kernel, so it needs an initrd with appropriate modules. For some reason, the default script loaded modules in the wrong order, causing some loads to fail with the preceding message.

We fixed the problem by changing the load order in the initrd; specific directions would depend on your distro.

A Constant Stream of 4GiB seg fixup Messages

Sometimes, on booting a newly installed i386 domain, you'll be greeted with screens full of messages like this:

```
4gb seg fixup, process init (pid 1), cs:ip 73:b7ec2fc5
```

These are related to the */lib/tls* problem: Xen is complaining because it's having to emulate a 4GiB segment for the benefit of some process that's using negative offsets to access the stack. You may also see a giant message at boot, reminding you to address this issue.

To solve this problem, you want to use a glibc that does not do this. You can compile glibc with the -mno-tls-direct-seg-refs option or install the appropriate libc6-xen package for your distribution (both Red Hat–like and Debian-like distros have created packages to address this problem).

With Red Hat (and its derived distros), you can also run these commands:

```
# echo 'hwcap 0 nosegneg' > /etc/ld.so.conf.d/libc6-xen.conf
# ldconfig
```

This will instruct the dynamic loader to avoid that particular optimization. For Debian-based distros (using the 2.6.18 kernel), you can simply run:

```
# apt-get install libc6-xen
```

If all else fails (or if you are just too lazy to find a version of gcc with no-tls-direct-seg-refs), you can do as the error message advises and move the TLS library out of the way:

```
# mv /lib/tls /lib/tls.disabled
```

In our experience, there isn't any problem with moving the library. Everything will continue to function as expected.

The Importance of Disk Drivers (initrd Problems)

Often when using a distro kernel, a Xen domU will boot but be unable to locate its root device. For example:

```
VFS: Cannot open root device "sda1" or unknown-block(0,0)
Please append a correct "root=" boot option
Kernel panic - not syncing: VFS: Unable to mount root fs on unknown-block(0,0)
```

The underlying problem here—at least in this case—is that the domU kernel doesn't have the necessary drivers compiled in, and the ramdisk was not specified. A look at the boot output confirms this, with the messages:

```
XENBUS: Device with no driver: device/vbd/769
XENBUS: Device with no driver: device/vbd/770
XENBUS: Device with no driver: device/vif/0
```

Nearly all distro kernels come with a minimal kernel and require an initrd with the disk driver to finish booting. These messages may simply come from the kernel before the initrd has loaded, or they can indicate a serious problem if the initrd doesn't contain the necessary drivers.

If the kernel managed to load its initrd correctly and failed to switch to its real root, you'll find yourself stuck in the initrd with a very limited selection of files. In this case, make sure that your devices exist (/dev/sda1 in this example) and that you've got the Xen disk frontend kernel module.

We also commonly see this within PyGRUB domUs after a kernel upgrade (and new initrd) if the modules config (*/etc/modules* on Debian, */etc/modprobe.conf* on Red Hat) didn't specify xenblk. For RHEL/CentOS domUs, you can solve this problem by running mkinitrd with the --preload xenblk switch.

If you use an external kernel and want to use a distro kernel, you must specify a ramdisk= line in the domain config file, and specify a ramdisk that includes the xenblk (and xennet, if you want network before boot) drivers.

Another solution to this problem would be to compile Xen from source and build a sufficiently generic domU kernel, with the xenblk and xennet drivers already compiled in. Even if you continue to boot the dom0 from the distro kernel (probably a good idea), this will sidestep the distro-specific issues found with both Red Hat and Debian kernels.

This may cause problems with some domU distros because the expected initrd won't be there. Sometimes it can be difficult to build an initrd against a kernel with disk drivers built in. However, the generic kernel will usually at least boot.

We often find it useful to keep these generic kernels as a secondary rescue boot option within the domU PyGRUB config because they work no matter how badly the initrd is messed up.

XenStore

Sometimes the XenStore gets corrupted, or xenstored dies, or for various other reasons the XenStore ceases to store and report information. For example, this may happen if the block device holding the XenStore database becomes full.

The most obvious symptom is that xm list will report domain names incorrectly, for example:

```
# xm list
Name                                 ID Mem(MiB) VCPUs State   Time(s)
Domain-0                              0     2554      2 r-----  16511.2
Domain-10                            10      127      1 -b----   1671.5
Domain-11                            11      255      1 -b----    442.0
Domain-14                            14       63      1 -b----   1758.2
Domain-15                            15       62      1 -b----   7507.7
Domain-16                            16      127      1 -b----  11194.9
Domain-6                              6       94      1 -b----   5454.2
Domain-7                              7       62      1 -b----    270.8
Domain-9                              9      127      1 -b----   1715.7
```

Obviously, this is problematic. For one thing, it means that all commands that can take a name or ID, such as xm console, will no longer recognize names.

Unfortunately, xenstored cannot be restarted, so you'll have to reboot. If you're running a version of Xen prior to 3.1 (including the RHEL 5.x version), you'll have to remove */var/lib/xenstored/tdb* first, then reboot.

Xen's Logs

These error messages make a good start for Xen troubleshooting, but sometimes they're not helpful enough to solve the problem. In these cases, we need to dig deeper.

dmesg and xm dmesg

Although the output of xm dmesg isn't a log in the usual sense of a log file, it's an important source of diagnostic output. If you've got a problem whose source isn't obvious from the error message, begin by looking at the Xen kernel message buffer. As you probably know, the Linux dmesg command prints out the Linux kernel's message buffer, which ordinarily contains all kernel messages since the system's last boot (or, if the system's been up for a while, it displays a succession of boring status messages).

Because Xen could be said to act as a kernel in its own right, it includes an equivalent tool, xm dmesg, to print out messages from the hypervisor boot (the lines that begin with (XEN) in the startup messages). For example:

```
# xm dmesg | tail -3

(XEN) (file=platform_hypercall.c, line=129) Domain 0 says that IO-APIC
REGSEL is good
(XEN) microcode: error! Bad data in microcode data file
(XEN) microcode: Error in the microcode data
```

In this case, the errors are harmless. The processor simply runs on its factory-installed microcode.

NOTE   *Like the kernel, Xen retains only a fixed-size message buffer. Older messages go off into oblivion.*

Logs and What Xen Writes to Them

If xm dmesg isn't enlightening, Xen's next line of communication is its extensive logging. Let's look at the various logs that Xen uses and what we can do with them.

We can summarize Xen's logs as follows, in rough order of importance:

- */var/log/xen/xend.log*
- */var/log/xen/xend-debug.log*
- */var/log/xen/xen-hotplug.log*
- */var/log/syslog*
- */var/log/debug*

Most of your Xen troubleshooting will involve the first two logs. *xend.log* is the main xend log, as you might suppose. It records domain startups, shutdowns, device creation, debugging whatever, and occasionally includes giant incomprehensible Python dumps. It's the first thing to check.

xend-debug.log has information relating to more experimental features of Xen, such as the framebuffer. It'll also have verbose tracebacks when Xen runs into trouble.

Because xend uses the syslog facility, messages from Xen also show up in the system-wide */var/log/syslog* and */var/log/debug*.

NOTE *We hasten to add that syslog is almost humorously configurable. Even the term system-wide only applies to the default configuration; syslog can consolidate logs across multiple hosts, categorize messages into various channels, write to arbitrary files, and so on, but we're going to assume that, if you've configured syslog, you can translate what we say about Xen's use of it to apply to your configuration.*

Finally, if you're using HVM, qemu-dm will write its own logs. By and large, you can safely ignore these. In our experience, problems with HVM domains haven't been the fault of QEMU's device emulation.

If the kernel messages prove to be unenlightening, it's time to take a look at the log files. First, let's configure Xen to ensure that they're as round, firm, and fully packed as possible.

THE IMPORTANCE OF A DEBUG BUILD

For troubleshooting (and, in fact, general use) we recommend building Xen with all of its debugging options turned on. This makes the error messages more informative and plentiful, making it easier to figure out where problems are coming from and, with any luck, eliminate them.

Although it might seem that copious debugging output would cause a performance hit, in our experience it's negligible when running Xen normally. A debug build gives you the option of running Xen with excessive debugging output, but it performs about as well as a normal build when you're not using that mode. If you find that the error messages are unhelpful, it might be a good idea to make sure that you have all the the debugging knobs set to **full**. To enable full output for the hypervisor, add the options loglvl=all guest_loglvl=all to your hypervisor command line (usually in */boot/grub/menu.lst*).

See Chapter 14 for more information on building Xen, including how to set the debugging options.

Applying the Debugger

If even the maximum-verbosity logging isn't enough, it's time to attack the problem at the Python level, with the debugger.

One investigation to try is to run the xend server in the foreground and watch its debug output. This will let you see somewhat more information than simply following the logs.

With current versions of Xen, the debug functionality is included in the releases.[2] Enable the debug output with the following:

```
# export XEND_DEBUG=1
# export XEND_DAEMONIZE=0

# xend start
```

This will start xend in the foreground and tell it to print debug messages as it goes along.

You can also get copious debugging information for the XenStore by setting XENSTORED_TRACE=1 somewhere where xend's environment will pick it up, perhaps at the top of */etc/init.d/xend* or in root's *.bashrc*.

Xen's Backend Architecture: Making Sense of the Debug Information

Of course, all this debugging output is more useful with some idea of how Xen is structured.

If you take a look at the actual xend executable, the first thing you'll notice is that it's really very short. There's not much to it; all of the heavy lifting is done in external Python libraries, which live in */xen/xend/server* in one of the Python library directories. (In the case of the system I'm sitting in front of, this is */usr/lib/python2.4/site-packages/xen/xend/server*.)

Likewise, xm is also a short Python script. The take-home message here is that most of the error messages that you'll see emanate from somewhere in this directory tree, and they'll helpfully print the responsible file and line number so you can examine the Python script more closely. For example, look at this line from */var/log/xen/xend.log*:

```
[2007-08-07 20:14:26 6008] WARNING (XendAPI:672) API call:
VM.get_auto_power_on not found
```

At the beginning is the date, time, and xend's Process ID (PID). Then comes the severity of the error (in this case, WARNING, which is merely irritating). After that is the file and line number where the error occurred, followed by the contents of the error message.

---

[2] Once upon a time you had to download a patch and rebuild. Thankfully, this is no longer the case.

Armed with this information, you can do several things. To continue our earlier example, we'll open */usr/lib/python2.5/site-packages/xen/xend/XendAPI.py* and add a line near the top of the file to import the debugger module, pdb.

```
import pdb
```

Having done that, you can set a breakpoint. Just add a line near line 672:

```
pdb.set_trace()
```

Then try rerunning the server (or redoing whatever other behavior you're concerned with) and note that xend starts the debugger when it hits your new breakpoint.

At this point you can do everything that you might expect in a debugger: change the values of variables, step through a function, step into subroutines, and so forth. In this case, we might backtrace, figure out why it's trying to call VM.get_auto_power_on, and maybe wrap it in an error-handling block.

Domain Stays in Blocked State

This heading is a bit of a misnomer. The reality is that the "blocked" state reported by tools like xm list simply means that the domain is idle. The true problem is that the domain seems unresponsive.

Usually we find that this problem is related to the console; for example:

```
[root@localhost ~]# xm create -c sebastian.cfg
Using config file "/etc/xen/sebastian.cfg".
Going to boot Fedora Core (2.6.18-1.2798.fc6xen)
  kernel: /vmlinuz-2.6.18-1.2798.fc6xen
  initrd: /initrd-2.6.18-1.2798.fc6xen.img
Started domain sebastian
rtc: IRQ 8 is not free.
i8042.c: No controller found.
```

(and then an indefinite hang). Upon breaking out and looking at the output of xm list, we note that the domain stays in a blocked state and consumes very little CPU time.

```
[root@localhost ~]# xm list
Name                        ID  Mem(MiB) VCPUs State  Time(s)
Domain-0                     0    3476     2   r-----   407.1
sebastian                   13     499     1   -b----    19.9
```

A quick look at */var/log/xen/xend-debug.log* suggested an answer:

```
10/09/2007 20:11:48 Autoprobing TCP port
10/09/2007 20:11:48 Autoprobing selected port 5900
```

Port 5900 is VNC. Aha! The problem was that Xen wasn't using the virtual console device that xm console connects to. In this case, we traced it to user error. We specified the framebuffer and forgot about it. The kernel, as instructed, used the framebuffer as console rather than emulated serial console that we were expecting. When we started a VNC client and connected to port 5900, it gave us the expected graphical console.

NOTE *If we had put a getty on xvc0, even though we wouldn't have seen boot output, we'd at least get a login prompt when the machine booted.*

Debugging Hotplug

Xen makes extensive use of udev to create and destroy virtual devices, both in the dom0 and the domU. Most of its interaction with Linux's hotplug subsystem gets logged in */var/log/xen/xen-hotplug.log.* (We're going to treat hotplug as synonymous with udev because we can't think of any system that still uses the pre-udev hotplug implementation.)

First, we examine the effects of the script. In this case, we use udevmonitor to see udev events. It should show an add event for each vif and vbd as well as an online event for the vif. These go through the rules in */etc/udev/rules.d/ xen-backend.rules*, which executes appropriate scripts in */etc/xen/scripts.*

At this point you can add some extra logging. At the top of the script for the device you're interested in (e.g., blktap), put:

```
set -x
exec 2>>/var/log/xen-hotplug.log
```

This will cause the shell to expand the commands in the script and write them to *xen-hotplug.log*, enabling you (hopefully) to trace down the source of the problem and eliminate it.

Hotplug can also act as a bit of a catchall for any virtual device problem. Some hotplug-related errors take the form of the dreaded Hotplug scripts not working message, like the following:

```
Error: Device 0 (vkbd) could not be connected. Hotplug scripts not working.
```

This seems to be associated with messages like the following:

```
DEBUG (DevController:148) Waiting for devices irq.
DEBUG (DevController:148) Waiting for devices vkbd.
DEBUG (DevController:153) Waiting for 0.
DEBUG (DevController:539) hotplugStatusCallback
/local/domain/0/backend/vkbd/4/0/hotplug-status
```

In this case, however, these messages turned out to be red herrings. The answer came out of *xend-debug.log*, which said:

```
/usr/lib/xen/bin/xen-vncfb: error while loading shared libraries:
libvncserver.so.0: cannot open shared object file: No such file or
directory
```

As it developed, libvncserver was installed in */usr/local*, which the runtime linker had been ignoring. After adding */usr/local/lib* to */etc/ld.so.conf*, xen-vncfb started up happily.

strace

One important generic troubleshooting technique is to use strace to look at what the Xen control tools are really doing. For example, if Xen is failing to find an external binary (like xen-vncfb), strace can reveal that problem with a command like the following:

```
# strace -e trace=open -f xm create prospero 2>&1 | grep ENOENT | less
```

Unfortunately, it'll also give you a lot of other, entirely harmless output while Python proceeds to pull in the entirety of its runtime environment based on crude guesses about filenames.

Another example of strace's usefulness comes from when we were setting up PyGRUB:

```
# strace xm create -c prospero
(snipped)
mknod("/var/lib/xen/xenbl.4961", S_IFIFO|0600) = -1 ENOENT (No such file or
directory)
```

As it turned out, we didn't have a directory required by PyGRUB's backend. Thus:

```
# mkdir -p /var/lib/xen/
```

and everything works fine.

Python Path Issues

The Python path itself can be the subject of some irritation. Just as you've got your shell executable path, manpath, library path, and so forth, Python has its own internal search path that it examines for modules. If the path doesn't include the Xen modules, you can wind up with errors like the following:

```
# xm create -c sebastian.cfg
Using config file "/etc/xen/sebastian.cfg".
Traceback (most recent call last):
  File "/usr/bin/pygrub", line 26, in ?
    import grub.fsys
ImportError: No module named fsys
```

Unfortunately, the mechanisms for adjusting the search path aren't exactly intuitive. In most cases, we just fall back to either creating some symlinks or moving the Xen files into some directory that's already in Python's path.

The correct solution is to add a *.pth* file to a directory that's already in Python's path. This *.pth* file should contain the path of a directory with Python modules. For example:

```
# echo "/usr/local/lib/python2.5/site-packages" >>
/usr/lib/python2.5/local.pth
```

Confirm that the path updated correctly by starting Python:

```
# python

>>>> import sys
>>>> print sys.path
['', '/usr/lib/python25.zip', 'usr/lib/python2.5' (etc)
'/usr/local/lib/python2.5/site-packages']
```

Mysterious Lockups

Mysterious lockups are among the most frustrating aspects of dealing with computers; sometimes they just don't work.

If Xen (or the dom0) hangs mysteriously, chances are you have a kernel panic in the dom0. In this case, you have two problems: first, the crash; second, your console logging isn't adequate to its task.

A serial console improves your life immensely. If you're using serial, you should see an informative panic message on the serial console. If you don't see that, you may want to try typing CTRL A three times on the console to switch the input to the Xen hypervisor. This will at least confirm that Xen and the hardware are still up.

If you don't have a serial console, try to keep your VGA console on tty1 because often the panic message won't go anywhere else. Sometimes a digital camera is handy for saving the output of a kernel panic.

If the box reboots before you can see the panic message on your console, and serial isn't an option, you can try adding panic=0 to the module line that specifies your Linux kernel in the domU *menu.lst* file. This has the obvious disadvantage of hanging your computer rather than rebooting, but it's good for test setups because it'll at least let you see the computer's final messages.

Kernel Parameters: A Safe Mode

If even the hypervisor serial console doesn't work—that is, if the machine is *really* frozen—there are some kernel parameters that we've had good luck with in the past.

The ignorebiostables option to the Linux kernel (on the module line) may help to avoid hangs when under I/O stress on certain Intel chipsets. If your machine is crashing—the hardware is full-on ceasing to function—it might be worth a shot. (I know, it's only one step removed from waving a dead chicken over the server, but you work with what you've got.)

In a similar vein, acpi=off and nousb have been reported to improve stability on some hardware. You may also want to disable hyperthreading in the BIOS. Some Xen versions have had trouble with it.

If you want to add all of these options at once, your */boot/grub/menu.lst* entry for Xen will look something like this:

```
root hd0(0)
kernel /boot/xen-3.0.gz
module /boot/vmlinuz-2.6-xen ignorebiostables acpi=off noapic nousb
```

Getting Help

You can, of course, email us directly with Xen-related questions. No guarantee that we'll be able to help, but asking is easy enough. There's also a list of Xen consultants on the Xen wiki at *http://wiki.xensource.com/xenwiki/Consultants.* (If you happen to be a Xen consultant, feel free to add yourself.)

Mailing Lists

There are several popular mailing lists devoted to Xen. You can sign up and read digests at *http://lists.xensource.com/.* We recommend reading the Xen-users mailing list at least. Xen-devel can be interesting, but the high volume of patches might discourage people who aren't actively involved in Xen development. At any rate, both lists are good places to look for help, but Xen-users is a much better place to start if you have a question that involves *using* Xen, rather than hacking at it.

The Xen Wiki

Xen has a fairly extensive wiki at *http://wiki.xensource.com/*. Some of it is out of date, but it's still a valuable starting point. Of course, new contributors are always welcome. Take a look, poke around, and add your own experiences, tips, and cool tidbits.

The Xen IRC Channel

There's a fairly popular Xen IRC channel, *#xen* on *irc.oftc.net*. Feel free to stop by and chat.

Bugzilla

Xen maintains a bug database, just like all software projects above a certain size. It's publicly accessible at *http://bugzilla.xensource.com/*. Type keywords into the search box, press the button, and read the results.

Your Distro Vendor

Don't forget the specific documentation and support resources of your vendor. Xen is a complex piece of software, and the specifics of how it's integrated vary between distros. Although the distro documentation may not be as complete as, say, this book, it's likely to at least point in the correct direction.

xen-bugtool

If all else fails, you can use xen-bugtool to annoy the developers directly. The purpose of xen-bugtool is to collect the relevant troubleshooting information so you can conveniently attach it to a bug report or make it available to a mailing list.

Simply run xen-bugtool on the affected box (in the dom0, of course). It'll start an interactive session and ask you what data to include and what to do with the data.

The xen-bugtool script collects the following information:

1. The output of xm dmesg
2. The output of xm info
3. */var/log/messages* (if desired)
4. */var/log/xen/xend-debug.log* (if desired)
5. */var/log/xen/xen-hotplug.log*
6. */var/log/xen/xend.log*

xen-bugtool will save this data as a *.tar.bz2*, after which it's up to you to decide what to do with it. We recommend uploading it somewhere web-accessible and sending a message to the Xen-devel mailing list.

Some Last Words of Encouragement

This chapter describes a troubleshooting work flow that works for us. In general, we try to hit the obvious stuff before escalating to more invasive and labor-intensive methods.

We've also tried to list error messages that we've seen, along with possible solutions. Obviously, we can't be encyclopedic, but we've probably hit most of the common error messages in our years working with Xen, and we can at least give you a decent starting point.

Don't get depressed! Concentrate! Remember that the odds are very good that someone has seen and solved this problem before. And, don't forget: There's no shame in giving up occasionally. You can't beat the computer all the time. Well, maybe you can, but we can't. Good luck.

A

XM REFERENCE

The xm command is probably the first thing to know about Xen. It's your primary interface to Xen's control-plane functionality. Using xm, you can create, query, and destroy domains. You can send certain instructions (e.g., shut down) to guest domains. You can attach and detach storage and network devices and dynamically adjust resource consumption.

In short, knowing xm is *important*. That's why we've documented xm's subcommands here, with references to the rest of the book.

NOTE *Some of these commands—the ones introduced with Xen 3.1 or later—may not work with the Xen version included in RHEL 5.x because Red Hat's priority is to maintain compatibility within major releases, rather than support new features. These commands are marked with an asterisk.*

All of xm's commands work by sending instructions to xend, the Xen control daemon. This is a Python program that runs in domain 0. It receives requests and sends replies to client applications, like xm.

If xend isn't running, xm will return an error and exit. Much of xm's functionality relies on the XenBus, which is a shared communication channel between all domains on the machine, and the XenStore, which is a centralized configuration database that xend uses to hold domain configuration information and states. For more information on the XenStore and XenBus, take a look at Chapter 14.

That said, let's look at the general form of an xm command.

xm's Syntax

xm's syntax is fairly simple and consistent:

```
xm <subcommand> <domain specifier> [options]
```

Options can go either before or after the domain specifier, but we usually put them at the end. For example, to order domain 10 to shut down cleanly:

```
xm shutdown 10
```

Here we're not specifying any options, and we're referring to the domain by numeric ID rather than name. The domain specifier may be either a domain number or domain name—the names will be internally translated to numbers. (Note that this won't work if the XenStore isn't up, but in that case, you have bigger problems.)

xm commands are usually asynchronous, which means that the command may return before it's actually completed. In the case of a command like xm shutdown, it may take the domain several minutes to actually shut down. In that case, we ordinarily poll xm list to make sure that the domain has stopped running.

xm Subcommands

Here's a list of the various xm subcommands. We use some of them frequently, and we don't use some of them at all. New commands with version 3.1 are marked with an asterisk (*) because version 3.1 marks a substantial change in Xen's approach to domain management. As we mentioned earlier, this means they might also not work with RHEL 5.x. Although RHEL 5.2, for example, uses the 3.1 version of the Xen hypervisor, it uses the 3.0.3 versions of the userspace tools, such as xend.

addlabel, cfgbootpolicy, dumppolicy, getlabel, labels, loadpolicy, makepolicy, resources, and rmlabel

These subcommands interface with Xen's security policy infrastructure. As we mention in Chapter 14, we haven't seen any practical use for Xen's security policies. If you're interested in more information about the security modules (which are themselves the subject of ongoing work), we suggest looking at the sample policies included with the Xen source distribution.

`block-attach`, `block-configure`, `block-detach`, and `block-list`

The various `block` subcommands manage storage devices that are attached to domains. These commands are handled in more detail in Chapter 4.

`console`

The console subcommand attaches to the given domain's console. Note that this is only useful if the domain is set up to use Xen's virtual console.

Even if everything is set up correctly, you may need to press ENTER to make it give you a login prompt. (This can be puzzling for new users, who type `xm console` and see a blank screen, because nothing's been added to the console buffer since the last time they used it.)

`create`

The `xm create` subcommand, in recent versions of Xen, is a synonym for `xm new` followed by `xm start`. It's the subcommand we use throughout the book to make domains go.

Create expects the name of a config file. If you don't specify a file, it uses the default, */etc/xen/xmdefconfig*.

The create subcommand takes these options:

- `-h`: Prints help.
- `-q`: Quiet mode.
- `--path`: Base path for domain configuration files (*/etc/xen* by default).
- `-n`: Dry-run mode. Prints the configuration that would be generated. This is used to debug Python code in domain configurations. If you're autogenerating a domain config, it's nice to have some way to test it.
- `-x`: Similar to `-n` but outputs a domain definition in XML. Note that, as of Xen 3.3, this option still relies on the deprecated `xml.dom.ext` module and thus does not work with many Python installations.
- `-c`: Connect automatically to the console. This is necessary to interact with PyGRUB.
- `-s`: Skip DTD checking for XML domain configurations.

If you don't give `xm create` a full path, it will default to looking for the config file in */etc/xen*. You can change that with the `--path` option.

`debug-keys` *

The debug-keys subcommand interacts with the GDB stub built into Xen, enabling you to send magic keystrokes to control the stub's output. It is likely to be useful only if you're hacking Xen's internals.

Note that this will only have an effect if you've built Xen with the GDB stub.

delete *

The xm delete subcommand removes a domain from Xen's management. If the domain is running, the delete subcommand shuts it down, then removes its definition.

destroy

> Before you think UNIX is family oriented, note that all children must die.
> —Eric Foster-Johnson, *Cross-Platform Perl*

The xm destroy command is the equivalent of yanking the power plug on a physical machine. If the domU has locked up completely, it may be necessary to ask xend to terminate it forcefully. All resources are immediately returned to the hypervisor.

dmesg

Like the dmesg system command, the xm dmesg subcommand prints out diagnostic messages from the kernel boot. We talk more about these messages in Chapter 15.

domid and domname

The domid and domname commands look up a domain's ID when you have its name, or vice versa. Each subcommand takes a single argument, the domain name or ID respectively, and returns the ID or name as appropriate. They're handy if you've got a lot of domains floating around.

dry-run

Although the dry-run subcommand, in theory, tests whether Xen can successfully find and use its virtual devices, we've had mixed luck because it's not very good at predicting whether we'll be successful in starting a domain. One important use for it is to debug Python code that is included in domain configurations, as described in Chapter 14.

This subcommand is also a suboption for xm create, which creates the domain in dry-run mode.

dump-core

The dump-core subcommand triggers an immediate memory dump.

Ordinarily, it pauses the domain, dumps its memory to the specified file, and then unpauses. You can, however, specify the -L (--live) option to make it dump in a fashion similar to live migration, without pausing and unpausing the domain (or, at least, without pausing it for any noticeable amount of time).

info

The info subcommand prints a lot of useful information about the Xen host, including the precise version of Xen you're using, the capabilities of the processor, and the memory that's available for domUs.

list

The xm list subcommand, in its simplest form, just lists domains in a table. However, it can also print out general information about domains, including a complete s-expression (if given the --long option).

The short form of the list subcommand will also show the state for each domain.

- 'b' (blocked): The domain is waiting for something, either for I/O or scheduling reasons. Idle domains will show up in a blocked state. This is normal; when they have something to do, they'll be unblocked.

- 'p' (paused): This state means that the domain's been paused by xm pause.

- 'c' (crashed): The domain has crashed.

- 'd' (dying): The domain is in shutdown and in the process of being destroyed by the hypervisor. If a domain remains in this state, the odds are good that it's a bug.

- 's' (shutdown): The domain is in the process of shutting down, whether because of a command issued from within the domain (e.g., halt) or from dom0 (e.g., xm shutdown). This state is also used for domains that are known to Xen but are not started. If you use xm new, the imported domain definition will show in xm list as shutdown until you start it with xm start.

- 'r' (running): The domain is presently executing on the physical computer. Note that, on a single-processor machine, xm list will always show dom0 as the only running domain because dom0 is generating and displaying the xm list output.

log

The xm log command simply prints out */var/log/xend.log*. We go into more detail about Xen's various log files in Chapter 15.

mem-max

The mem-max subcommand specifies the maximum amount of memory that the domain can use in megabytes. This is identical to the maxmem directive in the domain config file. Right now, this subcommand has no effect on running domains; changes take effect when the domain reboots.

mem-set

The xm mem-set subcommand works by sending messages to the balloon driver in the target domU. Altering the domain's memory allocation in this way requires cooperation from the domU's operating system and thus is not guaranteed. It also raises the possibility of taking too much memory from the domain, which will make it unstable.

We prefer to avoid using this subcommand. However, for more information about the balloon driver, see the relevant discussion in Chapter 14.

migrate

The migrate subcommand, as one might suppose, migrates domains. Migration is fairly complicated. Chapter 9 is devoted entirely to the subject.

network-attach, network-detach, and network-list

As you might guess, these subcommands manage virtual network devices (*vifs*, in Xen parlance, rather than networks per se). With these subcommands, you can attach, detach, and list vifs. We address these subcommands in Chapter 5.

new *

The new subcommand adds a domain to Xen's management; that is, it defines the domain but doesn't actually allocate resources or run it. Having imported the domain into Xen, you can start it with the xm start subcommand.

You'll probably want to run new with the -f option, specifying a file that describes the domain. This can be XML or the standard Python config format.

pause

This subcommand pauses the domain. While paused, the domain continues to occupy memory and hold a lock on its devices, but it won't be scheduled to run on the CPU.

reboot

The reboot subcommand orders the domain to reboot itself cleanly. Note that, if you're using PyGRUB, xm reboot will not load a new kernel; for that you'll need to shut down and re-create the domain. The same applies to, for example, shutdown -r from within the domU.

rename

The xm rename subcommand allows the administrator to change the human-readable name associated with the domain ID.

restore and save

The xm restore and save subcommands complement each other. As we describe in Chapter 9, xm save causes a domain to relinquish its resources and save state to a save file, and xm restore causes it to restore itself from a previously created save file. This is very much like hibernation.

resume *

The resume subcommand instructs a domain to return from a suspended state. Note that this only applies to domains managed by xend *lifecycle support*, which is essentially the ability to have xend manage inactive domains.

sched-credit

The credit scheduler is the default scheduler for Xen. The sched-credit subcommand configures the credit scheduler, allowing you to display or adjust a domain's weight and cap. We describe its use at some length in Chapter 7.

sched-sedf

The sedf scheduler, of course, is obsolete. However, if you find yourself using it, you can use the sched-sedf subcommand to adjust the scheduling parameters for a domain.

shell *

The shell subcommand is a bit interesting. It starts an interactive shell, nicknamed *The Xen Master*, from which you can issue the various xm subcommands.

shutdown

Like xm reboot, the shutdown subcommand orders the domain to shut down, with the difference that it doesn't immediately restart it. This subcommand requires domU cooperation; if the domain doesn't shut down, xend won't forcefully terminate it. If xm shutdown doesn't work, you may want to try xm destroy.

start *

The start subcommand starts a managed domain. Note that this subcommand, like new and suspend, only exists as of Xen 3.1, which adds xend lifecycle support.

suspend *

The xm suspend subcommand suspends a managed domain.

sysrq

The sysrq subcommand sends one of the magic sysrq keys to the domU. Note that this can't be done via xm console because the dom0 won't pass a sysrq through to the domU. It's a useful last resort if the domain seems catatonic. For more information about sysrq, see the kernel documentation (*Documentation/sysrq.txt* in the Linux kernel source tree).

top

The xm top subcommand presents status information for the running Xen domains in a format similar to that of the top(1) subcommand.

trigger *

The trigger subcommand sends a CPU event to a domain. It can trigger a Non-Maskable Interrupt (NMI), reset, or init event (although the latter two fail with a function not implemented message on Xen 3.2/i386). This subcommand is useful mostly for debugging.

unpause

The xm unpause subcommand resumes a domain that's been paused with xm pause.

uptime

The xm uptime subcommand will print the uptime for the selected domain or for all VMs if no domain is specified.

vcpu-list, vcpu-pin, and vcpu-set

The vcpu- subcommands control which cpus a domain will use in an SMP system. For more information, see Chapter 7.

vnet-create, vnet-delete, and vnet-list

These three vnet- subcommands interact with Xen's VLAN support. We don't cover the VLAN support because we've never had occasion to use it and we've never seen anyone else use it. If you're finding it useful, drop us an email.

vtpm-list

The vtpm-list subcommand allows you to list the virtual TPMs (trusted platform modules) that are attached to a domain. Although we don't go into much detail about the TPM, we do refer to it a bit in Chapter 14.

B

THE STRUCTURE OF THE XEN CONFIG FILE

The domain config file is the conventional way to define a Xen domain (and the method that we've used throughout this book). It works by specifying Python variables in a config file, conventionally kept in */etc/xen/<domain name>*. When the domain is created, xend executes this file and uses it to set variables that will eventually control the output of the domain builder.

Note also that you can override values in the config file from the xm command line. For example, to create the domain *coriolanus* with a different name:

```
xm create coriolanus name=menenius
```

The config file—and it would be difficult to overstate this point—is executed as a standard Python script. Thus, you can embed arbitrary Python in the config file, making it easy to autogenerate configurations based on external constraints. You can see a simple example of this in the example HVM config shipped with Xen, */etc/xen/xmexample.hvm*. In this case, the library path is selected based on the processor type (i386 or x86_64).

The *xmexample2* file takes this technique even further, using a single config file to handle many domains, which are differentiated by a passed-in vmid variable.

Python in the config file isn't limited to domain configuration, either. If you're using Xen for hosting, for example, we might suggest tying the domain configuration to the billing and support-ticketing systems, using some Python glue to keep them in sync. By embedding this logic in the config files, or in a separate module included by the config files, you can build a complex infrastructure around the Xen domains.

First, let's start with the basic elements of a domain configuration. Here's a basic config file, specifying the VM name, kernel image, three network cards, a block device, and a kernel parameter:

```
name = coriolanus
kernel = "/boot/linux-2.6-xen"
vif = ['','','']
disk = ['phy:/dev/corioles/coriolanus-root,sda,rw']
root = "/dev/sda ro"
```

Here we're setting some variables (name, kernel, disk, and so on) to strings or lists. You can easily identify the lists because they're enclosed in square brackets.

String quoting follows the standard Python conventions: a single quote for noninterpreted strings, double quotes for strings with variable substitution, and three single quotes to begin and end a multiline string.

Whitespace has significance just as in standard Python—newlines are significant and spacing doesn't matter, except when used as indentation.

NOTE *Although these syntax rules are usually true, some external tools that parse the config file may have stricter rules. pypxeboot is an example.*

Here's another, more complex example, with an NFS root. In addition, we'll specify a couple of parameters for the vif:

```
name = coriolanus
kernel = "/boot/linux-2.6-xen"
initrd = "/boot/initrd-xen-domU"
memory = 256
vif =
['mac=08:de:ad:be:ef:00,bridge=xenbr0','mac=08:de:ad:be:ef:01,bridge=xenbr1']
netmask = '255.255.255.0'
gateway = '192.168.2.1'
ip = '192.168.2.47'
broadcast = '192.168.2.255'
root = "/dev/nfs"
nfs_server ='192.168.2.42'
nfs_root = '/export/domains/coriolanus'
```

Your kernel must have NFS support and your kernel or initrd needs to include xennet for this to work.

Finally, HVM domains take some other options. Here's a config file that we might use to install an HVM FreeBSD domU.

```
import os, re
arch = os.uname()[4]
if re.search('64', arch):
    arch_libdir = 'lib64'
else:
    arch_libdir = 'lib'
kernel = "/usr/lib/xen/boot/hvmloader"
builder='hvm'
memory = 1024
name = "coriolanus"
vcpus=1
pae=1
acpi=0
vif = [ 'type=ioemu, bridge=xenbr0' ]
disk = [
        'phy:/dev/corioles/coriolanus_root,hda,w',
        'file:/root/8.0-CURRENT-200809-i386-disc1.iso,hdc:cdrom,r'
]
device_model = '/usr/' + arch_libdir + '/xen/bin/qemu-dm'
boot="cd"
vnc=1
vnclisten="192.168.1.102"
serial='pty'
```

Here we've added options to specify the QEMU-based backing device model and to control certain aspects of its behavior. Now we pass in a boot option that tells it to boot from CD and options for a virtual framebuffer and serial device.

List of Directives

Here we've tried to list every directive we know about, whether we use it or not, with notes indicating where we cover it in the main text of this book. We have, however, left out stuff that's marked *deprecated* as of Xen version 3.3.

There are some commands that work with the Xen.org version of Xen but not with the version of Xen included with Red Hat Enterprise Linux/ CentOS 5.*x*. We've marked these with an asterisk (*).

Any Boolean parameters expect values of true or false; 0, 1, yes, and no will also work.

bootargs=string

This is a list of arguments to pass to the boot loader. For example, to tell PyGRUB to load a particular kernel image, you can specify bootargs= 'kernel=vmlinuz-2.6.24'.

bootloader=string

> The `bootloader` line specifies a program that will be run within dom0 to load and initialize the domain kernel. For example, you can specify `bootloader=pygrub` to get a domain that, on startup, presents a GRUB-like boot menu. We discuss PyGRUB and pypxeboot in Chapter 7 and Chapter 3.

builder=string

> This defaults to "Linux", which is the paravirtualized Linux (and other Unix-like OSs) domain builder. Ordinarily you will either leave this option blank or specify HVM. Other domain builders are generally regarded as historical curiosities.

cpu_capp=int *

> This specifies a maximum share of the CPU time for the domain, expressed in hundredths of a CPU.

cpu=int

> This option specifies the physical CPU that the domain should run VCPU0 on.

cpu_weight=int *

> This specifies the domain's weight for the credit scheduler, just like the `xm sched-credit -w` command. For example, `cpu_weight = 1024` will give the domain twice as much weight as the default. We talk more about CPU weight in Chapter 7.

cpus=string

> The `cpus` option specifies a list of CPUs that the domain may use. The syntax of the list is fairly expressive. For example, `cpus = "0-3,5,^1"` specifies 0, 2, 3, and 5 while excluding CPU 1.

dhcp=bool

> This directive is only needed if the kernel is getting its IP at boot, usually because you're using an NFS root device. Ordinary DHCP is handled from within the domain by standard userspace daemons, and so the DHCP directive is not required.

disk=list

> The `disk` line specifies one (or more) virtual disk devices. Almost all domains will need at least one, although it's not a requirement as far as Xen's concerned. Each definition is a stanza in the list, each of which has at least three terms: backend device, frontend device, and mode. We go into considerably more detail on the meaning of these terms and the various types of storage in Chapter 4.

extra=string

The extra option specifies a string that is appended, unchanged, to the domU kernel options. For example, to boot the domU in single user mode:

```
extra = "s"
```

Many of the other options listed here actually append to the kernel command-line options.

hpet

This option enables a virtual high-precision event timer.

kernel=string

This option specifies the kernel image that Xen will load and boot. It is required if no bootloader line is specified. Its value should be the absolute path to the kernel, from the dom0's perspective, unless you've also specified a bootloader. If you're using a bootloader and specify a kernel, the domain creation script will pass the kernel value to the bootloader for further action. For example, PyGRUB will try to load the specified file from the boot media.

maxmem=int

This specifies the amount of memory given to the domU. From the guest's perspective, this is the amount of memory *plugged in* when it boots.

memory=int

This is the target memory allocation for the domain. If maxmem isn't specified, the memory= line will also set the domain's maximum memory. Because we don't oversubscribe memory, we use this directive rather than max-mem. We go into a little more detail on memory oversubscription in Chapter 14.

name=string

This is a unique name for the domain. Make it whatever you like, but we recommend keeping it under 15 characters, because Red Hat's (and possibly other distros') *xendomains* script has trouble with longer names. This is one of the few non-optional directives. Every domain needs a name.

nfs_root=IP
nfs_server=IP

These two arguments are used by the kernel when booting via NFS. We describe setting up an NFS root in Chapter 4.

nics=int

> This option is deprecated, but you may see it referenced in other documentation. It specifies the number of virtual NICs allocated to the domain. In practice, we always just rely on the number of vif stanzas to implicitly declare the NICs.

on_crash
on_reboot=string
on_shutdown

> These three commands control how the domain will react to various halt states—on_shutdown for graceful shutdowns, on_reboot for graceful reboot, and on_crash for when the domain crashes. Allowed values are:

- destroy: Clean up after the domain as usual.
- restart: Restart the domain.
- preserve: Keep the domain as-is until you destroy it manually.
- rename-restart: Preserve the domain, while re-creating another instance with a different name.

on_xend_start=ignore|start
on_xend_stop=ignore|shutdown|suspend

> Similarly, these two items control how the domain will react to xend exiting. Because xend sometimes needs to be restarted, and we prefer to minimize disruption of the domUs, we leave these at the default: ignore.

pci=BUS:DEV.FUNC

> This adds a PCI device to the domain using the given parameters, which can be found with lspci in the dom0. We give an example of PCI forwarding in Chapter 14.

ramdisk=string

> The ramdisk option functions like the initrd line in GRUB; it specifies an initial ramdisk, which usually contains drivers and scripts used to access hardware required to mount the root filesystem.
>
> Many distros won't require an initrd when installed as domUs, because the domU only needs drivers for extremely simple virtual devices. However, because the distro expects to have an initrd, it's often easier to create one. We go into more detail on that subject in Chapter 14.

root=string

> This specifies the root device for the domain. We usually specify the root device on the extra line.

rtc_offset

> The rtc_offset allows you to specify an offset from the machine's real-time clock for the guest domain.

sdl=bool

> Xen supports an SDL console as well as the VNC console, although not both at the same time. Set this option to true to enable a framebuffer console over SDL. Again, we prefer the vfb syntax.

shadow_memory=int

> This is the domain shadow memory in MB. PV domains will default to none. Xen uses shadow memory to keep copies of domain-specific page tables. We go into more detail on the role of page table shadows in Chapter 12.

uuid=string

> The XenStore requires a UUID to, as the name suggests, uniquely identify a domain. If you don't specify one, it'll be generated for you. The odds of collision are low enough that we don't bother, but you may find it useful if, for example, you want to encode additional information into your UUID.

vcpu_avail=int

> These are active VCPUs. If you're using CPU hotplugging, this number may differ from the total number of VCPUs, just as max-mem and memory may differ.

vcpus=int

> This specifies the number of virtual CPUs to report to the domain. For performance reasons, we strongly recommend that this be equal to or fewer than the number of physical CPU cores that the domain has available.

vfb=list

```
vfb = [type='vnc' vncunused=1]
```

> In this case, we specify a VNC virtual framebuffer, which uses the first unused port in the VNC range. (The default behavior is to use the base VNC port plus domain ID as the listen port for each domain's virtual framebuffer.)
>
> Valid options for the vfb line are: vnclisten, vncunused, vncdisplay, display, videoram, xauthority, type, vncpasswd, opengl, and keymap. We discuss more details about virtual framebuffers in Chapter 14 and a bit in Chapter 12. See the vnc= and sdl= options for an alternative syntax.

videoram=int

> The videoram option specifies the maximum amount of memory that a PV domain may use for its frame buffer.

vif=list

> The vif directive tells Xen about the domain's virtual network devices. Each vif specification can include many options, including bridge, ip, and mac. For more information on these, see Chapter 5.
>
> Allowable options in the vif line are backend, bridge, ip, mac, script, type, vifname, rate, model, accel, policy, and label.

vnc=bool

Set vnc to 1 to enable the VNC console. You'll also want to set some of the other VNC-related options, such as vncunused. We prefer the vfb syntax, which allows you to set options related to the vfb in a single place, with a similar syntax to the vif and disk lines.

vncconsole=bool

If vncconsole is set to yes, xend automatically spawns a VNC viewer and connects to the domain console when the domain starts up.

vncdisplay=int

This specifies a VNC display to use. By default, VNC will attach to the display number that corresponds to the domain ID.

vnclisten=IP

This specifies an IP address on which to listen for incoming VNC connections. It overrides the value of the same name in *xend-config.sxp*.

vncpasswd=string
vncpasswd="Swordfish"[1]

These options set the password for the VNC console to the given value. Note that this is independent of any authentication that the domU does.

vscsi=PDEV,VDEV,DOM *

This adds a SCSI device to the domain. The paravirtualized SCSI devices are a mechanism for passing a physical SCSI generic device through to a domain. It's not meant to replace the Xen block driver. Rather, you can use pvSCSI, the SCSI pass-through mechanism, to access devices like tape drives or scanners that are hooked up to the machine's physical SCSI bus.

vtpm=['instance=INSTANCE,backend=DOM,type=TYPE']

The vtpm option, just like the vif or disk options, describes a virtual device—in this case, a TPM. The TPM instance name is a simple identifier; something like 1 will do just fine. The backend is the domain with access to the physical TPM. Usually 0 is a good value. Finally, type specifies the type of the TPM emulation. This can be either pvm or hvm, for paravirtualized and HVM domains, respectively.

HVM Directives

Certain directives only apply if you're using Xen's hardware virtualization, HVM. Most of these enable or disable various hardware features.

---

[1] Terry Pratchett, in *Night Watch*, has this to say on the subject of passwords: "Every password was 'swordfish'! Whenever anyone tried to think of a word that no one would ever guess, they always chose 'swordfish.' It was just one of those strange quirks of the human mind."

acpi=bool

> The `acpi` option determines whether or not the domain will use ACPI, the Advanced Configuration and Power Interface. Turning it off may improve stability, and will enable some versions of the Windows installer to complete successfully.

apic=bool

> The APIC, or Advanced Programmable Input Controller,[2] is a modern implementation of the venerable PIC. This is on by default. You may want to turn it off if your operating system has trouble with the simulated APIC.

builder=string

> With HVM domains, you'll use the HVM domain builder. With most paravirtualized domains, you'll want the default Linux domain builder. The domain builder is a bit more low level than the parts that we usually work with. For the most part, we are content to let it do its thing.

device_model=string

> The `device_model` directive specifies the full path of the executable being used to emulate devices for HVM domains (and for PV domains if the framebuffer is being used). In most situations, the default `qemu-dm` should work fine.

feature=string

> This is a pipe-separated list of features to enable in the guest kernel. The list of available features, fresh from the source, is as follows:

```
[XENFEAT_writable_page_tables]       = "writable_page_tables",
[XENFEAT_writable_descriptor_tables] = "writable_descriptor_tables",
[XENFEAT_auto_translated_physmap]    = "auto_translated_physmap",
[XENFEAT_supervisor_mode_kernel]     = "supervisor_mode_kernel",
[XENFEAT_pae_pgdir_above_4gb]        = "pae_pgdir_above_4gb"
```

> We have always had good luck using the defaults for this option.

hap=bool

> This directive tells the domain whether or not to take advantage of Hardware-Assisted Paging on recent machines. Implementations include AMD's *nested paging* and Intel's *extended paging*. If the hardware supports this feature, Xen can substantially improve HVM performance by taking advantage of it.

loader=string

> This is the path to HVM firmware. We've always been completely satisfied with the default.

---

[2] "It's not stupid, it's advanced." —Invader Zim

pae=bool

> This enables or disables PAE on an HVM domain. Note that this won't enable a non-PAE kernel to run on a PAE or 64-bit box. This option is on by default.

Device Model Options

There are some directives that specify options for the device model. As far as we know, these are specific to the QEMU-based model, but, because no others exist, it seems safe to consider them part of Xen's configuration.

access_control_policy=POLICY,label=LABEL

> The access_control_policy directive defines the security policy and label to associate with the domain.

blkif=bool
netif=bool
tpmif=bool

> These three variables are all Booleans. If they are enabled, the builder will make the domain a backend for the specified device type.
>
> To use a non-dom0 backend, specify the backend parameter in the definition for your device of choice.

boot=string

> Set boot to one of a, b, c, or d to boot from the first floppy, second floppy, hard drive, or CD drive, respectively.

fda
fdb=string

> This option specifies the disk image or device file used to emulate the first or second floppy drive—fda and fdb, respectively.

guest_os_type=string

> This is the type of the guest OS. It's a free-form identifier, limited to eight characters.

ioports=FROM-TO
irq=IRQ

> These two options instruct Xen to forward a range of (real) ioports and an IRQ to the domU. The main use for this option that we've seen is for serial ports, so that the domU has access to a physical serial port on the server.

keymap=string

> The keymap option specifies a keymap file by name. Xen (or rather, the device model) keeps its keymaps under */usr/share/xen/qemu/keymaps*. On our machines, the default is en-us.

localtime=bool

> This is a simple Boolean option indicating whether the hardware clock is set to local time or GMT.

monitor=string

> If monitor is set to yes, the device model will attach the QEMU monitor, which you can use to give commands to the device model. Use CTRL-ALT-2 to break out to the monitor. From there, you can issue commands—try help.

nographic=bool

> This indicates whether the device model should use graphics.

serial

```
serial='file:/filename'
serial='/dev/pts/n'
serial='pty'
serial='stdio'
```

> The serial option specifies a file (or file-like object, such as a named pipe) to use as an emulated serial port. Other options are to have Xen pick a pty, or use STDIN and STDOUT for its serial port; none is also a valid option.

soundhw=bool

> This indicates whether to emulate an audio device.

stdvga=bool

> If stdvga is set to yes, the device model will use standard VGA emulation. If it's set to no or omitted, it'll use emulated Cirrus Logic graphics instead. Ordinarily, the default is just fine.

usb=bool

> This is a Boolean value that indicates whether to emulate USB.

usbdevice=HOST:id:id

> This item indicates the name of the USB device to add.

INDEX

reliance on trusted guest OS, 5
role of, *9*
use of shadow page tables by,
176–*177*

I

i386-PAE dom0, running, 221
ignorebiostables option, 239
incoming traffic, shaping, 96–*97*
INFO message, 235
info subcommand, 246
initialization lines, outputting, 16
initrd problems, troubleshooting,
230–231
INPUT chain, role in networking, 67
instance, explained, xxi
instructions, performing, 1–2
interrupts, interception of, 7
I/O, performing to physical
devices, 45
I/O devices, 10–11
IOMMU (I/O Memory Manage-
ment Unit), 178, 195
ionice command, regulating disk
access with, 99–100
IP address
avoiding conflicts, 64
specifying for virtual network,
66–67
IP masq, setting up iptables rule for,
70–71
iptables
troubleshooting, 227–228
using with antispoofing rules, 66
using with HTB qdisc, 98
using with network-nat, 70–71
iSCSI
vs. AoE (ATA over Ethernet), 136
portals, 138
sda and *sdb* exports in, 138
targets and initiators, 136
iscsiadm, 138
iSCSI database, updating
nodes in, 138
iscsid iSCSI daemon, using, 138
iSCSI Enterprise Target
implementation, 136

iSCSI storage migration, 136–139
iterative precopy, beginning in live
migration, 129

J

jails vs. zones, 3

K

kernel parameters
safe mode, 239
specifying, 27
kernels. *See also* distro kernel
building and installing, 202
building separately for dom0
and domU, 203
configuring, 201
loading, 33
specifying for domU image,
24–25
uncompressed on Red Hat–
derived distros, 153
Kickstart
provisioning systems with, 39–41
specifying with virt-manager, 84
koan client, using with virtual
machines, 39–41
kpartx command, using with
partitions, 47
KQEMU, incompatibility with Xen,
30, 36
KQEMU kernel module, 3
KVM virtualization technology,
30, 180

L

labels subcommand, 244
LDoms, use on UltraSparc
systems, 110
libfsimage, limitation of, 117
/lib/tls problem, cause of, *9*
libvirt
advantages of, 81
creating virbr0 with, 61
suite of tools based on, 81–82
web page, 31
Liguori, Anthony, 30

Y

Z

The Electronic Frontier Foundation (EFF) is the leading organization defending civil liberties in the digital world. We defend free speech on the Internet, fight illegal surveillance, promote the rights of innovators to develop new digital technologies, and work to ensure that the rights and freedoms we enjoy are enhanced — rather than eroded — as our use of technology grows.

PRIVACY EFF has sued telecom giant AT&T for giving the NSA unfettered access to the private communications of millions of their customers. eff.org/nsa

FREE SPEECH EFF's Coders' Rights Project is defending the rights of programmers and security researchers to publish their findings without fear of legal challenges. eff.org/freespeech

INNOVATION EFF's Patent Busting Project challenges overbroad patents that threaten technological innovation. eff.org/patent

FAIR USE EFF is fighting prohibitive standards that would take away your right to receive and use over-the-air television broadcasts any way you choose. eff.org/IP/fairuse

TRANSPARENCY EFF has developed the Switzerland Network Testing Tool to give individuals the tools to test for covert traffic filtering. eff.org/transparency

INTERNATIONAL EFF is working to ensure that international treaties do not restrict our free speech, privacy or digital consumer rights. eff.org/global

EFF.ORG

ELECTRONIC FRONTIER FOUNDATION

Protecting Rights and Promoting Freedom on the Electronic Frontier

EFF is a member-supported organization. Join Now! www.eff.org/support

NAGIOS, 2ND EDITION
System and Network Monitoring

by WOLFGANG BARTH

Nagios, which runs on Linux and most *nix variants, can be configured to continuously monitor network services such as SMTP, POP3, HTTP, NNTP, SSH, and FTP. It can also supervise host resources (processor load, disk and memory usage, running processes, log files, and so on) and environmental factors, such as temperature and humidity. *Nagios, 2nd Edition* is your guide to getting the most out of this versatile and powerful monitoring tool.

OCTOBER 2008, 728 PP., $59.95
ISBN 978-1-59327-179-4

PRACTICAL PACKET ANALYSIS
Using Wireshark to Solve Real-World Network Problems

by CHRIS SANDERS

Practical Packet Analysis shows how to use Wireshark to capture and then analyze packets as you take an in-depth look at real-world packet analysis and network troubleshooting. *Practical Packet Analysis* teaches you how to use packet analysis to tackle common network problems, such as loss of connectivity, slow networks, malware infections, and more. You'll also learn how to build customized capture and display filters, tap into live network communication, and graph traffic patterns to visualize the data flowing across your network.

MAY 2007, 172 PP., $39.95
ISBN 978-1-59327-149-7

LINUX FIREWALLS
Attack Detection and Response with iptables, psad, and fwsnort

by MICHAEL RASH

Linux Firewalls discusses the technical details of the iptables firewall and the Netfilter framework that are built into the Linux kernel, and it explains how they provide strong filtering, Network Address Translation (NAT), state tracking, and application layer inspection capabilities that rival many commercial tools. You'll learn how to deploy iptables as an IDS with psad and fwsnort and how to build a strong, passive authentication layer around iptables with fwknop. Concrete examples illustrate concepts such as firewall log analysis and policies, passive network authentication and authorization, exploit packet traces, Snort ruleset emulation, and more.

OCTOBER 2007, 336 PP., $49.95
ISBN 978-1-59327-141-1

THE BOOK OF™ IMAP
Building a Mail Server with Courier and Cyrus

by PEER HEINLEIN AND PEER HARTLEBEN

IMAP (the Internet Message Access Protocol) is powerful and flexible, but it's also complicated to set up; it's more difficult to implement than POP3 and more error-prone for both client and server. *The Book of IMAP* offers a detailed introduction to IMAP and POP3, the two protocols that govern all modern mail servers and clients. You'll learn how the protocols work as well as how to install, configure, and maintain the two most popular open source mail systems, Courier and Cyrus.

MAY 2008, 368 PP. $49.95
ISBN 978-1-59327-177-0

BUILDING A SERVER WITH FREEBSD 7
A Modular Approach

by BRYAN J. HONG

The most difficult part of building a server with FreeBSD, the Unix-like operating system, is arguably software installation and configuration. Finding the software is easy enough; getting everything up and running is another thing entirely. If you're a small business owner looking for a reliable email server, a curious Windows administrator, or if you just want to put that old computer in the closet to work, *Building a Server with FreeBSD 7* will show you how to get things up and running quickly. You'll learn how to install FreeBSD, then how to install popular server applications with the ports collection. Each package is treated as an independent module, so you can dip into the book at any point to install just the packages you need, when you need them.

APRIL 2008, 288 PP., $34.95
ISBN 978-1-59327-145-9

PHONE:
800.420.7240 OR
415.863.9900
MONDAY THROUGH FRIDAY,
9 A.M. TO 5 P.M. (PST)

FAX:
415.863.9950
24 HOURS A DAY,
7 DAYS A WEEK

EMAIL:
SALES@NOSTARCH.COM

WEB:
WWW.NOSTARCH.COM

MAIL:
NO STARCH PRESS
555 DE HARO ST, SUITE 250
SAN FRANCISCO, CA 94107
USA

The Book of Xen is set in New Baskerville, TheSansMonoCondensed, Futura, and Dogma.

The book was printed and bound at Malloy Incorporated in Ann Arbor, Michigan. The paper is Glatfelter Spring Forge 60# Antique, which is certified by the Sustainable Forestry Initiative (SFI). The book uses a RepKover binding, which allows it to lay flat when open.

UPDATES

Visit *http://www.nostarch.com/xen.htm* for updates, errata, and other information.